David B. Moore and Gerald M. Schmitz (*editors*)
DEBATING DEVELOPMENT DISCOURSE: Institutional and Popular
Perspectives

Juan Antonio Morales and Gary McMahon (*editors*)
ECONOMIC POLICY AND THE TRANSITION TO DEMOCRACY: The Latin
American Experience

Paul J. Nelson
THE WORLD BANK AND NON-GOVERNMENTAL ORGANIZATIONS:
The Limits of Apolitical Development

Archibald R. M. Ritter and John M. Kirk (*editors*)
CUBA IN THE INTERNATIONAL SYSTEM: Normalization and Integration

Ann Seidman and Robert B. Seidman
STATE AND LAW IN THE DEVELOPMENT PROCESS: Problem-Solving and
Institutional Change in the Third World

Tor Skålnes
THE POLITICS OF ECONOMIC REFORM IN ZIMBABWE: Continuity and
Change in Development

John Sorenson (*editor*)
DISASTER AND DEVELOPMENT IN THE HORN OF AFRICA

Howard Stein (*editor*)
ASIAN INDUSTRIALIZATION AND AFRICA: Studies in Policy Alternatives
to Structural Adjustment

Deborah Stienstra
WOMEN'S MOVEMENTS AND INTERNATIONAL ORGANIZATIONS

Larry A. Swatuk and Timothy M. Shaw (*editors*)
THE SOUTH AT THE END OF THE TWENTIETH CENTURY: Rethinking the
Political Economy of Foreign Policy in Africa, Asia, the Caribbean and Latin
America

Sandra Whitworth
FEMINISM AND INTERNATIONAL RELATIONS

David Wurfel and Bruce Burton (*editors*)
SOUTHEAST ASIA IN THE NEW WORLD ORDER: The Political Economy
of a Dynamic Region

Lessons in Economic Policy for Eastern Europe from Latin America

Edited by

Gary McMahon
Senior Specialist
International Development Research Centre
Ottawa, Canada

Foreword by Doug Daniels
Director
Office for Central and East Europe Initiatives

First published in Great Britain 1996 by
MACMILLAN PRESS LTD
Houndmills, Basingstoke, Hampshire RG21 6XS
and London
Companies and representatives
throughout the world

A catalogue record for this book is available
from the British Library.

ISBN 0–333–64270–8

First published in the United States of America 1996 by
ST. MARTIN'S PRESS, INC.,
Scholarly and Reference Division,
175 Fifth Avenue,
New York, N.Y. 10010

ISBN 0–312–12647–6

Library of Congress Cataloging-in-Publication Data
Lessons in economic policy for Eastern Europe from Latin America /
edited by Gary McMahon.
p.   cm. — (International political economy series)
Includes bibliographical references and index.
ISBN 0–312–12647–6 (cloth)
1. Europe, Eastern—Economic policy—1989–   2. Latin America–
–Economic policy.   3. Economic policy.   4. Comparative economics.
I. McMahon, Gary.   II. Series.
HC244.L456   1996
338.947—dc20   95–2566
                                                                          CIP

Printed and bound in Great Britain by
Antony Rowe Ltd, Chippenham, Wiltshire

To **Ada** and **Patrick**

Contents

List of Tables and Figures

Foreword

The magnitude of the transformation required in Eastern Europe and the former Soviet Union is unprecedented in modern history. No other societies have embarked on such massive change in terms of societal values, organisation and economic structure. These countries have been launched on an arduous and very uncertain path that will involve considerable social dislocation and economic stress. The experience of the first few years after the break-up of the Soviet Union demonstrates how very different the conditions and development prospects are for the countries of this region.

Unfortunately this means there are no models elsewhere to serve as close parallels. Certainly none of the industrial countries have had to deal with such major changes in the postwar period. The experiences of some countries in the south, however, have some similarities where instances exist of inefficient and unprofitable public sectors, high levels of underemployment and inflation, currency depreciation and low debt servicing capability. The IDRC thought it would be useful to encourage an assessment of the experience with structural adjustments programme in Latin America to see what approaches might be useful for Central and Eastern Europe.

The IDRC has operated on the premise that successful development requires the creation of a national capacity to make choices and that there is a limit to what outsiders can do, no matter how well informed or well intentioned. Thus the idea was born of inviting Central and Eastern European economists to look at the experiences of Latin American countries in their structural adjustment programmes over the last decade. They could then draw on their results to help define the policies they believe would be useful in their own countries.

The Latin American institutions that were approached to support the work of these economists readily agreed, and we are most grateful to them for their considerable support. Four economists were invited from Hungary, Poland, Russia and then Czechoslovakia to look at the experiences of Argentina, Chile, Brazil and Mexico. The review began with an initial joint workshop in Santiago, followed by two-week tours in the individual countries. The key Latin American counterparts were then invited to a final workshop in Prague, where the Central and Eastern European economists presented and defended their conclusions.

The results are presented in this book, along with a covering essay by Gary McMahon of the IRDC and José María Fanelli of CEDES, Argentina. Thanks are due to Gary McMahon for his considerable input in guiding the development of this project as well as to Tom Bartos of the IDRC for his support in organising the study. We would also like to thank the Latin American participants, who have, in addition to their other assistance, coauthored two chapters of this book. Finally, thanks are due to the other four authors of this study for undertaking the exercise at short notice and meeting the publication deadlines.

The IDRC is committed to promoting the sharing of experience across regions and we believe there are opportunities in other areas to share experiences for mutual benefit. The experience of Central and Eastern Europe in addressing their serious industrial pollution problems is one area where developing countries could benefit in future, as many of these countries have increasing problems in this area as well. The IDRC has already become involved with an environmental programme on the Dnipro in Ukraine, with the sharing of information as one of its objectives.

We hope that the results of this exercise will prove useful in informing East and Central Europeans about the choices they can make, and that it will contribute to a greater appreciation of the benefits of sharing experiences with other regions of the world.

DOUG DANIELS
Director
Office for Central and East Europe Initiatives

List of Abbreviations

BNDES	Banco Nacional de Desenvolvimiento Social e Economico
CEDES	Centro de Estudios de Estado y Sociedad
CETES	Certificados de la Tesorería (treasury bonds)
CIEPLAN	Corporación de Investigaciones Económicas para Latinoamerica
CMEA	Council for Mutual Economic Assistance
CODELCO	Corporación del Cobre
COMECON	See CMEA
CORFO	Corporación del Fomento
CSFR	Republic of Czechoslovakia
CSK	Czechoslovakian crowns
CTC	Comparñía de Teléfonos de Chile
CVG	Corporación Venezolana de Guayana
EC	European Community
ENDESA	Empresa Nacional de Electricidad S.A.
ENTEL	Empresa Nacional de Telecommunicaciones
ESOP	Employee Share Ownership Programme
EU	European Union
GATT	General Agreement on Tariffs and Trade
GDP	Gross domestic product
GDR	German Democratic Republic
GNP	Gross national product
HUF	Hungarian forints
IDRC	International Development Research Centre
IMF	International Monetary Fund
KCS	See CSK
LIB	Latvian Investment Bank
OECD	Organisation for Economic Cooperation and Development
PECE	Pact of Stability and Economic Growth
PEMEX	Petroleos de Mexico
PSBR	Public sector borrowing requirement
PSE	Pact of Economic Solidarity
SIBRA	Electrosiderúrgica Brasileira
SOE	State owned enterprise
SOQUIMICH	Sociedad Química y Minera de Chile
SPA	State Property Agency
TELMEX	Telecommunicaciones Mexicanas

UNCTAD	United Nations Commission for Trade and Development
US	United States
USSR	Union of Soviet Socialist Republics
VAT	Value added tax

Notes on the Contributors

Marcelo de Paiva Abreu is Professor of Economics at the Pontifical Catholic University of Rio de Janeiro. He received his MSc from the London School of Economics and his PhD from the University of Cambridge. He has been a visiting professor at the universities of Cambridge, Illinois, Modena and Venezia. His publications include books and articles in academic journals and collected volumes on contemporary and historical aspects of links between Brazil and the world economy.

José María Fanelli is currently Director of the Economics Department at the University of Buenos Aires. Since 1984 he has been Senior Researcher at CEDES (Centre for the Study of State and Society) and CONICET (the National Research Council) in Buenos Aires. He has specialised in macro-economics and monetary economics, and has published several books and articles on stabilisation, structural reform and the financial system in Latin America. He has also worked as a consultant for ECLA, UNCTAD, OECD and IDRC.

János Hoós is Professor of Economics at Budapest University of Economic Sciences, where he teaches public economics and economic forecasting. He also works as Consultant to the Hungarian Finance Ministry. He has more than twenty years' practical experience in national economic management, having been President of the Hungarian Planning Office and the Hungarian Central Statistical Office. His research interests are public economics and economic forecasting, and he has published ten books and more than a hundred scientific articles.

Vratislave Izák has been a lecturer at the Economics Institute of the Academy of Sciences, Prague, Czech Republic since the mid-1960s. His previous research interests include economic integration of Western Europe, Keynesian macroeconomics and, later, theory of optimal planning of the socialist economy, planning models, input/output and, most recently, macroeconomics theory and policy, especially monetary and fiscal policies. His doctoral dissertation in 1973 on Keynesian multiplier theory was published as a book in Prague. He is also Associate Professor at the University of Economics in Prague.

Gary McMahon is Senior Specialist at the International Development Research Centre in Ottawa, Canada. He holds a PhD in economics from the University of Western Ontario, London, Canada. Dr McMahon has published articles in the area of general equilibrium models and macro-economics, both applied to the problems of developing countries. His most recent work is on fiscal policy and environmental economics.

Raúl E. Sáez holds a MS in economics from the University of Chile and a PhD in economics from Boston University. He has been Consultant for the IDRC, the UN Economic Commission for Latin America and the Caribbean (ECLAC), the Ministry of Finance and the Ministry of Foreign Relations of Chile. He has also worked as an advisor on trade policy and negotiations to the Undersecretary of the Economy of Chile. Dr Sáez has published articles on international trade issues and privatisation in journals and books. He is currently Senior Researcher at the Centre for Economic Research for Latin America and Assistant Professor of Economics at the University of Chile.

Andrzej Slawinski is a lecturer at Warsaw School of Economics, where he teaches monetary policy and financial markets. He also works for the Research Department of the National Bank of Poland. Since the late 1980s Dr Slawinski has been involved in the process of reforming the Polish banking system. He is the author of a book on adjustment policies and of more than fifty papers on exchange rate policy, balance of payments, financial reforms and Poland's emergency money and foreign exchange markets.

Carlos M. Urzúa is Professor of Economics at El Colegio de México. He is the editor of *Estudios Economicos*, and was President of the Latin American Chapter of the Econometric Society (1993–4). His interests range from macroeconomics to econometrics.

Map of Latin America

Commonwealth of Independent States and surrounding countries

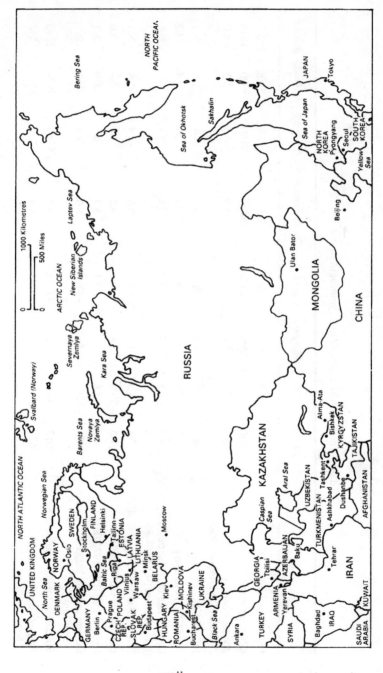

Latin America and Eastern Europe: general indicators for 1980

	Brazil	Chile	Mexico	Argentina	Czech Republic[1]	Hungary	Poland	Russia[2]
Population (millions)	118.7	11.1	69.8	27.7	15.3	10.8	35.8	265.5
GNP/capita ($)	2050	2150	2090	2390	5820	4180	3900	4550
Average annual growth rate of GNP/capita 1960–80	5.1	1.6	2.6	2.2	4.0	4.5	5.3	4.0
Inflation rate 1970–80	36.7	185.6	19.3	130.8	NA	NA	NA	NA
% of GDP in industry	37	37	38	NA	75	59	64	62
Growth rate of domestic, investment (%) 1970–80	9.7	-1.8	7.4	2.9	NA	NA	NA	NA
Fiscal balance S/D (% of GDP)[3]	-2.5	5.6	-3.1	-5.3	NA	-2.9	NA	NA
Exports (% GDP) 1970–80	7.5	10.9	13.4	9.3	6.5	8.2	6.7	5.6
Imports (% GDP) 1970–80	4.2	2.8	7	2.1	5.7	6.1	6.0	8.3
Current account balance (millions $)	-12871	-1784	-7466	-4700	NA	NA	NA	NA
Total external debt (millions $)[4]	71012	12081	57378	27157	NA	9764	8894	2240
Aggregate net resource flows (millions $)[5]	6621	2312	8991	3535	NA	728	3143	252

Latin America and Eastern Europe: general indicators for 1980 (*Continued*)

	Brazil	Chile	Mexico	Argentina	Czech Republic[1]	Hungary	Poland	Russia[2]
Total external debt as % of GNP	16.7	18	20.6	7.2	NA	NA	NA	NA
Life expectancy (at birth)	63	67	65	70	71	71	72	71
Total adult literacy (%), 1977	76	NA	81	93	NA	99	98	100
Infant mortality per 1000 live births	NA	NA	NA	NA	NA	NA	NA	NA
% Total secondary school enrollment, 1979	32	55	45	56	43	69	54	100
% Total tertiary school enrollment, 1978	11	12	12	22	16	12	18	21

Notes:
[1] Former Czechoslovakia.
[2] Former USSR.
[3] Taken from World Bank, 1994, Table 10.
[4] Taken from World Bank, 1994, Table 20.
[5] Taken from World Bank, 1994, Table 14.

Source: World Bank, 1982, 1994.

Latin America and Eastern Europe: general indicators for 1986

	Brazil	Chile	Mexico	Argentina	Czech Republic[1]	Hungary	Poland	Russia[2]
Population (millions)	138.4	12.2	80.2	31	15.5	10.6	37.5	281.1
GNP/capita ($)	1810	1320	1860	2350	NA	2020	2070	NA
Average annual growth rate of GNP/capita, 1965–86	4.3	-0.2	2.6	0.2	NA	3.9	NA	NA
Inflation rate (%) 1980–86	157.1	20.2	63.7	326.2	NA	5.4	31.2	NA
% of GDP in industry	39	NA	39	40	NA	41	NA	NA
Growth rate of domestic investment (%), 1980–86	-2.7	-7.4	-7.6	-12.6	NA	-3.2	-0.8	NA
Fiscal balance S/D (% GNP)	-11.6	-1.1	-9.2	-8.0	NA	-3.3	-0.3	NA
Exports % GDP, 1980–86	4.3	3.9	7.7	1.5	NA	NA	NA	NA
Imports % GDP, 1980–86	-5.1	-9.3	-9.2	-13.8	NA	NA	NA	NA
Current account balance (millions $)	-4930	-1091	-1270	-2864	NA	-1287	-1109	NA
Total external debt (millions $)	110675	20741	101722	48908	NA	17218	36638	NA
Aggregate net resource flows	106	728	955	635	NA	1064	-228	NA
Total external debt as % of GNP	37.6	120.1	76.1	51.7	NA	59.6	48.5	NA
Life expectancy (at birth)	65	71	68	70	70	71	72	70
Total adult literacy (%)	NA	NA	NA	NA	NA	NA	NA	NA
Infant mortality per 1000 live births	65	20	48	33	14	19	18	30
% Total secondary school enrollment	35	69	55	70	39	72	78	99
% Total tertiary school enrollment	11	16	16	36	16	15	17	21

Notes:
[1] Former Czechoslovakia.
[2] Former USSR.

Source: World Bank, 1988.

Latin America and Eastern Europe: general indicators for 1992

	Brazil	Chile	Mexico	Argentina	Czech Republic¹	Hungary	Poland	Russia
Population (millions)	153.9	13.6	85	33.1	10.3	10.3	38.4	149
GNP/capita ($)	2770	2730	3470	6050	2450	2970	1910	2510
Average annual growth rate of GNP/capita, 1980–92	0.4	3.7	-0.2	-0.9	NA	0.2	0.1	NA
Average annual inflation rate, 1980–92	370.2	20.5	62.4	402.3	NA	11.7	67.9	NA
% of GDP in industry	37	NA	28	31	61	30	51	49
Growth rate of domestic investment, 1980–92	-0.3	9.2	-0.8	-2.6	NA	-2.3	-1.0	NA
Fiscal balance S/D	-0.9	2.4	0.8	NA	NA	0.8	NA	NA
Exports (% of GDP), 1980–92	5.0	5.5	1.6	2.2	NA	1.6	3	NA
Imports (% of GDP), 1980–92	1.5	3.5	3.8	-1.7	NA	0.5	1.8	NA
Current account balance	6266	-940	-22924	-8370	454	337	-3357	-4600
Total external debt (millions $)	121110	19360	113378	67569	NA	21900	48521	78658
Aggregate net resource flows	7151	1506	10309	5019	NA	1273	933	14401
Total external debt as % of GNP	31.2	48.9	34.1	30.3	NA	65	55.2	NA
Life expectancy (at birth)	66	72	70	71	72	69	70	72
Total adult illiteracy (%), 1990	19	7	13	5	NA	NA	NA	NA
Infant mortality per 1000 live births	57	17	35	29	10	15	14	20
% Total secondary school enrollment, 1991	39	72	55	NA	NA	81	83	NA
% Total tertiary school enrollment, 1991	12	23	15	43	NA	15	22	NA

Note:
¹Includes Slovakia

Latin America and Eastern Europe: general indicators for 1992 (*Continued*)

	Brazil	Chile	Mexico	Argentina	Czech Republic[1]	Hungary	Poland	Russia[2]
Real GDP per capita (adjusted $), 1991	5240	7060	7170	5120	6570	6080	4500	6930
Human development index	0.756	0.848	0.804	0.853	0.872	0.863	0.815	0.858
Years of schooling (mean)	4	7.8	4.9	9.2	9.2	9.8	8.2	9
% Population with access to health services, 1985–91	NA	97	90	NA	NA	NA	NA	NA
% Population with access to safe water, 1988–91	86	88	77	89	NA	NA	NA	NA
% Population with access to sanitation, 1988–91	78	88	55	87	NA	NA	NA	NA
Urban population as % of total population	77	85	74	NA	NA	NA	NA	NA
Gini coefficient, 1975–88	0.57	0.46	0.5	NA	NA	NA	NA	NA

Source: UNDR, 1994.

1 Economic Lessons for Eastern Europe from Latin America

José María Fanelli and Gary McMahon

1.1 INTRODUCTION

Most of the countries of Eastern Europe are currently going through the same process of economic and social transformation that many Latin American countries began in the early 1980s.[1] Given the large variety of Latin American experiences, it would seem, therefore, that Eastern Europe could learn a great deal by studying Latin America. However, few Eastern European eyes seem to have turned to the south-west. While one can only conjecture why this is so, it is likely that most of the attention has fallen on Western Europe – due to its proximity and for historical reasons – and on South-East Asia – because of the recent spectacular success stories. It may also be due to a general ignorance of Latin America, a region about which few economists in Eastern Europe have much knowledge, and the tendency to think of it as a somewhat wealthier Africa.

Very roughly speaking, Latin America (especially the larger countries) is the region in the world with which Eastern Europe has the most similarities. Income levels are in the same general area, as is infrastructure development, industrialisation and the levels of human capital. Of course, there are also at least three major differences. Eastern Europe does not have a large, marginalised, indigenous group, as do many countries of Latin America. Also, state ownership of the means of production, while pervasive in Latin America, never reached anywhere near the levels of Eastern Europe. The social safety net – largely due to guaranteed employment – was also much stronger in Eastern Europe, although this is no longer the case in much of that region.

Another important feature common to the two regions is the significant level of macroeconomic instability. However, while this is a relatively recent phenomenon in Eastern Europe, Latin America has had a long tradition of macro instability. Consequently the countries of the latter region have accumulated ample experience of stabilisation policies and this could be valuable for Eastern Europe, which has much less experience in the design and implementation of adjustment policies in the market economy.

1

A country such as Russia, for example, which was recently on the brink of hyperinflation, could learn a lot from the virtues and flaws of the anti-inflationary policies implemented in Bolivia or Argentina to stop high inflation processes. There are also valuable lessons to be learned about the relationship between structural reform and stabilisation. Since the mid-1980s, in the context of high instability created by the debt crisis, many Latin American countries have launched structural reforms aimed at reducing the role of the state and liberalising the economy. Given that in Eastern Europe the transformation process is also bound to be carried forward in a highly unstable macroeconomic context, the analysis of the sequence of stabilisation and structural reform measures in Chile, Mexico or Argentina in recent years can be highly relevant for the former socialist countries. Indeed the experience of Latin America may be valuable not only regarding the relationship between reform and stabilisation, but also for the design of the sequencing of the structural reform process itself. The analysis of the successes and failures of the Southern Cone liberalisation attempts of the late 1970s, for example, can be especially illuminating for the avoidance of the perverse interactions among the opening of the capital account, trade liberalisation and financial deregulation that were observed in Argentina, Chile and Uruguay, and that ultimately led to the collapse of the liberalisation attempts in those countries in the early 1980s.

Given this mix we believed that there was a lot for Eastern Europe to learn from Latin America in economic policy, but we had some misgivings. While both regions were quickly moving from state-directed, closed economies of varying degrees to market-based, open economies, it may well be that the differences noted above were more important than this broad similarity.

Nevertheless we decided to invite four economists from Eastern Europe to different countries in Latin America for two weeks in December 1992. Each spent one week in a sister institution and then went to Santiago for a two-day conference, followed by another week in the sister institution. This allowed them to become quickly immersed in the Latin American economic literature and to see for themselves the degree of development of much of Latin America. The latter was even more important than we thought it would be in breaking down misconceptions and making the researchers receptive to the comparison.

Each researcher focused on a different aspect of economic policy. The pairings and topics were Hungary–Chile – privatisation; Poland–Brazil – external trade and finance; Czech Republic–Mexico – fiscal policy; and Russia–Argentina – monetary policy and stabilisation. In April 1993 the East Europeans presented their papers at a conference in Prague. Their counterparts made comments, which were later expanded and used to form two additional papers. The first groups together fiscal policy and privatisation; the second consists of a discussion on monetary policy and stabilisation.

The way of attacking the problem varied considerably, however, with regard to both thematic scope and country coverage. While all of the Europeans tended to focus on their counterpart country in Latin America, they all to some degree touched on other countries in the region. However, while all focused to a large degree on their own country on the Eastern European side of the comparison, two of the researchers did so almost exclusively (Poland and Russia) while the others were more eclectic. In addition, on the thematic side there was a tendency to look at the whole package of stabilisation and structural policies and stray away from narrow concentration on their thematic topic. This was especially true in the cases of Russia and Poland, fairly true in the case of the Czech Republic, but much less so in the case of Hungary. Nevertheless it would only be slightly incorrect to say that we have four case studies on stabilisation and structural reform, each attacking the problem from a different entry point.[2]

This chapter is a summary and synthesis of the papers that make up the chapters of this book, and is organised as follows. Section 1.2 contains summaries of what we perceived to be the main results from each of the studies, including the two shorter papers by the Latin Americans. It is divided into four parts – privatisation, fiscal policies, stabilisation and monetary policy, and the role of the external sector and finance. In each part, after presenting the results of the papers, we evaluate the issues concerned, incorporating some of the more recent literature on reforms in Latin America and Eastern Europe. Section 1.3 makes a general assessment of the lessons learned from Latin America regarding stabilisation and structural reform and presents some conclusions. Before we begin, however, we would like to emphasise that this chapter is not a survey of the literature on the subject, rather it concentrates on the IDRC-funded study and a few other selected documents.

1.2   THE CASE STUDIES

Privatisation

The first section of Chapter 2, by Janós Hoós of Hungary, examines the reasons for and the process of privatisation in Latin America in the last two decades. Hoós begins with an examination of the experiences of Latin America. He follows this with a discussion of privatisation in Eastern Europe, with the emphasis on Hungary, Czechoslovakia and Poland. The chapter concludes with a section on the lessons that Eastern Europe can learn from Latin America.

The two overriding reasons for privatisation in Latin America were economic efficiency and fiscal balance considerations. The ideological shift in Latin America in the 1980s meant that the government is now seen by many as only responsible for what the private sector cannot or will not do. Greater efficiency can be achieved by leaving production largely in the hands of the private sector. Moreover greater equity can be achieved with the social participation that occurs through the democratisation of capital. That is, public enterprises are inherently inefficient as they do not have to worry about making profits, and they are inherently inequitable as they are captured by the better-off classes in society.

Losses generated by state owned enterprises (SOEs) have often accounted for significant portions of the fiscal imbalance within a given country. Therefore privatisation will help the long-run fiscal balance of the government. Nevertheless the short-run fiscal deficit is often one of the driving forces behind privatisation. At the heart of much of the macroeconomic instability that plagued Latin America in the 1980s were large fiscal deficits. Significant parts of these resulted from new expenditures in the form of debt payments to domestic and international bondholders; another important cause was the decline in tax revenues that accompanied the instability.[3] With few other short-run options to close the fiscal deficit, some governments began to sell off their assets – that is, to privatise. In Mexico, Chile and Argentina, for example, proceeds for privatisation played a major role in meeting fiscal needs until other sources of revenue could be obtained. In fact Argentina (and Mexico, to a lesser extent) will soon have to face the problem of how to replace these privatisation revenues on a long-term basis.

Hoós also documents a number of other reasons for the emphasis on privatisation in Latin America. Specific divestments are often undertaken more for ideological reasons than on efficiency grounds. They are seen as giving signals to the private sector that they are to play the lead role in economic growth and that the government is serious about 'market friendly' reform. On similar grounds, in a climate of great uncertainty the government may choose to privatise some firms in order to give the private sector relatively easy sources of investment. There may be no need for major start-up costs and monopoly profits can be obtained, at least in the short run. Privatisation can also lead to a deepening of stock markets, especially when some type of popular capitalism is used in the divestiture process. Finally, privatisation also tends to improve relations with international financial agencies and commercial banks, which can play an important role in building up investor confidence in a country.

In this chapter Hoós describes in some detail the many different forms that divestiture assumed in Latin America. These included direct sale, partial sale to employees, stock market sales, popular capitalism, partial sales to foreigners and sales to pension funds. The main point here is that privatisation can take many different forms and a country should not feel bound to follow just one or two of them. The type of privatisation undertaken will very much depend on the type of firm and economic and institutional situation of the country.

Nevertheless privatisation has often run into serious problems in Latin America, the biggest of which has been a lack of transparency and the regulation of non-competitive industries. Chile in the 1970s is the most prominent example of SOEs being sold off in a very non-transparent manner, resulting in catastrophe. By allowing a very high concentration of ownership, the government exposed the country to enormous economic risk, especially as firms and commercial banks were owned by the same conglomerates. In fact the money to buy the companies was often loaned by the conglomerates to themselves. This concentration of ownership was one of the prime factors for the enormous depression in 1982–3.

The regulation of the noncompetitive industries has often been implicitly done by liberalising trade at the same time as privatisation is occurring. However this remedy can be very ineffective if the goods are nontradables or if the regulatory body has little experience or power of enforcement. The problem is often exacerbated by the generous conditions used to attract the buyers in the first place.

Privatisation in Eastern Europe has had similar objectives to those in Latin America, but with greater emphasis on the need to spread and promote ownership. Nevertheless the efficiency and fiscal balance objectives have been just as prominent as in Latin America. The magnitude of the problem, however, is much larger than in Latin America. Generally, one is speaking of privatising firms worth about 50 per cent of GDP in three to four years versus firms worth 10 per cent of GDP in eight to ten years in Latin America. Moreover, while Eastern European governments face some of the same problems experienced by Latin America, they have many other difficulties to confront.

The three main additional difficulties in Eastern Europe are lack of capital, the absence of clear property rights and a very inadequate legal and institutional framework. In general in Latin America finding buyers for privatised firms has not been a problem; the question was more how to go about it. In Eastern Europe, given the poor institutional framework, the lack of property rights and the paucity of domestic capital, it is often difficult to find a buyer at any price. Until financial responsibilities are clarified, including the problem of bad debts to the banking system and between firms, this may continue to be the case. As in Latin America, Eastern European countries also have protected markets, especially the European Union, but unlike in Latin America the newly privatised firms in Eastern Europe very frequently have to begin exporting goods very quickly, due to the small size of the internal market and the collapse of the former export market of COMECON.

The three main techniques of privatisation in Eastern Europe are (1) spontaneous or from below (2) active or driven by the state or (3) voucher plans with free mass transfer. The second and third of these are similar to the experience of Latin America although Eastern European countries have tended to resort to voucher plans of one sort or another more frequently than was the case in Latin America, primarily due to the objective of 'spreading capitalism'. The first technique refers to the process by which workers and managers more or less take over the SOE and buy it out. While this sounds fine in principle, the reality has been that it has led to enormous abuse. First, managers and workers generally have inside information about the true worth of their company and have often 'sold to themselves' at fire-sale prices. Second, given that the privatised firms often need to be restructured, one of the main ingredients of which is significant 'labour shedding', this is impeded by workers controlling the companies. The end result has often been that the nomenklatura ends up with bargain-priced companies that continue to operate as they always have.

Privatisation in Eastern Europe to date has been much less then envisaged. While it has been relatively easy to privatise small firms via auctions, larger firms remain largely in the hands of the state. Hoós emphasises that this is due to constraints on both the supply and the demand side. That is, there is a need to clarify the legal and institutional framework before putting firms on the block and a need to find buyers. The demand-side problem is particularly severe with regard to domestic buyers, a problem exacerbated by the understandable reluctance of governments to sell everything off to foreigners. Connecting both constraints is the difficulty of valuing enterprises in a country with no financial markets to spread of and tremendous uncertainty in all markets.

In a section on lessons for Eastern Europe from Latin America, Hoós begins by noting some of the most important differences: public ownership in Eastern Europe is 80–90 per cent versus 10–20 per cent in most Latin

American countries; in Latin America prices bear some relation to scarcity; and Latin America has well-established concepts of property, ownership, title and contracts. Nevertheless he believes that Eastern Europe has a lot to learn from the Latin America 'experiment' of the 1980s.

First, privatisation is an integral part of an economic reform package. It is a means, not an end. It should be seen as part of the redefinition of the state by the government. In this respect the Eastern European governments should not aim at short-term revenue maximisation but adopt a longer-term perspective. It must also be consistent with other reforms. For example, privatisation without price liberalisation should be avoided as it becomes impossible to place a value on the assets of the firms.

Second, privatisation should be approached slowly. If it is undertaken without the proper institutions there is a possibility of widespread corruption and chaos, as has happened in Latin America. In Eastern Europe the damage from ill-conceived privatisation is likely to be much worse. In addition, trying to move too quickly can result in the situation experienced by Brazil, where the government totally missed its targets and lost credibility in the process. Third, a stable macroeconomic situation should be a prerequisite for an ambitious privatisation programme. Again, without a stable economy it is very difficult to place a value on the assets of a firm and gain a good idea of the potential profitability.

Fourth, due to regulatory problems Eastern European governments should first concentrate on the traded goods sector. At the same time they should build up their regulatory capacities in anticipation of more difficult privatisation. Fifth, they should be flexible in their methods of privatisation. There is no method that is superior in all situations. It is likely that each country will wish to have a portfolio of divestiture processes. There are two things, however, that they should all adopt – transparency and a reliance on cash, not debt.

Finally, on both humanitarian and political grounds there is a need to deal adequately with workers that lose their jobs. In many cases privatisation will lead to large-scale lay-offs. If unemployed workers are not certain of reintegration into the economy they are likely to resist the privatisation process, and perhaps derail it.

Raúl Sáez and Carlos Urzúa (Chapter 4) largely agree with Hoós assessment of the similarities and differences between the two regions. However they think that two further differences should be added. First, Latin America has a long experience in dealing with foreign investors. Second, economies in Latin America are not structured on the basis of large vertically and horizontally integrated monopolies, thus making the regulation problem even more pressing in Eastern Europe. Despite the differences they found that the regions are facing many of the same issues: optimal sequencing, methods of divestiture, choice of buyers, financing of the purchase, transparency and the resulting market structure. In all these areas, Eastern Europe has much to learn from Latin America experience.

While they agree in theory with Hoós' timetable of privatising small firms first, followed by those in tradable sectors and then larger service-type firms, they believe that in practice it will probably be necessary to tackle several fronts at the same time. It is also essential to break up monopolies before privatisation and to 'renationalise' SOEs in countries in which workers and management have taken them over de facto. Sáez and Urzúa stress that once property rights are allocated it is very difficult to undo them; accordingly it is necessary to get them right before privatisation and not try to sort them out later.

Along the same lines, they emphasize the importance of regulation, especially of the financial system. Particular care needs to be taken with the large investment funds that are springing up in countries that employed the voucher system (or 'mass privatisation'). Once again, if governments try to regulate after the fact, special interest groups will have formed that will try to block them. Finally, Sáez and Urzúa note that the type of divestiture often plays a significant role in the final market structure. Therefore it is necessary to consider the instruments to be used when looking at the regulatory process.

Three important conclusions follow from our summary of Hoós' chapter. First, the most important reasons for privatisation in Latin America – economic efficiency, fiscal balance, ideology, market deepening and the spread of capitalism – are also playing a prominent role in Eastern Europe. Second, the problems faced in Latin America have their counterparts in Eastern Europe – concentration of ownership and regulation, methods of divestiture, asset valuation and transparency being the four most important. Third, the major differences are related to the lack of capital, property rights and an adequate legal and institutional framework in Eastern Europe. With regard to these last items, it is not clear that Latin America has a lot to offer Eastern Europe that cannot be more easily obtained elsewhere.

With regard to the challenges and problems that are similar in the two regions, the question becomes one of scope. Given the much bigger privatisation effort needed in Eastern Europe, does the Latin American experience really offer concrete lessons? We think that it does for two reasons. First, the difference in magnitude, while very large, is not as large as it first appears. Much of the private sector in Latin America depended (and often continues to depend) on government regulation and procurement.

One wit neatly summed it up by saying that in Latin America it is necessary to privatise the private sector first.[4] Second, while privatisation is proceeding much more slowly than envisaged in Eastern Europe, in some Latin American countries (for example Argentina) the opposite has been the case; therefore the magnitude of privatisation in any given year may not be too different, and hence the Latin American experience could be valuable.

At the very least, Latin America can offer many lessons on how to go about the job. Almost all imaginable types of privatisation have been tried, so there is a large pot to draw from. Two additional features that make the Latin American experience valuable are that the sequencing and scope of the privatisation process have shown a wide diversity, and that the macroeconomic context within which this process has taken place has greatly varied from country to country.

Mexico, as Hoós has noted, probably has a lot to teach with regard to the sequencing of privatisation. Its relatively successful experience was based on privatising small firms first, and then moving on to larger ones. Cardoso (1992) notes that this 'learning by doing' experience has been quite successful. The case of Bolivia, on the other hand, can give some insights into the relationship between stabilisation and privatisation. Although, as Hoós emphasised, stability makes privatisation easier, this has not been the case in Bolivia. Bolivia succeeded in stabilising the economy in the mid-1980s but, as Morales (1991) describes, its privatisation process has been very slow for a number of familiar reasons: small stock markets, high interest rates, problems of valuation, and worries about the concentration of ownership. A more in-depth study of Bolivia could give some insights into the problems that lie ahead for some of the smaller Eastern European countries, such as Bulgaria and Romania, where privatisation is progressing very slowly.

The recent Argentine experience may be another important source of relevant lessons for Eastern Europe, especially regarding the problem of the trade-off between speed of divestiture on the one hand, and equity and efficiency on the other. Unlike the majority of Latin American countries, Argentina adopted a kind of 'big bang' approach to privatisation, which has been highly effective in rapidly reducing the role of the state in direct production. Since 1990 practically all existing public enterprises have been sold. The assets divested from 1990–3 amounted to $16.2 billion, which represents around 7 per cent of GDP (Fanelli and Machinea, 1994). There was no well-defined sequencing in terms of small/large firms or tradable/non-tradable products and there were no worries about the participation of foreign investors. Given the considerable magnitude of the public property divested compared with the small size of domestic capital markets, foreign investors have had a prominent role. Foreign investment accounted for 60 per cent of the total proceeds from privatisation. The Argentine authorities gave priority to minimising the duration of the process while maximising revenues, which were in turn used to finance the restructuring of the government balance sheet. The bulk of the revenues from privatisation were used to reduce the stock of public debt and to finance the public deficit (especially at the beginning of the stabilisation plan launched in early 1991). Undoubtedly the costs incurred in terms of efficiency and equity have been important. Specifically, there was no time to define a sound regulatory framework and the process has led to a greater concentration of property.

It could be argued that, given the lack of capital in Eastern Europe, many of the Latin American experiences are not too relevant and that it seems likely that the heavy reliance on the voucher system, which has been used only marginally in Latin America, will continue – not so much so as to spread capitalism, but because there are no ready buyers. While this argument is basically correct, even in this regard there are at least two lessons to be learned from Latin America. First, as Borensztein (1993) argues (and Sáez and Urzúa warn), mass privatisation can result in powerful investment funds with large equity positions in the banking sector. Without proper regulatory controls over their behaviour, a situation akin to the one that led to the Chilean debacle of the early 1980s could occur. Second, the Latin American experience shows that if the international situation is favourable, investment funds can be, to a certain extent, endogenously generated by the privatisation process. This is obvious with regard to foreign direct investment, which has played a key role in Latin America, but funds for investment can also be endogenously generated if the reform contributes to changing the portfolio decision of domestic investors by opening new investment opportunities. In Latin America, during the debt crisis of 1980s the high level of international interest rates fuelled capital flight and discouraged investment in domestic real assets. This aggravated the lack of investment funds in most Latin American countries and was one of the most important factors restraining structural reforms. Nonetheless in the 1990s, when the international situation changed, in countries such as Argentina the privatisation process gained momentum because the fall in the international interest rate rendered investment in domestic real assets much more profitable. In a favourable international setting, then, privatisation can be a means to stop capital flight by creating investment opportunities in the domestic economy.

It is obvious that privatisation, by allowing the private sector to buy existing assets, could divert capital from new, profitable projects. However if such projects are few or are perceived to be very risky, privatisation could be a good way of channelling funds that would otherwise be invested abroad. This role of privatisation in stopping capital flight could be very important in some Eastern European countries. In Russia, for example, capital flight is absorbing a significant part of the foreign exchange generated by exported raw materials, as Karagodin highlights in Chapter 5 of this volume.

Fiscal revenues generated by privatisation have been a major concern in many Latin American countries as they have been crucial in closing the fiscal gap in the short-term. However it is not clear that they have such a strong role to play in Eastern Europe, partly due to the general lack of capital and partly to problems of valuation, which have posed large difficulties even in Latin America. Some of the difficulty lies in the fiscal deficit itself. Given the macroeconomic instability that usually accompanies large fiscal deficits and the uncertainty about future tax liabilities, it can be very difficult to assess the profitability of a firm. Needless to say these problems are magnified tremendously in Eastern Europe, where the equilibrium relative price structure and real exchange rate are largely unknown quantities.

Indeed, if the recent German experience is taken into account, it seems that there is a trade-off between the speed of privatisation and the importance of its contribution to budget equilibrium. The rapid divestiture process in Germany has generated a mounting fiscal deficit, which in 1992 was around 1.2 per cent of GDP (see Schwartz and Silva Lopes, 1993). In summary despite the enormous fiscal problems facing many countries in Eastern Europe, it does not seem likely that privatisation will play a major role in closing any short-term gaps.

The experience of the Latin American countries also shows that the need to maintain fiscal equilibrium can, indeed, put additional constraints on privatisation. In Chapter 2 and the literature on privatisation, a point that is generally missing is that even successful privatisers such as Chile and Mexico have not sold state-owned firms that process natural resources such as copper and petroleum. That is so because these public enterprises play a key role in financing the government and their privatisation would have required a major change in the tax and expenditure structures. In the case of Chile, for example, during the debt crisis a huge part of public expenditure was directly or indirectly financed by the proceeds from the copper industry.

The alternative to privatisation chosen by the Chilean government was that of decisively improving efficiency in copper production via significant increases in public investment. In the context of the 1980s, which were marked by a severe shortage of private investment funds, it seems to have been a wise decision. The Chilean experience can be very relevant for the case of Russia, for example, where oil and other natural resources show great growth potential if the required investment is made. The current institutional disarray in Russia nonetheless differs greatly from that of Chile, and consequently the first problem to be solved seems to be the regaining of government control over the rents generated by natural resources in order to finance both investment and the stabilisation process in general. Beyond the differences in the institutional situation in Latin America and Eastern Europe, nonetheless, the preceding argument tries to highlight the point that it is very important to analyse not only why public firms were privatised but also the reasons (primarily macroeconomic) why some state-owned enterprises were not divested.

Finally, we would like to mention an area we think could have been discussed in greater detail – the privatisation of banks and the related problem of bad debts. One of the biggest challenges facing Eastern Europe is how to privatise banks, given the large portfolio of bad debts they usually hold. Similar situations have occurred in Latin American countries – most notably Chile, Argentina and Uruguay in the early 1980s – with a slight twist; that is, the banks were private but had to be bailed out by the government to avoid the destruction of the entire financial system. A comparable response in Eastern Europe would be for governments to assume the bad debts of firms by, for example, issuing government bonds to the banks when the latter are privatised. As Levine and Scott (1993) argue, despite the obvious implications for the fiscal deficit the fact is that governments will in any case have to bail out many of the failing state banks. Their proposed solution could greatly reduce uncertainty and increase the credibility of the reform programme. What does seem clear is that until at least some banks are privatised and some competition exists in financial markets, state banks will continue to issue credits ('new bad loans') to their debtors in order to keep them afloat. Consequently, sustained macro-economic stability partially hinges on resolution of this problem.[5]

Fiscal Policy

In Chapter 3 Vratislave Izak (1993) of the Czech Republic analyses the lessons that Eastern Europe, with a strong emphasis on the Czech and Slovak Republics, could learn from Latin America, with an emphasis on

Mexico, in the realm of fiscal policy. He begins with the role of fiscal policy in stabilisation, then looks at revenue and expenditure policies in the two regions, and finally discusses tax reform.

Izak finds two main lessons that Eastern Europe should learn from Latin America with regard to fiscal policy and stabilisation. First, tight fiscal policy is a necessary but not sufficient condition for macroeconomic stability. Fiscal balance has never been enough to reduce inflation to acceptable levels as inertial forces have proven resistant to purely orthodox schemes. Generally, some heterodox elements such as 'social pacts' or a nominal anchor are necessary. Second, for countries undergoing deep structural changes, attempts to reactivate unused capacity by running a fiscal deficit are likely to result in high inflation and even lower output. In Eastern Europe the cost of macro imbalances is likely to be even greater, given the large degree of uncertainty that exists.

The second part of Chapter 3 looks in detail at the course of public revenues and expenditures in Mexico and Czechoslovakia. While the details are included, some aspects need to be highlighted. First, the reduction of Mexico's fiscal deficit was due more to a reduction in government spending than to an increase in tax revenues. This reduction was largely in public investment, transfers and subsidies. In general, investment in health and education fared relatively well. In the late 1980s a large decrease in debt servicing was also crucial for fiscal balance in the light of the drop in international interest rates, debt rescheduling under the Brady Plan and the fact that the proceeds from privatisation were largely used to retire some of the domestic debt.

Second, attempts by Mexico in the mid-1980s to move from inflation tax to a financial repression tax (by forced savings of government bonds at negative interest rates) led to financial disintermediation. When the government moved to market rates in 1987 the real interest rates were very high, with strong negative consequences for future fiscal deficits. Only when it was decided to use the proceeds from privatisation to alleviate this debt were the fiscal accounts put on a solid footing. Izak sees an important lesson for Eastern Europe in the Mexican experience as there is a strong temptation for Eastern European countries to move away from money financing into debt financing. If interest rates are unrealistic, the development of financial markets will be hampered; if they are realistic, there will be repercussions for future fiscal deficits. Eastern European countries could then find themselves in the situation of many Latin American countries in having to sell their assets to pay off past debts.

In the area of tax reform, both Eastern Europe and Latin America are trying to copy OECD systems. However the initial conditions are very different. Latin American tax systems, despite their narrow bases, are anchored in market-based economies. Their main problems have to do with a plethora of exemptions, high inflation and vulnerability to external shocks. Eastern European tax systems generally treat income very differently, depending on its sources, and are greatly lacking in transparency. Moreover the capability of administering the types of tax commonly found in market economies is almost completely lacking. In this respect, Izak considers that one of the main lessons to be learned from Latin America is that administrative and evasion issues have to be dealt with right from the start. In some cases they should even be given first priority.

In their companion chapter (Chapter 4) Raúl Sáez and Carlos Urzúa emphasize institutional and cultural factors. For example, with regard to tax evasion they believe that public reception of the government as honest is perhaps the most important factor. They also think that VAT may not work well in the less industrialised and less centralised countries of Eastern Europe and the former USSR. The administrative demands of VAT are relatively high, and it will be difficult to implement in countries that are undergoing a vast number of large structural reforms at the same time.

Sáez and Urzúa stress the equity implications of tax systems. Although Eastern European countries may feel that their taxes are already quite equitable, and therefore they do not have to worry about the distributional implications of their tax system, stabilisation and structural reforms can have very large distributive effects. As seems to be happening in Russia, for example, the distribution of income at the end of the process can be very different from that at the beginning. Mcreover instability can generate large swings in income distribution. VAT, in particular, may have significant regressive effects. Unfortunately no good studies have been carried out on its welfare impact in Latin American countries and East Europeans would do better to look to Western Europe for advice on the matter.

From our point of view, the main lessons emphasised by Izak in Chapter 3 regarding the role of fiscal policy in stabilisation are highly relevant. We agree with the danger of debt financing the government budget, the necessity for simplification of the tax system and the importance of tax administration. We also believe that one of the main lessons coming out of Latin America is that tight fiscal policy is a necessary but not sufficient condition for stabilisation. Indeed these conclusions are consistent with most analyses in the literature on stabilisation in developing countries.

It must be taken into account, however, that, although there seems to be a certain consensus in the literature on the fact that inertial forces are generally too strong to be tackled by fiscal policy alone, this by no means downgrades the importance of fiscal balance. In a paper in which he compares some of the experience of Eastern Europe, Latin America, South Korea and China, Solimano (1992) notes that the last two have often had large current account deficits, like Latin America, but have always kept the fiscal deficit within manageable bounds. Fanelli *et al.* (1992) also show that the stability and growth performance of Latin America countries during the debt crisis was highly correlated with the evolution of the fiscal deficit and the quality of fiscal policies. During the 1980s Chile and Colombia, which performed much better in terms of stability and growth, were able to bring the fiscal deficit under control and administer taxes and expenditure in a more efficient way than either Brazil or Argentina. The latter two countries did not succeed in sufficiently reducing the fiscal deficit and were therefore unable to stabilise their economies, in spite of the significant adjustment effort made in terms of reducing domestic absorption.

One point that deserves to be emphasised is that control of the fiscal deficit in Latin America is important because of the weaknesses of the financial structure. Even ignoring the possible negative effects of large deficits on the real side of the economy, fiscal disequilibrium cannot be large if there is a low degree of financial deepening. Given the smallness of the market for government bonds in the typical Latin American scenario, debt financing causes a rise in interest rates, which has strong repercussions on future deficits as well as crowding out private investment. In a situation where credit is rationed, the latter factor becomes all the more important. Dornbusch (1990) has argued that tight money is no substitute for fiscal reform. A restrictive monetary policy in the presence of a high deficit tends to increase interest rates, which makes the deficit worse because of the interest that must be paid on outstanding government debt and any new borrowing. If we take into account the fact that financial deepening and financial fragility are worse in the typical Eastern European country than in Latin America, it is clear that there is a lot to learn from both the mistakes and the achievements of Latin American countries regarding the coordination of fiscal and monetary policy.

The lack of independence between fiscal and monetary policy in a context of low financial deepening suggests that the implementation of fiscal reform in Eastern Europe cannot imply the generation of (even temporarily) large fiscal deficits. As has been the case in many Latin American countries in the past decade, this indicates that effective tax collection must be given priority over efficiency. Izak noted that much of the success of Latin American tax reform was coupled to administrative changes. Despite the intent, it seems likely to us that it will be some time before most Eastern European countries have a similar structure to the OECD countries. Even VAT, which is the centrepiece of many fiscal systems in Latin America, can be quite difficult to administer and typically has a long gestation period. Numerous authors, including Burgess and Stern (1993), argue that a country should only move away from trade taxes towards VAT if the administrative capability exists. Given that the World Bank estimates that the administration costs of tariffs are 1–3 per cent versus 5 per cent for VAT and 10 per cent for income taxes in a typical developing country, this appears to be good advice.[6]

One would expect, in particular, that VAT administration costs would be much higher than average in most Eastern European countries. One of the conclusions of an IMF seminar on transition economies was that it is very difficult to move to an optimal tax structure. In the short term such countries should gather taxes in whatever way they can.[7] Once again Bolivia may provide an important lesson here. The Bolivian government managed quickly to bring down hyperinflation by imposing very heavy taxes on petroleum products in order rapidly to reduce the enormous fiscal deficit. These taxes have been replaced slowly over time by more conventional ones.

Indeed the necessity for tight control over the fiscal deficit can put severe constraints not only on fiscal reforms but on other structural reforms as well. Given the underdeveloped administrative capabilities of the tax bureau in Bolivia, if the government had privatised the petroleum company it would have lost its only available instrument to achieve improved and better controlled tax collection. According to Solimano (1992), there are liberalisation measures acting in favour of budget equilibrium – such as the conversion of quotas to tariffs – that must be implemented at an earlier stage; but there are others, such as financial liberalisation, that – via increased interest rates and/or a financial crisis – can have huge fiscal costs and must therefore be postponed.

One point we would like to emphasise in addition to those raised by Izak in Chapter 3 is that the quality of fiscal reform not only affects stability but also the growth potential of the economy. Particularly important is the fact that in Latin America after the debt crisis, countries that were able to avoid severe and sudden reductions in public investment during the adjustment process grew at a faster rate (Fanelli *et al.* 1992). For example, Colombia and Chile recovered growth earlier and grew more rapidly than Argentina and Mexico, even though the latter two implemented policies aimed at curtailing the fiscal deficit that were as severe as those implemented in Chile and Colombia. The crucial difference was that Colombia and Chile managed to maintain the level of tax collection throughout the crisis, and consequently were able to maintain a reasonable level of public investment without disturbing the budget equilibrium.

In Argentina and Mexico, on the other hand, the crisis induced a severe reduction in tax collection, and the only way to reduce the fiscal deficit was to slash public spending. Public investment suffered the greatest cutback because reductions in other current expenditures were politically much more difficult and contentious. It seems that in countries lacking a good infrastructure, such as those in Latin America and Eastern Europe, public investment plays a crucial role in supporting private efforts during the growth process.

In addition to the constraints imposed by the necessity to avoid the collapse of public investment, in some Eastern European countries, and particularly in Russia, there is likely to be strong pressure to increase expenditure because of two factors. The first is environmental protection. For decades the Eastern European countries have been following a development strategy that has largely ignored ecological considerations, and as a consequence environmental problems have reached a critical point. In a recent paper Zhukov (1994) estimated that a Russian programme to dispose of dangerous nuclear and chemical weapons and protect the population from Chernobyl-type reactors would cost around 3.5 per cent of Russia's GDP per year. Total direct environmental expenditure in Russia at present is only 1.2 per cent of GDP.

A second factor that will probably have a strong effect on budget equilibrium during market transition and political democratisation is the allocation of fiscal responsibilities between central and local governments. The experience of Latin America can again be valuable. Chile has achieved a sustainable fiscal equilibrium, but expenditure and tax policies are designed and implemented in a highly centralised way. Brazil, on the other hand, is undergoing a period of strong fiscal disarray, largely due to the fact that – following the reform of the Constitution in 1988 – there was a dramatic increase in local government autonomy over expenditure decisions. In the case of Russia in particular, designing a new and sustainable financial base for federalism (that is, for the relationship between the Oblasti and the central government) is surely one of the most important issues on the fiscal reform agenda (Litvack and Wallich, 1993).

Finally, we would like to stress two items that are not given prominence in Chapter 3 – the interaction between macroeconomic and tax reform and the quasi-fiscal deficit. Tanzi (1989) has argued that the effects of macroeconomic reform on the fiscal deficit can easily swamp any changes arising from tax reform. In particular, this can be the case if there is a change in the real exchange rate, given that many government assets (rents on raw materials) and liabilities (foreign debt) are tightly linked to this variable. For example Perry (1992) reports that devaluation in Argentina, whose government was a net external debtor, from 1980–3 directly caused the fiscal deficit to rise by 3.2 per cent of GDP. On the other hand, devaluation in (net creditor) Chile from 1982–5 directly caused the fiscal deficit to fall by 7.1 per cent of GDP! Likewise, price liberalisation oriented towards correcting relative prices can result in the acceleration of inflation, as has been the case in many Eastern European countries, particularly Poland and Russia. Via the Olivera–Tanzi effect there could be sizeable reductions in the tax burden. In Argentina during the 1980s, for example, the Olivera–Tanzi effect induced reductions in tax collections of more than 2 per cent of GDP in periods of inflation acceleration.

The deficit generated by the Central Bank due to such actions as subsidising foreign exchange and interest rates or supporting failing commercial banks was often enormous in Latin America in the 1980s. However, one suspects that, given the bad-loan problem referred to above with respect to privatisation, this quasi-fiscal deficit problem will really come into its own in Eastern Europe. There are two obvious lessons from Latin America on the subject, both somewhat facile. First, governments should not try to hide it by not presenting consolidated accounts that include the financial sector. Second, they should take it very seriously right from the start. However, it is not clear that Latin America has any more concrete lessons for Eastern Europe on the subject, given that the magnitude of the problem, both with regard to bad debts and the lack of financial institutions, is far beyond anything that countries in the former region had to deal with.

Monetary Policy

Nikolay Karagodin of Russia authored a paper on the lessons that Eastern Europe, with a strong emphasis on Russia, could learn from Latin America in the area of monetary policy. This is presented here as Chapter 5. His analysis focused very much on stabilisation policy as a whole and much less on structural adjustment. He begins by examining the different types of stabilisation policy in Latin American – orthodox, heterodox and what he calls a pragmatic combination. He then analyses in more detail the Southern Cone experience of the late 1970s. The last two sections are on the conditions for a sustainable stabilisation and the failed monetary reform in Russia in 1992.

Karagodin asks whether austerity is sufficient to achieve stabilisation and finds that in Latin America the answer was no. Inflation inertia and the related problems of credibility and coordination prevented inflation from reaching the desired levels. As people often expected the programme to fail, prices and wages were set on this basis. Moreover, no one wanted to be the first to reduce the rate of increase of prices or wages. To make matters worse, stabilisation plans were often accompanied by programmes of structural reform, in particular trade liberalisation. Generally this led to real exchange rate depreciation, which not only increased pressure on the rate of inflation but also affected the fiscal deficit, which is often closely tied to the exchange rate.[8] The main lessons Eastern Europe can learn from the experience of Latin America with orthodox programmes are: (1) money-based stabilisation plans have a high cost in terms of output and employment; (2) in countries with a long tradition of indexation, attempts to prevent moderate inflation by use of an orthodox plan are unlikely to be successful; and (3) floating exchange rates are not very compatible with price stabilisation due to their direct effect on inflation, their effect on the fiscal deficit and the instability they are likely to generate, including speculative runs on the local currency.[9]

Before looking at more obvious heterodox plans, Karagodin analyses a number of exchange-rate-based orthodox stabilisation plans. While these have often been more successful than the first group, they have usually led to problems because of the real appreciation they entail. As domestic inflation in Latin America generally has not fallen to the level of international inflation rates, exchange rates have slowly and surely appreciated. There have often been booms of import consumption in anticipation of future depreciation. While generally in favour of such plans, Karagodin's main conclusion is that a fixed nominal exchange rate cannot be used as an anchor for too long and eventually it must be replaced with other instruments, such as a crawling peg combined with more traditional monetary and fiscal instruments.

Finally, on the subject of orthodox stabilisation plans, he notes that there were very definite reasons for the success of two of these. First, Bolivia – which had no history of high inflation – was suffering from hyperinflation. As the country had become almost completely dollarised, fixing the exchange rate was almost sufficient to remedy the situation. Second, the Chilean success of 1983–4 not only followed a long period of austerity but was greatly helped by the fact that a depreciation of the currency had very positive repercussions for the fiscal deficit due to the importance of the state copper enterprise, CODELCO. Stabilisation in both countries was greatly aided by large inflows of external aid (Bolivia) or debt rescheduling (Chile), which gave the respective governments more time to deal with the problem of their long-term fiscal deficits.

In the section on heterodox stabilisation Karagodin mainly discusses the failed Austral and Cruzado Plans of the mid-1980s. He notes that the early success of these incomes policy based plans was soon lost due to the misalignment of relative prices. Nevertheless there is a lesson to be learned in that the plans were able to bring down inflation quickly and without the customary recession. However fiscal and monetary restraint were required to support the plans. Little was done in either Argentina or Brazil during the terms of these plans to address the problem of the fiscal deficit.

The next section looks at two plans that contained (or contain) a pragmatic combination of heterodox and orthodox elements – the Mexican stabilisation of 1987 and the Cavallo Plan, which began in 1991. The plans had a number of similarities, including nominal exchange rate anchors (although a crawling one in the case of Mexico), an emphasis on trade liberalisation to keep inflation down, and tight monetary and fiscal policies. The main differences were the importance of a tripartite social pact in Mexico and the introduction of the Convertibility Law in Argentina. This law obliged the government to convert Argentinean pesos one for one for American dollars and was designed to boost confidence in the peso and the continuity of the plan. While both plans have achieved a great deal of success, they have also led to real appreciation of the exchange rates in both countries and very large current account imbalances. The lessons that Karagodin draws for Eastern Europe are: (1) a stabilisation plan needs to use all the available tools at the country's disposal and should be tailor made; (2) while it may be necessary to limit the flexibility of some key prices, this should not be overdone; (3) a social pact is a useful way of distributing the costs of stabilisation; and (4) too much import liberalisation can threaten external equilibrium and ultimately destroy the stabilisation plan.

In his discussion of the Southern Cone experience of the late 1970s, Karagodin highlights a couple of elements. First, full liberalisation of interest rates during a period of high inflation generally leads to very high real interest rates. Second, liberalisation of external capital flows before domestic stabilisation can lead to enormous swings in the capital account of the balance of payments, depending on the current state of expectations. When real interest rates are also high, the situation becomes especially destabilising.

In the next section Karagodin discusses the social and political aspects that are necessary to sustain stabilisation. First, stabilisation is an exercise in coalition building. Second, there are generally severe or significant effects on output and employment, so it is necessary not to alienate too many important social groups. Third, strong executive power is required in order to persuade unwilling social groups to make the necessary sacrifices.

Fourth, while type of government does not seem to be very important, those leading the transition to democracy must carry the extra burden of dealing with pent-up distributive expectations. Finally, some groups will probably have to be compensated for their losses. On all of these fronts, stabilisation is made easier if there is sustained external financing.

In his analysis of the monetary reform of Russia that began in January 1992, Karagodin first points out that it followed very similar lines to orthodox plans in Latin America, with many of the same results. The failure of the tight monetary policy to bring down inflation was due to a number of reasons: (1) a high degree of monopolisation – in monopolised sectors prices went up and quantities down; (2) the prices of raw materials, which historically had been held well below international prices, rose rapidly; (3) very tight credit policy resulted in a huge increase in real interest rates; (4) given the uncertainty and the general lack of credit, investment fell dramatically; and (5) in military industries demand fell enormously.

Instead of inefficient producers closing down there was merely a large accumulation of arrears to suppliers. In fact other industries were not allowed to stop supplying bankrupt customers. Finally, in mid-1992 there was a need for a massive monetary injection to provide credit to these bankrupt firms and inflation soared.

Karagodin sees a number of lessons that Russia can learn from Latin America. First, stabilisation via monetary instruments is not enough – it is also necessary to obtain fiscal balance and stabilise the exchange rate. However, these are both very difficult to achieve in present-day Russia as much of the economy – and accordingly much of taxable income and foreign exchange – has gone underground. Even in primary products, which are the main source of foreign exchange, most of the profits are going through illegal channels and ending up in foreign bank accounts. It is imperative, according to Karagodin, for Russia to curtail capital flight.

Second, given the giant fall in production that is inevitable during the transition process, Russia will need large amounts of external aid. Without such resources the cost will be too high and there will be too much opposition to the reforms.

The third lesson from Latin America that seems especially pertinent to Russia is the need for a strong executive power. Since the transition process began, Russia has been plagued by a series of weak governments that have been unable to push reforms through without seriously compromising their goals. Only an executive that is able to unite disparate elements into some form of social coalition seems likely to succeed in the foreseeable future.

In their companion chapter (Chapter 7) Marcelo Abreu and José María Fanelli first note that while external support is often necessary to the success of a stabilisation plan, in Latin America it has only been forthcoming when the plan has been orthodox – and such plans do not have a very good track record. They argue that the sustained stability that many Latin American countries have recently experienced has been due to the renewed availability of external credit, much of which is due to low US interest rates. Moreover innovation in policy making – that is, the implementation of heterodox plans – has usually only been possible when the country has had sufficient reserves to 'go it alone'. Until Russia is able to establish some control over foreign exchange flows (and reduce capital flight), it is not likely to be able to move significantly away from traditional orthodox plans. Abreu and Fanelli also think that Karagodin could have put greater emphasis on the breakdown of the CMEA trading bloc, which meant that Russia had completely to reorganise its commercial flows at a time of extreme macroeconomic instability.

Abreu and Fanelli agree with Karagodin's emphasis on the need for political stability. Like Russia, Brazil's inability to reach a satisfactory fiscal position – a prerequisite for enduring macroeconomic stability – has been strongly influenced by the political instability of the 1980s. In fact the experience of Brazil and other Latin American countries suggests that the sequencing of political and economic reforms can be as important as the sequencing of strictly economic measures.

They also believe that Russia has much to learn from Latin America on sequencing as it is structurally adjusting in a situation of macroeconomic disequilibrium, a juggling act often performed in Latin America. In such situations structural reforms are often pursued primarily because they reduce macro imbalances. Structural reforms are often at odds with market liberalisation – for example the Convertibility Plan in Argentina, the de facto nationalisation of Chile's financial system in the early 1980s and the Mexican social pact, with its tight controls on prices and wages. In summary, a strong lesson coming out of Latin America for policy makers in Russia and other Eastern European countries is that stabilisation and structural reforms are interdependent, with complicated interactions between them.

Finally, they argue that Russia should put its efforts into market creation, not market liberalisation. In a country where there are, for example, no short-run financial assets to hedge against inflation or long-run assets for the smoothing of government expenditure, it is a bit facile to speak of freeing markets and many of the questions traditionally examined under the heading of stabilisation policy are rendered rather meaningless. To meet these challenges the state will have to play a large role in the coming years; hence Karagodin's emphasis on the need for a strong executive power.

We will now discuss some qualifications and extensions to Karagodin's chapter. Given the underdeveloped character of financial systems in Eastern European countries, monetary policy has a limited role to play and financial liberalisation is almost reduced to the liberalisation of external capital flows. However there are a few more specific points that we would like to bring out.[10]

Karagodin, in particular, stressed the fact that money-based stabilisation has had little success in Latin America and has incurred a very high cost in terms of employment and output. Inertial factors have usually been so important that monetary brakes have not worked. Whether this will be the case in Eastern Europe will depend on the importance of inertial factors in these countries coupled with the expectations generated. While in general one would expect the former to be much less serious in Eastern Europe, the negative expectations caused by any further deepening of the current depression could be disastrous.

The most pressing problem faced by most Eastern European countries in the monetary sphere was the large monetary overhang caused by years of queuing and rationing. These overhangs caused price shocks of various sizes when prices were liberalised. The belief (or hope) was that these would be once-and-for-all jumps that would result in a new equilibrium when the demand and supply of money reached equilibrium. However in many cases this has only happened slowly or, as in the case of Russia, is barely happening at all. Latin America has only one good example to offer with regard to this problem – Chile in 1973. With a monetary overhang of about 500 per cent the government tried to get rid of it via price liberalisation but without monetary reform. There was a large price jump, followed by several years of high and moderate inflation. Inertial factors proved too strong and the relatively closed economy of the time meant that international prices did not play a decisive role in keeping down inflation.[11]

Even if the problem of monetary overhang were to be resolved and/or the inertial factors were not important, one question would still remain: is it possible for Eastern European countries to have a monetary policy in the sense in which this policy tool is usually conceived of in a capitalist economy? In order to assess this question, three features of the financial system in the Eastern European countries are likely to be present for a long time and hence must be taken into account.

The first is the lack of a developed market for government bonds. As mentioned before, it is very difficult to think of an independent monetary policy in a context in which the reduced size of the bond markets render unfeasible open-market operations and/or the financing of the deficit via bonds. The Latin American experience – characterised by difficulty in developing wide bond markets – teaches us that, beyond the obstacles posed by inertial factors, more often than not monetary restraint fails simply because monetary authorities cannot keep the monetary base under control.

The two most frequent reasons for this are as follows. First, tough monetary policies tend to be recessionary and the fall in the activity level widens the fiscal deficit. This is reinforced by the fact that in the typical stabilisation package, monetary restraint is normally accompanied by devaluation, which has usually been contractionary in Latin America, at least in the short run. Under such circumstances the impossibility of fulfilling government borrowing needs in the domestic credit market ultimately leads to the monetisation of the deficit and hence to the loosening of monetary policy. Second, it is normal for monetary restraint to result in marked increases in interest rates. In a context of very low financial deepening, this usually induces large financial disequilibria in the banking system and the Central Bank is obliged to act as lender of last resort, thereby relaxing the control of monetary aggregates. In Latin America this monetary trap could only be bypassed when the stabilisation package was supported by foreign credit – making it possible to finance the deficit by means of increasing foreign indebtedness – and/or if the devaluation had a positive effect on the fiscal budget. Brazil and Argentina – with their tax structures tightly related to the domestic activity level – provide the best examples of the difficulty of having an independent monetary policy, while Chile – and to a lesser extent Mexico – represent the opposite case because of the positive fiscal consequences of devaluation. If one takes this into account, Sachs's recent complaints about the lack of external support for Russia's stabilisation effort can be easily understood (Sachs, 1994).

The second feature of the Eastern European economies that casts doubt on the effectiveness of monetary policy is the lack of a suitable definition of property rights. The existence of a 'grey zone' with regard to property rights implies that there is no clear definition of the agent's budget constraints, creating an economy populated by agents facing a soft budget constraint. Given that monetary contraction can only restrain effective demand by tightening the budget constraint, if the latter is ambiguously defined contractionary monetary policy is unlikely to reduce expenditure. The 'bad loans' problem is the most important manifestation of this fact. In the textbook example, monetary contraction creates an excess demand for loanable funds in the banking system, which is supposed to generate a deflationary trend by inducing an excess supply for goods. However, if agents can finance their expenditure by forcing state banks or other public enterprises to accommodate any demand for credit, it is obvious that the excess demand for loanable funds will never occur. The failure of the Gaidar stabilisation attempt in 1992 in Russia is a good example of this. The programme, based on monetary restraint as a means of stabilisation, led first to the accumulation of bad debts and afterwards to the loss of control of monetary expansion by the authorities, which were ultimately obliged to validate inflation (Ofer, 1992).

The third characteristic we would like to highlight – as a constraint to monetary policy – is the tendency for many Eastern European countries to increase the level of dollarisation in the absence of domestic assets that can act as an effective hedge against inflation. The question of whether to dollarise is one that many countries in Latin America and Eastern Europe have had to confront. One of the main reasons for dollarising is to reduce capital flight. However dollarisation and capital flight have similar results in that they both reduce the domestic monetary base – either by increases in velocity or simple substitution – and reduce the amount of inflation tax. Therefore a country dependent on revenues from this source will have to be careful about how it moves. Although the end result may be similar, the higher transaction costs of capital flight may make this the preferred option. Dornbusch and Reynoso (1989, p. 89) also argue that dollarisation makes the domestic banking system very vulnerable to devaluations and tends to lead to an overvalued exchange rate. The experience from Latin America suggests that dollarisation can be very helpful for stabilisation, but it generally means that most bank deposits will be in foreign currencies until full credibility is restored to the economy.

However it must be taken into account that the authorities are not likely to be free to choose whether to dollarise the economy or not. The Latin American experience of the 1980s seems to show that some degree of dollarisation is an inherent feature of highly unstable situations and that, more importantly, dollarisation tends to remain even after stabilisation has been achieved. In many Latin American countries (Uruquay, Argentina, Peru and Bolivia) during the years of high inflation that followed the debt crisis, there was a huge reduction in the demand for money and a permanent increase in the demand for foreign currency. This feature did not disappear in Bolivia and Argentina after inflation had been dramatically reduced.

The Argentine case is particularly relevant in this context. After three years of stability the inflation rate is now around 5 per cent per year. The fall in the inflation rate induced a marked remonetisation of the economy.

The process of remonetisation has nonetheless revealed two important features that suggest that the consequences of the previous crisis have been only partially reversed. First, the liquidity coefficient in pesos is currently lower than it was when the inflation rate was 100 per cent per year. Second, the most dynamic component of the demand for domestic assets is the demand for dollar-denominated deposits (the so-called 'argendollars'), and therefore the major part of the newly generated credit is also denominated in dollars. As a consequence dollar-denominated financial assets at present account for more than 50 per cent of total domestic financial assets. In summary, a kind of hysteresis effect acting against the recovery of the demand for domestic assets seems to be present in the post-stabilisation period. A similar story could be told in relation to Bolivia and, *mutatis mutandis*, for the cases of Uruguay and Peru.

The irreversibility of the dollarisation process – and of its counterpart, a fall in the demand for domestic assets – puts a further constraint on the implementation of an effective monetary policy. Since the Central Bank only controls the supply of pesos, the greater the degree of dollarisation, the lower the capacity to implement an independent 'national' monetary policy.

From what has been said above it follows that it is necessary to bring about a profound change in the Eastern European countries' financial structures, not only to ensure improved allocation of resources but also to make stabilisation easier. Is financial liberalisation a feasible alternative? From our point of view, financial liberalisation does not appear to offer much promise in the current situation of most Eastern European countries, and it will have to proceed very slowly at first, with a strong emphasis on institution building.

The Southern Cone experience of financial liberalisation resulting in high interest rates has been similar in a number of Asian countries, with widespread bankruptcy and the need for a government bail-out of the banking system. In their extensive study of financial liberalisation in Asia, Cho and Khatkhate (1989) argue that it should never be used as a stabilisation device as it just makes things worse. The question for us is how relevant is this for Eastern Europe, with its very underdeveloped financial system. Leite and Sundararajan (1990) argue that, if there are many other market imperfections, interest rate liberalisation will result in a very wide spread. It is also likely to be necessary to restructure the many banks that would fail due to a liberalisation of interest rates. The speed of the reform should depend partly on the ability of the government to recapitalise weak institutions and design and introduce new monetary instruments, particularly those that can act as a hedge against inflation.

Attempts to liberalise the financial systems in Eastern Europe appear to have stumbled upon other more important obstacles.[12] First, as discussed above enormous difficulties have to be overcome before commercial banks can be privatised, the most notable of which is the great number of bad debts in their portfolios. Second, in countries that have broken up large state banks, the new smaller institutions have often become associated, officially or otherwise, with certain firms and sectors, resulting in a Chilean-like situation where firms are lending to themselves through the banks they control. That is, financial reform is associated with a significant principal-agent problem caused by the combination of an enormous number of bad loans and a lack of regulatory powers. In addition, credit restrictions have been circumvented, as noted by Karagodin in Chapter 5, by interenterprise trade credits. In Russia, for example, firms are afraid that if they do not provide these credits their suppliers will go bankrupt and they will be unable to continue as they do not have access to foreign exchange.[13] Once again it seems that the bad debt problem has to be cleared up before this difficulty can be adequately addressed. Perhaps Fanelli and Frenkel (1992) are correct when they comment that a well-developed financial sector is more an indicator of development than a causal factor.

External Trade and Finance

In Chapter 6 Andrzej Slawinski discusses the lessons that Eastern Europe, with a strong emphasis on Poland, can learn from Latin America in the areas of external trade and finance. Like that of Karagodin in Chapter 5, his analysis very much centres on stabilisation, emphasising however the role that the external sector might play in the stabilisation process. He looks first at adjustment policies in Latin America, then at those in Poland, and finally he discusses the lessons learned.

In his introduction, Slawinski says that 'The main lesson for Eastern Europe [with regard to the external sector] is that external liberalisation goes through a long period of stabilisation'. He bases this conclusion on the observation that whenever stabilisation has failed, there has been backsliding on the liberalisation of the external sector. He begins his analysis with a section on the Southern Cone experience of the late 1970s and early 1980s, focusing on Chile and Argentina. He sees a number of lessons for Eastern Europe in these 'experiments'. First, liberalisation where financial markets are underdeveloped can lead to misaligned relative prices, especially the exchange rate and interest rates. Second, capital market liberalisation – if it leads to inflows – can cause an exchange rate appreciation, which moves production to nontradables, the exact opposite of what is intended. Third, unless fiscal deficit is controlled, trade liberalisation has very little chance of success. Fourth, and by far the most important, the Southern Cone experiments show that an attempt to stabilise via external liberalisation and 'the law of one price' is much more difficult than was believed at the time due to the problem of overshooting and expectations.

Slawinski then turns to the cases of Brazil and Mexico in the 1980s. In the first half of the 1980s Brazil made a number of attempts at orthodox stabilisation based on tight monetary policy and large devaluations. Despite major success in the current account, indexation caused inflation to remain very high. That is, successful trade liberalisation did not stabilise the macroeconomy. A substantial part of the Mexican stabilisation plan of 1987 was trade liberalisation. Unlike in the Southern Cone about 10 years earlier, the law of one price seemed to hold. However, a great deal of this success was due to the tripartite social pact that was negotiated at the same time as trade liberalisation took place. In the earlier cases of Argentina and Chile there had been no agreement on how to distribute the costs of liberalisation and stabilisation. A lesson that comes out of the comparison of Brazil and Mexico, in addition to the importance of some sort of social consensus, was the important role that external debtors can play. Mexico was given substantial debt relief at the time of its stabilisation cum liberalisation policy, while Brazil found itself with no external support and no possibility of significant capital flows.[14]

In the 1990s we are seeing an increasingly successful integration of Latin American economies with the rest of the world. Trade liberalisation and stabilisation have been completed successfully (or almost so) in more and more countries of the region, and have usually reinforced one another. Their success has been such that large capital inflows have come to the region, significant portions of which are investment capital. The only large negative factor is that there has been a strong currency appreciation in many countries, supported by these inflows, which is making it more difficult to export. However in many cases this may be more a sign of maturity as the economy moves towards a new long-run external equilibrium, and should not cause undue alarm.

In the early 1990s Poland suffered many of Brazil's experiences on the external front. It had a huge foreign debt and high inflation, which was hidden in the form of a large monetary overhang. Large devaluations in the early 1980s substantially eased the trade balance, but the government was unable to bring the fiscal deficit and monetary situation under control. As in Brazil, debt servicing put an enormous burden on the fiscal deficit.

In 1989 the Polish government launched its first large-scale economic reform programme. In no time the country was experiencing hyperinflation due to the large rise in liberalised food prices, the introduction of wage indexation and, most importantly, the premature liberalisation of the foreign exchange market. The latter led to dollarisation, reducing tremendously the monetary base from which to obtain inflation tax.

In 1990 a tough adjustment called the Balcerowicz Plan was introduced. Wage indexation was restricted, financial policies were very restrictive and a convertible currency was introduced with a fixed rate of exchange with the US dollar. The intent of this plan was to reduce domestic absorption and free resources for export, very similar to what took place in Mexico and Brazil in the 1980s. By limiting wage indexation and restricting access to credit, firms were forced to export. However, the success of such a plan depends to a great extent on the ability of firms to redirect their sales from domestic to foreign markets as well as high mobility of factors of production between sectors. The recessions that characterised Latin America in the 1980s were partly due to the fact that these conditions were only partially fulfilled. In Eastern European economies such as Poland they were hardly fulfilled at all. The result was a very large fall in production. Nevertheless, inflation was greatly reduced and the current account moved from deficit to surplus.

Very shortly, however, the government had to deal with a predicament experienced by many Latin American countries – the exchange rate was slowly appreciating. To curtail both this and the deterioration of the current account, the government introduced a crawling peg. However the rate of devaluation was slightly less than inflation, so the problem persisted. The government was reluctant to devalue the currency as it had not been able to bring the fiscal deficit under control and devaluation would add to the cost of debt servicing. At the same time, expectations of a devaluation led to high real interest rates, pushing many firms toward bankruptcy. In many cases the only funds available to firms were their own export earnings. It was beginning to look like the Southern Cone syndrome all over again.

In April 1991 Poland received a debt reduction package equal to about 50 per cent of the present value. This greatly relieved pressure on the fiscal deficit and provided a very positive signal to foreign investors. The latter were especially important to Poland because at the time almost all domestic credit was going towards financing the fiscal deficit (as inflation tax was very much circumscribed by the convertibility of the currency). Because of the shortage of domestic credit, Poland is not able to act upon one of the lessons to be learned from Latin America; that is, capital market liberalisation should be undertaken last in the sequence of reforms. However, Poland should learn from Latin America that it must do its best to discourage very short-term, highly speculative inflows.

In Chapter 7 Marcelo Abreu and José María Fanelli note that while Brazil is currently the economic laggard in Latin America, it can provide some important lessons for Eastern Europe from its numerous failures of the 1980s: (1) pure monetarist policies are inefficient in a highly indexed economy; (2) it is much easier to overcome a foreign exchange constraint than a fiscal constraint; (3) the failure of one stabilisation plan makes the next one all the more difficult; and (4) high inflation makes it more difficult to persist with other elements of the reform package. For example, of the broad economic reforms implemented in Brazil in 1990, only trade liberalisation and privatisation survived to 1994, and they are under increasing pressure to be modified. As Slawinski notes, the way to external liberalisation is through a long period of domestic stabilisation.

Abreu and Fanelli also note that some of the countries in Latin America and Eastern Europe that have succeeded, or seem to be succeeding, have received favourable debt deals. Part of the relative success of Poland could no doubt be attributed to the very favourable deal it received from the Paris Club negotiations.

Of all of the contributors to this book, it is Slawinski who has put more emphasis on the problems of sequencing faced by reform policies. In the area of trade and financial flow liberalisation, he draws a number of very strong lessons from Latin America. These include the importance of first establishing macroeconomic stabilisation, the negative effects of the liberalisation of capital markets in terms of exchange-rate appreciation, the difficulties of stabilisation based on trade liberalisation, and the interdependence between the real exchange rate and the fiscal deficit.

The ironic part of his analysis is the conclusion that Poland cannot follow one of the most important lessons to be derived from the Latin American experience: it needs foreign capital so badly that it must extensively liberalise its capital markets, and it risks the danger of an exchange-rate appreciation that could offset its drive to increase exports. However the evidence to date in Eastern Europe suggests that capital inflows will be nowhere near the magnitude of those that entered Latin America in the late 1970s and early 1990s. A more real danger seems to be that of inflation rising significantly above zero with a fixed exchange rate (or rising higher than the sliding peg). Although it must be taken into account that, either by wisdom or by luck (that is, because macroinstability during the liberalisation process induced an overshooting of the real exchange rate in relation to its equilibrium level), the 'fixed' exchange rate in some Eastern European countries, such as the Czech Republic and Poland, seems initially to have been undervalued, which has considerably reduced any damage caused by a subsequent real appreciation.

We nevertheless believe that the dangers of real appreciation during the adjustment process should not be underestimated. It can determine the success or failure of important reform policies. This is particularly so with regard to trade liberalisation because there is one important lesson from Latin America that does not seem to have been learnt by Eastern European countries. In spite of the fact that in Latin America rapid trade liberalisation with regard to both imports and exports generally resulted in short-run current account deficits of considerable magnitude, Eastern European countries have put into practice ambitious programmes of trade liberalisation. Bruno (1992) and Solimano (1992) both argue that Eastern European countries should have moved more slowly on tariff reduction, a move that would probably have been politically acceptable, both domestically and internationally, given the frail nature of their economies and the OECD barriers faced by them.

In general, there has been excessive optimism about the speed of response to trade liberalisation on the export side. Perhaps the reason for moving so quickly on tariff reduction was to try to reduce inflation by the 'law of one price'. However, a fairly flat tariff structure could have done the same; that is, the law of one price plus, for example, 30 per cent. In discussing the adjustment of Russian defence-related enterprises, Kuznetsov (1993) also suggests that, during the restructuring process, some degree of protection via tariffs may be required.[15] Given that the reallocation of productive factors is not instantaneous, the idea is to encourage factor reallocation by giving firm signals that there will be strong tariff reductions in the future while maintaining some protection in the short run in order to minimise the costs in terms of unemployment and the loss of human capital. It could be argued that subsidising firms in the restructuring sectors would be better. However, in the present context of high fiscal deficits, institutional disarray and the low administrative capacity of the states concerned, this alternative does not seem to be feasible. Indeed it is precisely because of this latter reason that exchange-rate appreciation should be avoided. A high exchange rate – not costly from an administrative point of view – is a suitable tool to protect those parts of the industry that deserve to be restructured. Furthermore, the higher the real exchange rate, the lower the level of tariffs required to protect potentially viable sectors.

Regarding restructuring and competitiveness, two additional lessons for Eastern Europe from Latin America deserve to be mentioned here. First there is a general one, stressed by authors as diverse as Cooper (1991) and Helleiner (1990), that one of the most important factors in export expansion is the maintenance of a stable real exchange rate. Second, Meller

(1992) indicates the role that promotion of nontraditional exports – such as forest products, fruit and fish – has played in the adjustment of the Chilean economy.

In Chapter 6 Slawinski notes that Poland has found itself in an uncomfortable situation via-à-vis the relationship between the level of the exchange rate, the current account deficit and the fiscal deficit. As we have noted, one of the strongest lessons to come out of Latin America was the importance of the relationship between real devaluation and the fiscal deficit. Poland belongs to the group of countries with net external debt, which means that devaluation, which presumably helps the current account, hurts the fiscal deficit. Therefore, it has had to play a careful balancing act in this regard. The discussion by Abreu and Fanelli in Chapter 7 suggests that Poland should pay more attention to the fiscal deficit than to the current account deficit, as the latter is easier to rectify. Although good advice – especially if Brazil's experience is taken into account – it needs to be weighed very carefully.

As has been the case in Latin America, the policy dilemma regarding the 'correct' level of the exchange rate is very difficult to resolve, especially if political economy considerations are brought into the picture: a lagging exchange rate is tempting because it can improve the fiscal situation 'without visible social costs'. In spite of this the Polish authorities should not lose sight of the fact that, in the long run, social costs – particularly in terms of high unemployment – could be very high if real appreciation were to make the required restructuring of the industrial sector more difficult or lead to an unsustainable current account deficit.

Indeed the recent evolution of Latin America shows that this problem is far from easy to resolve. The question is not qualitative – that is, to choose between fiscal and current disequilibrium – but one of degree – to follow an exchange-rate policy capable of maintaining an acceptable degree of macrostability in terms of the fiscal gap and inflation without hurting the economy's competitiveness. The evolution of economic policy in the 1990s in Brazil and Argentina provides two polar cases in this respect. Brazil has chosen to favour external competitiveness via the maintenance of a high real exchange rate, and as a consequence it is the only important Latin American country today to show a sizeable trade surplus. The costs of this policy in terms of fiscal disequilibrium and inflation have been very high. Argentina, in contrast, has managed to bring about strong disinflation and to achieve fiscal equilibrium by following a policy based on a nominally constant exchange rate. The appreciation of the real exchange rate that has resulted from this policy has brought about a large and increasing current-account disequilibrium. This strategy is highly risky because the country's vulnerability to external shocks – that is, the reversal of large capital inflows – is very high. It seems that the optimal response to the trade-off between fiscal and current account equilibrium must lie somewhere between these polar cases.

1.3 CONCLUSION: STABILISATION, STRUCTURAL REFORM AND ECONOMIC POLICY

The project that led to this book was designed to cover the areas that *a priori* we believed to be most important for Eastern Europe – fiscal policy, privatisation, monetary and financial policy, and trade policy.[16] In this final section we will present what we consider to be the main conclusions that can be drawn from our work. By investigating each of the areas chosen we have naturally gone into the problem of the relationship between stabilisation and structural adjustment, although in a somewhat random fashion. Accordingly we present our conclusions on the subjects treated in this chapter by taking into account the problems posed by the interactions between stabilisation and structural reform. From the point of view of such problems, the most important issues are the order of implementation of the stabilisation and reform policies (the problem of 'sequencing') and the closely related question of the speed of the process (shock therapy versus gradualism).

Eastern Europe has some major problems to deal with that either did not exist or were much less important in Latin America. These include the general lack of institutions, the absence of an adequate legal framework, the massive scale of privatisation, the problem of commercial banks, and the enormous bad-loan problem. It is clear that a necessary condition for tackling the latter three problems is achieving some degree of success in solving the first two. Institutional building, then, must be given priority in the sequence, and it should begin with the reconstruction of the most important institution of capitalism: property. Without a clarification of property rights on the basis of a sound, clearly defined and enforceable legal system, it is unlikely that massive privatisation of large firms can take place or a financial system develop. If property rights are diffused, the badly needed contribution of foreign investors is unlikely to occur and national investors will prefer capital flight to financial or productive investment within the country.

Another necessary condition is achieving a minimum degree of macroeconomic stability. Nonetheless the common advice to stabilise first and then structurally adjust cannot be applied to Eastern Europe – it is impossible to wait for the latter as it is happening in front of our eyes, and in any case the former is probably dependent on it. Consequently some degree of overlap between stabilisation and structural reform seems to be unavoidable. This implies that the true problem is that of selecting which reforms should be encouraged and which should be delayed until stability is well-rooted. Given this caveat, perhaps the two most important lessons to be learned from Latin America in this regard are (1) that the fiscal deficit should be dealt with as soon as possible, and (2) that financial liberalisation should be effected very slowly. Nevertheless the repercussions of the bad-debt problem make this more complex than in Latin America. In some respects many Eastern European countries find themselves in an end game. Resolution of the fiscal deficit problem depends partially on the removal of subsidies to large firms, but these firms cannot be privatised until the first (major) steps of financial reform have been undertaken; that is, the restructuring, recapitalisation and privatisation of commercial banks. However these reforms are likely to have very strong effects on the fiscal deficit!

We also believe that fiscal reform will probably follow a sequence within the larger adjustment sequence as different possibilities reveal themselves. For example, early in the adjustment process very high taxes on goods such as petroleum may be necessary; privatisation revenues may be of some importance in the next stage and a more full-blown fiscal reform in the last stages. It is important to emphasise that an optimal tax system is not likely to be obtained for many years.[17]

Another important conclusion from our study is that, during the process of stabilisation and adjustment, the role of the exchange rate is often crucial. We have seen that devaluation of the real exchange rate can have a very strong effect on the fiscal deficit in either direction. It is of fundamental importance that this relationship is well known within a given country and that allowance is made for it. For example, if a devaluation has a strong negative effect on the fiscal deficit it is likely that trade liberalisation will have to proceed much more slowly than would otherwise be the case (or fiscal reform much faster, if feasible). The exchange rate may also pay a strong role in the stabilisation process, especially if it is used as an anchor. Once again this use of the exchange rate may be at odds with rapid trade liberalisation. The lesson from Latin America in this regard is not to rely on the exchange rate as an anchor for too long as a real appreciation is likely to occur. Nevertheless, if a government's fiscal accounts benefit from a real appreciation, *ceteris paribus* the duration of this anchor can be longer.

It is also important to begin trade liberalisation at an early stage, although we have noted above that it may have moved too rapidly. According to Corbo (1992), taking into account the Latin America experience, the initial stages of trade reform should be the replacement of managed trade for open trade, the replacement of quantitative restrictions for tariffs, and the reduction of extreme tariffs. More important than trade liberalisation *per se*, however, is the need to concentrate first on two or three sectors with high potential. These sectors can then provide an impetus (and surplus) to the economy at large. The World Bank (1992) country study on Russia, for example, notes the large potential of the oil and agricultural sectors in that country. In fact this seems to be precisely the strategy followed by Vietnam, one of the most successful transition economies in the world, which put a heavy reliance on oil and agriculture in the first stage of its structural adjustment.[18] In other words, the authorities should complement commercial policies with sectoral or industrial policies in order to make the opening of the economy more efficient and less painful with respect to employment.

Where does privatisation fit into the sequence? From our study it follows that the privatisation of small-scale firms should be sped up while the privatisation of large firms should be carefully planned, even at the cost of delaying the process. This conclusion seems to be in accordance with the recent literature. For example Fischer (1991) suggests that the key to the long-run transformation of the former socialist economies may lie less in the privatisation of very large industrial firms – many of them dinosaurs – than in the development of new firms and the growth of existing smaller firms. For that reason, rapid progress in other areas of the reform can be just as important to the development of a vibrant private sector as the privatisation of large firms. Solimano (1992) notes that massive privatisation of large-scale firms can have either stabilising or destabilising macroeconomic effects. Likewise, given the importance of some large enterprises in the industrial sector, as in the case of Russia's defence-related sector, the privatisation process should be coordinated with commercial and sectoral policies.

It does not seem likely that liberalisation of domestic financial markets can be undertaken until the commercial bank problem has been rectified. If the price to pay for the institutional reconstruction of the banking system is maintaining it under the partial control of the state and maintaining a certain degree of financial repression, such a price may be worth paying. The only caveat is that negative interest rates should be avoided. Even McKinnon, one of the founding fathers of the financial liberalisation approach, has recently acknowledged that the failure to recognise the need for official action to limit bank lending rates was partly responsible for the financial collapses in the Southern Cone (McKinnon, 1991). In the same vein, Stiglitz (1993) has recently called attention to the potentially positive role of the state in the financial system in developing countries. The rationale is that in such countries market failures are almost undoubtedly greater than in the more developed countries.

One of the most important lessons from Latin America is that full liberalisation of the capital account is fraught with dangers, and consequently should be delayed for as long as possible. We have seen, nonetheless, that the desperate need for capital may force countries into a less than optimal sequence. This tension between the objectives of preserving financial and macroeconomic stability on the one hand, and the need for capital on the other, could indeed be an important source of economic policy dilemmas and macroeconomic stress in Eastern Europe in the future. The main problem is that the increase in capital inflows that normally follows the opening of the capital account tends to induce both domestic currency appreciation and an excess of loanable funds, which the typically weak banking system cannot efficiently allocate.

Argentina and Mexico at present are good examples of this. In recent years these countries have received large capital inflows, and the greater availability of credit has stimulated important increases in investment. However, to the extent that capital inflows have also produced a misalignment of relative prices, a good part of the increase in investment has been allocated to producing nontradables. Likewise the increase in the credit supply has also encouraged consumption, damaging the badly needed recovery in national saving rates. Due to these effects on investment and savings, it is unclear whether these countries will be able to repay external credit in the future without significant macroeconomic adjustments.

One way out of this dilemma could be to rely on nonmarket sources of foreign capital. The availability of foreign aid and grants could play an important role in helping Eastern European countries to move to some sort of optimal sequence if they are committed to maintaining a sensible structure of relative prices. The successful experience of Chile in the 1980s – Chile received important amounts of nonmarket external credit stemming from multilateral organisations and simultaneously preserved a competitive exchange rate – can be a source of suitable lessons for both Eastern European policy makers and the advisors of multilateral organisations.

Note that we have not mentioned labour markets in the above sequence. The study by Horton, Kanbur and Mazumdar (1991) suggests that for better or worse labour markets tend to adjust themselves during major structural upheavals. Nevertheless it is likely that the Eastern European countries will ultimately have to pay much more serious attention to the development of modern, skilled labour forces.[19]

Shock therapy has not had a very happy experience in Latin America except in cases of hyperinflation, although it seems to have been, with the exception of Russia, good medicine for the monetary overhang problem faced by most Eastern European countries.[20] However, as in Latin America, it is questionable whether countries had much to gain from a big bang. The need for institutional development and creation was so strong that wherever a big bang was tried, the response was much slower than expected, as Bruno (1992) has noted. Bruno also commented that part of the highly imperfect CMEA structure should have been maintained in the early years of the adjustment, in order to soften the enormous blow that GDP suffered in all the countries of Eastern Europe.

Another point in favour of gradualism is that it seems to be much more 'growth friendly' than the big-bang strategy, as the recent experiences of China and Vietnam seem to show.[21] Within a gradual framework of structural adjustment, there is much more scope to implement industrial policies for key sectors in order to minimise the costs of adjustment. In economies such as Russia, a series of agreements with the main industries on targets for the contraction of output, levels of employment and credit levels is badly needed (Ofer, 1992). It should be kept in mind that the increase in the population's welfare is the ultimate goal of the process, and consequently growth should be the outcome of the present efforts to transform the economic structure. From the point of view of growth, the problem is how to ensure the formation of linkages from the leading and potentially booming sectors of the economy (such as oil, gas and forestry in Russia) to manufacturing (currently largely relegated to the former military complex) (Kuznetsov, 1993); and how to foster productivity increases in economies where in the past, as Solimano (1990) indicates, the low pace of technical progress has heavily contributed to the slowdown in secular growth.

Indeed it seems that after the first 'heroic' stage, during which the move towards capitalism was accelerated no matter what the price, a new consensus is emerging that is much more favourable to gradualism with regard to stabilization and structural reform. McKinnon has recently summed up the core of this new consensus. After praising the greater efficiency of the gradual strategy of China compared with the Russian big-bang approach, he concludes:

In the short run, successful macroeconomic stabilization requires a major (re)centralization of the government's control over money and credit – and a reassertion of the primacy of the state-controlled banking system with the elimination of independent 'wildcat' banks. Due to the special characteristics of socialist industry, price setting at the producer level – including the exchange rate – may also have to be recentralized as part of the stabilization package. So we have an unfortunate policy dilemma: to secure macroeconomic stabilization in the near term, important banking and commodity pricing policies may have to move counter to what most of us would like to see for the long-run liberalization of the Russian economy (McKinnon, 1993, p. 23).

Gradualism, on the other hand, does not mean that economic policy should passively adapt to the current situation. It should be appreciated that some of the countries of Eastern Europe and the former Soviet Union (including large parts of Russia) are moving so slowly in the adjustment process that it is more proper to call it incrementalism than gradualism. Such an incremental approach does not seem capable of obtaining sufficient momentum to make the process self-motivating.

From the economic policy point of view, the analysis contained in the case studies and this chapter suggests that Eastern Europe can learn many lessons from Latin America. Some of these lessons can be put to good use almost immediately, while others are not likely be relevant until the institutional and legal frameworks of Eastern Europe start to match those of Latin America. For example, while the importance of keeping the fiscal deficit under control is an obvious lesson to be drawn from Latin America, the sequence of fiscal reforms necessary is likely to be quite different in the two regions. The importance of financial deepening is also an obvious implication of the Latin American experience, but it is really only something that most Eastern European countries can dream about as they struggle to put together the most rudimentary financial markets.

Nevertheless we think that it is a mistake to say that the initial conditions are so different that nothing of much practical use can be learned. Most Eastern European countries are on the same road as Latin America, just a few steps (or kilometres) behind. The 'experiments' undertaken in Latin America since the mid-1970s should help Eastern European countries avoid many of the potholes along the route. Finally, despite the natural temptation of Eastern European countries to look to Eastern Asia for lessons, we think that this could be less beneficial. They are even further behind on that path; moreover the cultural context may be so different that it is hard to draw any practical lessons.

Notes

1. Note that when we speak of Eastern Europe in this chapter, we include Russia.
2. For the most part, the researchers concentrated on economic policy, although at times that was not practical and a more overt political economy stance was taken. Karagodin in particular remarked on the unique problems of a newly democratic, transition economy. For an analysis of the problems confronting economic policy makers during the democratic transition in Latin America, see Morales and McMahon (1995).
3. See Tanzi (1989) for an explanation of these revenue declines.
4. Glade, as quoted in Cardoso (1992, p. 86).
5. See Caprio and Levine (1994) for an in-depth discussion of the privatisation and development of the banking sector.
6. As reported in Greenaway and Milner (1991).
7. See IMF, 26 July 1993.
8. For a detailed discussion of this issue, see Tanzi (1989).
9. Note that at the end of each of the first five sections of his chapter, Karagodin includes a summary of the lessons that Eastern Europe can learn from Latin America.
10. We will not detail here the issues related to monetary and financial policy. Many of the pertinent issues will be covered in the next two subsections on the external sector and stabilisation and structural adjustment.
11. See Edwards (1991) for an analysis of this experience.
12. See Caprio and Levine (1994) for an extensive discussion on financial reform in transition countries.
13. See World Bank (1992).
14. The studies undertaken in this book were all completed before the Mexican peso crisis and, consequently, there is no analysis of this situation on Mexico or other Latin American countries. Despite the magnitude of the crisis, it is interesting to note that by July 1995 the Mexican trade account had turned around spectacularly, due almost exclusively to a rise in exports, and the Mexican government was already successfully selling new international bond issues. On the other hand, the effects on unemployment, growth and the financial sector continue to be severe.
15. In early 1994 the Russian government did exactly this and raised tariffs.
16. One area we had thought of covering but dropped, primarily due to financial limitations, was investment, both domestic and foreign. While the other topics cover aspects of this area, they do not go into it as fully as we would have liked. Obviously this is an important question in Eastern Europe, especially given the difficulties of attracting foreign investment and raising domestic investment. We also did not breach the area of labour market policy, which at the macro, institutional and micro levels will undoubtedly play a key role in the level and sustainability of economic growth in both regions. Nevertheless it is our belief that the labour market is an area where Eastern Europe has little to learn from Latin America (except for, perhaps, Chile). This is due to the general lack of reform of labour markets in Latin America, their very different nature from their Eastern European counterparts and the persistence of unemployment and underemployment in most

Latin American countries. With these exceptions, we believe that *ex-post* the main problems in economic policy facing Eastern Europe have been covered.

17. See McMahon and Schmidt-Hebbel (1995) for a discussion of the sub-sequencing of fiscal reforms as other reforms unfold.
18. For a summary of the Vietnam experience, see IMF, 26 July 1993.
19. See Standing (1994a, 1994b) for a discussion and analysis of the extent of the employment and skills problems in Russia.
20. See Ofer (1992) for a discussion of the Russian experience with shock therapy.
21. For a discussion of the Chinese experience, see McKinnon (1993). Borensztein (1993) disagrees with the argument that the Chinese and Vietnamese results offer lessons for Eastern Europe with regard to gradualism versus shock therapy. He emphasises that, given the revolutionary political changes in the countries of Eastern Europe, there was no political authority to steer through a gradualist programme. Moreover the small business sector in most Eastern European countries was much smaller than in China or Vietnam. It was precisely on this sector that the gradualist programmes of the latter countries was focused.

Bibliography

Abreu, Marcelo and José María Fanelli (1994) 'Stabilization Lessons for Eastern Europe from Latin America: The Perspective of Monetary and External Sector Policy', mimeo, Pontificia Universidade Catolica, Rio de Janeiro, Brazil and CEDES, Buenos Aires, Argentina.

Agrawal, Pradeep *et al.* (1995) *Economic Restructuring in East Asia and India: Lessons in Policy Reform* (London: Macmillan).

Borensztein, Eduardo (1993) 'The Strategy of Reform in the Centrally Planned Economies of Eastern Europe: Lessons and Challenges', Papers on Policy Analysis and Assessment series (Washington, DC: IMF).

Bruno, Michael (1992) 'Stabilization and Reform in Eastern Europe' *IMF Staff Papers*, volume 39, no. 4, pp. 741–77.

Burgess, Robin and Nicholas Stern (1993) 'Taxation and Development', *Journal of Economic Literature*, vol. 31, no. 2, pp. 762–830.

Caprio, Gerard Jr. and Ross Levine (1994) 'Reforming Finance in Transitional Socialist Economies', *The World Bank Research Observer*, vol. 9, no. 1, pp. 1–24.

Cardoso, Eliana (1992) 'La Privatización en América Latina', in J. Vial (ed), *Adónde Va América Latina: Balance de las Reformas Económicas* (Santiago, Chile: CIEPLAN), pp. 79–100.

Cho, Yoon-Che and Deena Khatkhate (1989) 'Lessons of Financial Liberalization in Asia: A Comparative Study', World Bank Discussion Paper no. 50.

Cooper, Richard N. (1991) 'Economic Stabilization in Developing Countries', International Center for Economic Growth Occasional Paper no. 14 (San Francisco).

Corbo, Vittorio (1992) 'Economic Transformation in Latin America, Lessons for Eastern Europe', *European Economic Review*, vol. 36.

Dornbusch, Rudiger (1990) 'Policies to Move From Stabilization to Growth', *World Bank Economic Review* (Supplement), pp. 19–56.

Dornbusch, R. and A. Reynoso (1989) 'Financial Factors in Economic Development', NBER Working Paper no. 2889.

Edwards, Sebastian (1991) 'Stabilization and Liberalization Policies in Central and Eastern Europe: Lessons from Latin America', NBER Working Paper no. 3816.

Edwards, Sebastian (1992) 'The Sequencing of Structural Adjustment and Stabilization', ICEG Occasional Paper no. 34 (San Francisco).

Fanelli, José María and Roberto Frenkel (1992) 'On Gradualism, Shock Treatment and Sequencing', *International Monetary and Financial Issues for the 1990s*, vol. 2 (New York: UNCTAD, United Nations), pp. 73–100.

Fanelli, J. R. Frenkel and G. Rozenwurcel (1992) 'Growth and Structural Reform in Latin America. Where we Stand', in A. Zini Jr., *The Market and the State in Economic Development in the 1990s* (Amsterdam: North Holland).

Fanelli, J. M. and J. Machinea (1994) 'Capital Movements in Argentina', mimeo (Santigao: ECLAC).

Fischer, Stanley (1991) 'Privatization in East European Transformation', NBER Working Paper no. 3703 (Cambridge MA).

Greenaway, David and Chris Milner (1991) 'Fiscal Dependence on Trade Taxes and Trade Policy Reform', *Journal of Development Studies*, vol. 27, no. 3, pp. 95–132.

Helleiner, G. K. (1990) 'Trade Strategy in Medium-Term Adjustment', *World Development*, pp. 879–97.

Horton, Susan, Ravi Kanbur and Dipak Mazumdar (1991) 'Labour Markets in an Era of Adjustment: An Overview', Economic Development Institute WPS 694 (Washington, DC: World Bank).

International Monetary Fund (1993) 'Transition to a Market Economy: Lessons from the IMF's Experience', *IMF Survey* (July 26).

Kuznetsov, Yevgeny (1993) 'Adjustment of the Russian Defence-Related Enterprises: Macroeconomic Implications', mimeo (Moscow: Institute for Economic Forecasting).

Leite, Sérgio Pereira and V. Sundararajan (1990) 'Issues in Interest Rate Liberalization', *Finance and Development*, pp. 46–8.

Levine, Ross and David Scott (1993) 'Old Debts and New Beginnings: A Policy Choice in Transitional Socialist Economies', *World Development*, vol. 21, no. 3, pp. 319–30.

Litvack, J. and I. Wallich (1993) 'Son decisivas para la transformación de Rusia las finanzas intergubernamentales', *Finanzas y Desarrollo* (June).

McKinnon, Ronald I. (1991) *The Order of Economic Liberalization. Financial Control in the Transition to a Market Economy* (London: John Hopkins University Press).

McKinnon, Ronald I. (1993), 'Gradual versus Rapid Liberalization in Socialist Economies: Financial Policies and Macroeconomic Stability in China and Russia Compared', Annual Bank Conference on Development Economics (Washington DC: World Bank).

McMahon, Gary and Klaus Schmidt-Hebbel (1995) 'Macroeconomic Adjustment and Tax Reform in Developing Countries', in G. Perry and J. Whalley (eds), *Fiscal Reform and Structural Change* (London: MacMillan).

Meller, Patricio (1992) 'La Apertura Comercial Chilena: Enseñanzas de Política', Working Paper no. 109, Banco Interamericano de Desarrollo, Washington, DC.

Morales, Juan Antonio A. (1991) 'Reformas Estructurales y Crecimiento Económico en Bolivia', Working Document no. 4 (IISEC).

Morales, Juan Antonio A. and Gary McMahon (eds) (1995) *Economic Policy in the Transition to Democracy in Latin America*, (London: Macmillan).

Ofer, Gur (1992) 'Macroeconomic Stabilization and Structural Change: Orthodox, Heterodox, or Otherwise?', mimeo (Washington, DC: World Bank).

Perry, Guillermo (1992) 'Finanzas Públicas, Estabilización, y Reforma Estructural en América Latina', mimeo, BID.

Sachs, Jeffrey (1994) 'La derrota reformista en Rusia es culpa del FMI', *Ambito Financiero* 25 January.

Schwartz, G. and P. Silva Lopes (1993) 'La privatización: expectativas, ventajas y desventajas, concesiones y resultados', *Finanzas y Desarrollo* (June).

Solimano, Andrés (1990) 'Macroeconomic Adjustment, Stabilization, and Growth in Reforming Socialist Economies', WPS 399 (Washington, DC: World Bank).

Solimano, Andrés (1992) 'Diversity in Economic Reform: A Look at the Experience in Market and Socialist Economies', WPS 981 (Washington, DC: World Bank).

Standing, Guy (1994a) 'Employment Restructuring in Russian Industry', *World Development*, vol. 22, no. 2, pp. 253–60.

Standing, Guy (1994b) 'Labor Market Implications of "Privatization" in Russian Industry in 1992', *World Development*, vol. 22, no. 2, pp. 261–70.

Stiglitz, Joseph E. (1993) 'The Role of the State in Financial Markets', Annual Bank Conference on Development Economics (Washington, DC: World Bank).

Tanzi, Vito (1989) 'The Impact of Macroeconomic Policies on the Level of Taxation and the Fiscal Balance in Developing Countries', *IMF Staff Papers*, vol. 36, no. 3, pp. 633–56.

World Bank (1992) *Russian Economic Reform: Crossing the Threshold of Structural Change*, A World Bank Country Study (Washington, DC: World Bank).

Zhukov, Stanislav (1994) 'Russian Ecological Challenges', mimeo (Moscow: Institute of World Economy and International Relations).

2 Privatisation in Latin America and Eastern Europe

János Hoós

2.1 INTRODUCTION

Privatisation has become a key part of Latin America's drive for modernisation and revived growth in the last decade of the twentieth century. Latin American governments have come to realise that they have had too large a role in the production of goods and services (Glade, 1991). With the exception of Chile, Latin American governments began the privatisation process slowly and selectively, with relatively minor enterprises targeted for transfer to the private sector. These governments, however, have become increasingly committed to accelerating and broadening privatisation, both as a matter of preference and as a response to fiscal realities. Among the elements that played a part in the intensification of government efforts to privatise are:

● Labour conflicts in state-owned enterprises.
● The inability to gain more substantial relief from the external debt service burden.
● The need to reduce inflationary government deficits by eliminating subsidies to unprofitable state-owned enterprises.
● The need to generate significant new resources to attack the massive 'social deficit' resulting from nearly a decade of economic crisis and austerity budgets.
● The huge capital investment needs of even profitable state-owned enterprises that are urgently in need of technological modernisation.

All of the Central and Eastern European countries are now committed to changing their economic systems to predominantly private market economies similar to those of Western Europe. The elements of such a system transformation can be grouped into four broad analytical categories, all of which interact strongly in the process (Gelb and Gray, 1991).

43

The first concerns internal and external macroeconomic stabilisation. The second is the introduction of competitive markets and attendant price reform. Price reform typically involves decontrolling and broadening markets for goods and services, which in turn requires a restructuring and demonopolisation of the trade and transport sectors. The creation of factor markets for both labour and financial resources is also essential. Reform of international trade and payments systems is considered an integral part of price reform and competition policy.

The third category of reform is enterprise reform and restructuring. A first important step in enterprise reform involves clarifying public ownership rights (and separating them from the regulatory functions of government) and implementing more effective control over the management of existing firms, in part through widespread privatisation. Establishing secure private property rights and facilitating the growth of new private firms is also critical. Enterprise restructuring may involve breaking up large monopolies, removing or reassigning redundant labour, closing loss-making operations and disposing of their assets, restructuring balance sheets, or other actions aimed at improving the efficiency of existing enterprises.

The fourth category of reform (closely related to the others) involves reorienting the role of the state in the economy, away from direct ownership and control over production and towards an indirect regulatory role that promotes adjustment and private economic activity. This challenge has many dimensions. Privatisation will help reduce the role of government in direct production.

Concurrent reforms are needed in the central institutions of government, including the Central Bank, tax administration, the expenditure budget and control system, and policy-making bodies. Another important role for the state is to redesign the social safety net to reduce the need for enterprises to perform wider social functions, to make benefits 'portable' to facilitate labour reallocation, and to cope with rising unemployment as firms become subject to greater financial discipline. The state also needs to provide a suitable legal framework for collective bargaining and private sector activity and to develop legal institutions to implement and enforce it.

This chapter provides an overview of privatisation in the two regions and focuses on lessons for Eastern Europe that can be drawn from the Latin American experience. Section 2.2 discusses privatisation in Latin America. In Section 2.3 a description of privatisation in Eastern Europe is presented. Section 2.4 contains the conclusions and the lessons.

2.2 PRIVATISATION IN LATIN AMERICA

Why Are the Countries Privatising?

The following discussion, which relies mainly on the papers of Devlin (1992) and Meller (1992), outlines some of the major factors that seem to be explicitly or implicitly driving privatisations in the regions. The weights for each of course are different among the countries.

According to Meller (1992), two key arguments are used to justify privatisation. The first is that private firms are considered to be more efficient than public firms as profits and the risk of losing their own capital provide incentives to private entrepreneurs to do their best in terms of efficiency. Moreover, bankruptcy puts a floor on the level of inefficiency of private firms. A public enterprise can be relatively inefficient and still earn positive profits, just as a public enterprise can be efficient and still have losses because of the government's rate-setting policy.

The second argument is related to the public deficit – given that public firms do not go bankrupt, this eventually becomes an important factor in increasing that deficit (see Table 2.1). The sale of public enterprises, therefore, will provide resources to finance the overall public deficit in the short

Table 2.1   Public enterprise expenditures and deficits, selected Latin American countries, 1970–85 (% GDP)

	Current expenditures			Overall deficit[1]		
	1970–1	1980–1	1984–5	1970–1	1980–1	1984–5
Argentina	8.3	10.8	15.2	1.9	2.2	2.9
Brazil	7.5	16.3	13.8	0.4	6.0	2.0
Chile[2]	10.2	15.3	19.8	3.3	0.6	–0.4
Mexico[2]	6.1	8.2	9.7	0.5	1.5	0.6
Peru	3.9	29.3	28.3	0.4	3.5	1.7
Venezuela[2]	5.6	12.2	n.a	3.9	9.0	n.a

Notes:
1. Includes current and capital accounts.
2. Excludes copper in Chile, and petroleum in Mexico and Venezuela.
Source: Situación Latinoamericana (1993).

run and will diminish it in the medium and long run. Moreover the increase in efficiency will generate higher growth rates (Meller, 1992).

Public enterprises have an important share of gross domestic product (GDP) in many Latin American countries. This share increased during the 1970s and at the beginning of the 1980s (Table 2.1). Even excluding the large Chilean state copper mines and the large petroleum firms of Mexico and Venezuela, public firms (expenditure) represented more than 10 per cent of GDP in Argentina, Brazil, Chile, Mexico, Peru and Venezuela by 1984–5.

After many years of a strong public sector presence in the productive sphere, there are many criticisms. Government failure is perceived as much larger than market failure, because of political assignments to top (and intermediate) positions in public firms, their large internal inefficiency because of lifetime job tenure and job rigidity, lengthy bureaucratic procedures and so on. Furthermore, a large public sector with a government that substitutes the market in many aspects induces a rent-seeking attitude by the private sector to increase (private) profits – having the right connection becomes much more important than increasing productive efficiency. This is especially valid in a highly protected economy (Meller, 1992).

There has been an ideological shift in the region that puts stress on private sector initiative. The central idea is the 'subsidiary state', that is, the public sector should be limited to essential developmental activities that the private sector cannot or will not perform competently.

The new focus has had growing theoretical support and has been encouraged by the political success of Britain's ambitious privatisation programme. The interpretation can be subtle and selective. It can also be more emphatic and quantitative, picturing government failure as nearly always worse than private market failure. Hence the requirement to reduce drastically the size of the state in absolute terms irrespective of the theoretical merits of public intervention. The benefits of the new strategy are purported to be greater efficiency through the freeing-up of market forces and greater equity and social participation through the democratisation of capital (Devlin, 1992).

The new ideology can be identified in virtually all the governments of the region, but it has not always been a first-order, or even second-order consideration in the decision to privatise. It was, however, clearly the main motivation of the Chilean privatisation of 1985–9. Moreover the programme had the hard-hitting edge of the military government's 'Chicago boys'. Mexico's programme has also had ideology as a first-order consideration. In effect, the emergence of a new generation of US-educated government bureaucrats, less emotionally linked to the statist tradition that emerged from the Mexican Revolution, brought with it the perception that the state-dominated economy needed fundamental rebalancing. Mexico's tone was subtle and selective, however, with government emphasising that the state would redeploy its efforts to the social sector (Devlin, 1992).

Experience in the region suggests that the public sector often has difficulty playing the dual role of principal and agent. It is generally accepted that the principal–agent problem can be more difficult when ownership is dispersed because of the limited access to information and the free-rider problem. In this situation, the exercising of 'voice' is costly, although a large part of the potential benefits of effective voice are bestowed on third parties. It is because of this that 'exit' is often the preferred response. Indeed it reflects an old Wall Street dictum: 'If you don't like the management you should sell your stock'. The traditional problem could be considered potentially much more serious for a public enterprise because, in this case, the dispersion of ownership is extreme as the public sector is permeated by society at large.

In this environment the principal's potential objectives cover the entire spectrum of interests that can be effectively voiced in that society. The use of choice, however, and the monitoring of performance have high costs. Consequently voice is likely to be exercised only by groups whose objectives have more tangible and concentrated benefits. This intensified principal–agent problem of public firms is by no means an insurmountable obstacle, as demonstrated by some countries with a tradition of efficient public enterprises.

Indeed there is evidence that market structure matters much more than ownership *per se*. Nevertheless it could be plausibly argued that, all things being equal, the cost (effort) of exercising the voice of efficiency is relatively less for the principals of a privatised firm than for those of a public firm. Exit (privatisation) and the reallocation, or reduction, of the state's net worth could therefore be proposed as an attractive and less costly option for the achievement of greater efficiency.

Where monopoly power is involved, allocative efficiency will require public regulation of the privatised firm. As public monitoring must now take place 'outside' the firm itself, there will be a rise in the public cost of gathering the information needed for effective regulation. Nevertheless a decision to privatise must mean that the new public costs of regulation are perceived to be less than the sum of the public costs that must be assumed if the state is to play effectively the triple role of principal, agent and public regulator of an enterprise. At least theoretically, privatisation creates a more transparent division of labour, which makes for potentially better accountability. Put simply, the private principals and agents must only pursue some mode of profit maximisation, whereas public regulators must only pursue allocative efficiency.

Meanwhile the state can reallocate its receipts from privatisation to other activities with returns that are socially high but too low to attract private capital. Alternatively the receipts can be allocated to the reduction of public debt. Roughly speaking, in either case the government's net worth remains constant (assuming no undervaluation of the firm sold). Or the state can retreat and reduce net worth by using sale receipts to finance current outlays.

It is generally accepted that most state-owned enterprises (SOEs) have traditionally confronted a proliferation of conflicting public objectives, for example investment, conduits for foreign savings, low prices to aid the poor or to support stabilisation efforts, creation of demand for domestic capital goods industries, regional development strategies, political largesse of different types and so on. Some of the objectives have been consistent with development, whereas others have not. But clearly the institutional arrangement was often inefficient, as one instrument (the SOE) was invariably used to accomplish multiple social objectives (Devlin, 1992).

In practice, efficiency criteria seem to have been an especially important motivating factor in countries such as Argentina, Peru and Venezuela, which have had notoriously inefficient SOEs and governmental apparatus that have been judged to be too weak to effect the reform needed to raise the voice of efficiency. The efficiency factor, however, may have been less of a driving force in a few countries with strong governmental apparatus and where the performance of SOEs was already generally at least acceptable.

The best example is Chile, where the military government had the power and proven capacity to reform enterprises. Aided by an extremely authoritarian setting, the authorities effectively created greater concentration of ownership in SOEs, lowering the costs and raising the benefits of exercising the voice of efficiency, even though the principal remained nominally public. As a consequence Chilean SOEs were relatively efficient and financially viable well before the decision to privatise them (Devlin, 1992).

Governments have assumed that deregulated markets are contestable and that foreign competition will cause the number of domestic monopolies and oligopolies in the tradeable goods sectors to decline markedly. In effect, regulation of rents by market forces reduces the need for direct regulation via public ownership (Devlin, 1992).

Many governments are of the opinion that changing technology and innovative administrative techniques have eroded, or at least put into question, the presence of natural monopolies in many public services. Indeed some technical support has emerged for depackaging certain major domestic public services. This has occurred in the Chilean and Argentine electrical sectors. For example, dividing former monopolies into duopolies, as in the case of Argentine telephones, makes it possible, at least in principle, to regulate externally via 'yardstick competition' between the two firms. These technical developments, coupled with deregulation and the formation of contestable markets, have reduced the perceived need for a public enterprise (Devlin, 1992).

Monopolistic and oligopolistic control of traded goods (including technologies) in the international market, as well as the dominant position of the US economy, has been sharply reduced by the great postwar expansion of the world economy. In effect, Latin American countries objectively face a more competitive world economy and complex geopolitical matrix than they did in the interwar period and in the 1950s and 1960s.

The active participation of European firms, including Spanish ones, in the privatisations of Argentina, Chile, Mexico and Venezuela, as well as the participation of Chilean electrical distribution and generation companies in Argentina's divestment of its electrical sector, is a testament to the dispersion of international economic power. In these circumstances it could be argued that there is less need for a strong countervailing force in the form of state ownership of productive enterprises (Devlin, 1992).

Developments in the world economy also have strengthened the apparent attractiveness of transferring property to the private sector. The state's debt crisis, plus its forced absorption of private sector debts, have combined to help make the latter a superior player in world capital markets. There is also some perception that more competitive world markets have allowed private sector firms to keep up with quickly changing technology and increased their attractiveness to foreign partners. These developments have caused governments to seek opportunities for realignment of public investment portfolios.

Governments have used privatisation as a signal of their commitment to the new ideological model, thereby attempting to improve the expectations of domestic and international economic agents. Although this motive is widespread in the region, it has been especially important for new governments that have become committed (by conviction or circumstances) to a liberal strategy, but have initially lacked the ideological credentials of the Washington Consensus or have encountered difficulties in pushing forward liberal reforms on other fronts, or both (Devlin, 1992).

Credibility had first-order importance in the emergence of Argentina's first round of privatisation in 1989–90. Assuming power in the middle of an economic crisis, the government's announcement of the privatisation of ENTEL and Aerolineas Argentinas was motivated in part by the need to transform a formerly populist image and stabilise expectations. Credibility also seems to have been a first-order consideration in Brazil's decision to privatise. In effect it produced some concrete forward movement in a troubled economic setting that has not been receptive to across-the-board reforms. Credibility also appears to have had significant weight in the privatisations carried out by the new governments in Venezuela and Peru, which also took power in the middle of a severe economic crisis. In the former government, it was part of a programme that erased an initially populist image, and in the latter it helped to give definition to a new political party that had lacked a clear image upon assuming power.

The sale of state assets can temporarily close macroeconomically destabilising fiscal gaps. The sale itself creates an immediate financial transfer to the government. It also affects future fiscal flows. If a firm is losing money, an annual negative fiscal transfer could be converted into a positive flow of tax revenue, assuming private ownership is profitable. If the public firm is already profitable, the net future flow depends on the trade-off between the taxes and dividends of the public firm and the taxes paid by the privatised firm.

The privatisation option becomes tempting when possibilities for expenditure reduction have been exhausted, when revenue cannot (or will not) be raised through increased tax collection or when noninflationary sources of finances have become exhausted. In these circumstances there is the option of capitalising the potential future receipts of a public enterprise through its privatisation.

A fiscal deficit that generates serious inflation and balance-of-payments problems obviously is a socially costly phenomenon. These situations can inhibit reforms, bring unwanted conditionality from the international financial markets, paralyse investment and growth and have regressive distributional effects. Hence a peso of additional revenue today, employed to close the fiscal gap, should have a very high social rate of return. Moreover, in a situation of severe macroeconomic disequilibria and recession, a peso of fiscal revenue will usually have a higher shadow price than a peso of private consumption or investment.

In these circumstances an increase in tax collection could be an attractive option, especially if the taxes involved are not regressive in character. In an open, highly deregulated economy with a recession and a weak political and institutional setting, however, greater tax collection, especially of a progressive type, can be very difficult to effect. Indeed in today's setting an increased tax burden can intensify capital flight and deepen the recession, with negative net consequences for fiscal income and stabilisation. In addition a more aggressive tax policy will frequently be accused of sending the wrong signals to the private sector. After all, the liberal strategy that is fashionable today views most taxes as distortionary and welfare reducing.

Privatisation clearly is an expedient way to bypass the foregoing dilemma, but using privatisation receipts to finance expenditure is analogous to borrowing. Thus, when financing current outlays, privatisation reduces public sector net worth. Moreover the latter strategy only postpones rather than eliminates the need for further fiscal adjustment in the form of increased taxes or cutbacks in expenditure (Devlin, 1992).

The desire to finance fiscal deficits has been an important consideration in the decision to initiate privatisation. As money is fungible, it is difficult to isolate the use of receipts from divestment. Nevertheless the existence of fiscal deficits during periods of privatisation is indicative of financing via divestment. Moreover deficits on current fiscal balances hint of some financing of current expenditures, inducing a direct loss of public sector net worth. On this basis privatisation appears to have been a financing instrument in Chile in 1985–6, in Argentina in 1989–91 and in Mexico from 1983–90 (Table 2.2).

Table 2.2   Latin America: fiscal balances for selected countries* 1983–91
(percentage of GDP)

	1983	1984	1985	1986	1987	1988	1989	1990	1991
Chile:									
Current savings	−0.5	0.3	3.6	4.8	5.3	8.0	7.0	5.6	5.5
Total balance	−3.5	−4.6	−2.9	−2.0	2.6	3.9	5.5	1.5	1.7
Mexico:									
Current savings	−2.8	−2.1	−3.4	−9.9	−12.2	−9.8	−5.7	−2.0	0.8
Total balance	−8.1	−7.1	−8.0	−14.5	−14.4	−9.7	−5.1	−2.9	3.4
Argentina:									
Current savings	–	–	−1.9	−0.5	−1.7	−3.5	−1.6	−2.9	−1.6
Total balance	–	–	−5.4	−4.1	−6.7	−8.6	−4.8	−5.1	−2.2
Brazil:									
Current savings	−1.4	−2.8	−8.1	−7.1	−6.1	−12.6	−20.1	−10.1	−10.0
Total balance	–	–	–	–	–	–	–	–	–
Venezuela:									
Current savings					8.1	4.0	10.4	12.6	10.7
Total balance	–	–	–	–	−4.4	−8.6	−1.1	0.2	1.2

* Consolidated public sector.
Sources: ECLAC, *Economic Survey for Latin American and the Caribbean*, various issues and CEDES, Buenos Aires, Argentina.

Also, the surpluses registered in Mexico and Venezuela in 1991 would have been deficits in the absence of privatisation receipts. As for the implicit financing of current outlays, this appears to have occurred in Argentina and Mexico up until 1991. Meanwhile, through a more specific tracking of income and outlays, it was also concluded that 50 per cent of the Chilean privatisation receipts in 1985–6 went to finance current outlays, thus reducing net worth. Finally, it should be mentioned that a primary motive for the recent privatisations in Venezuela and Peru has been the desire to relax severe fiscal constraints.

As a fiscal situation stabilises, a country has more opportunities to use privatisation receipts to finance reductions of public debt and promote an overall improvement of net worth. In late 1990 Mexico began to earmark privatisation receipts for a special fund and a considerable amount of these resources has apparently been channelled into debt reduction. Domestic public debt was reduced by US$7 billion in 1991 and by US$5 billion in the first quarter of 1992. Moreover in 1992 the government quietly effected buybacks of US$7 billion of public foreign commercial bank debt (equivalent to nearly 10 per cent of total public foreign debt) through the use of privatisation receipts.

Total public debt, which in 1986 was equivalent to about 80 per cent of GDP, was expected to be 29 per cent of GDP by the end of 1992. Debt reduction became an important use of Chile's privatisation receipts, beginning in 1987. The receipts from Argentina's initial round of privatisation (1989–90) involved direct reduction of foreign debt as a considerable part of the payment was made in promissory notes bought on the secondary market. Much of the country's receipts in the second round of privatisation initially went towards general expenditure, but with an expected fiscal surplus in 1992 more funds were being earmarked for the reduction of foreign public debt (Devlin, 1992).

It is not easy to determine whether privatisation has acted as a direct substitute for taxation. In Chile, however, it can be stated rather emphatically that privatisation financed the military government's fiscal reforms of 1984 and 1988, which sharply lowered direct and indirect taxes.

The fiscal crisis during the 1980s is viewed as a serous obstacle to new investment in public firms and social infrastructure. When the crisis broke, the investment plans of SOEs could easily be postponed, and were postponed, to improve short-term financial balances (Table 2.3). Even profitable public firms became prisoners of the central government's financial crisis. As the decade progressed the investment lag became intolerable, especially in public services with a higher degree of visibility.

Table 2.3 Latin America: savings and deficits of public enterprises, 1980–1 and 1986–7 (percentage of GDP)

	D^1 1980–1 (1)	D^1 1986–7 (2)	D^{*2} 1980–1 (3)	D^{*2} 1986–7 (4)	DH^3	Absolute variation in D^* (5)=(4)–(3)
Argentina	–3.39	0.59	–4.92	–2.75	–3.21	2.17
Bolivia	0.10	–2.90	3.65	7.95	7.70	4.30
Brazil	–1.69	0.10	–3.10	–2.10	–4.22	1.00
Chile*[4]	–1.33	0.78	5.47	10.33	11.93	4.86
(excluding CODELCO[5])	–	–	–	–	–	–
Colombia	–2.00	–1.41	–3.16	0.08	–0.21	3.24
Costa Rica	–2.37	0.97	–1.55	3.46	4.11	5.01
Ecuador (non-oil exporters)	–0.63 (–1.6)	–1.77 (–0.55)	4.60 (–1.92)	4.09 (–0.67)	4.46 (–1.44)	–0.51 (1.25)
Mexico (non-oil exporters)	–1.30 (–1.57)	0.25 (–0.26)	1.49 (–6.22)	4.62 (–4.97)	3.53 (–5.77)	3.13 (1.25)
Uruguay	0.26	0.10	2.69	3.14	3.00	0.45
Venezuela	–2.33	–2.62	11.08	5.16	–0.05	–5.92
Total[6]	–1.48	–0.74	1.20	2.63	1.68	1.43
Subtotal[7]	–1.14	–0.32	–0.80	1.22	0.90	2.02

Notes:
1. D = Total income less total expenditure.
2. D* = D–T (T = transfers with the central government, registered in its accounts).
3. DH = D* plus difference in net capital account between 1980–1 and 1986–7.
4. For the period 1986–7 the values used were those for 1985, which is the last year for which figures are available.
5. CODELCO = Chilean Copper Corporation, a state enterprise.
6. Simple average, excluding Chile.
7. Simple average excluding Chile, Venezuela and the petroleum enterprises of Ecuador and Mexico.
Source: ECLAC, Economic Development Division.

As the public sector debt problem persisted, privatisation came to be perceived as a way of easing the public enterprises' growing investment bottleneck. In effect, through privatisation a public firm could escape the central government's fiscal restraint, and thus have greater freedom to invest. Moreover the receipts from privatisation could potentially allow the state to reinvigorate public social investment or reduce debt.

Investments bottlenecks have often been used as justification for privatisation, even in countries such as Chile where many SOEs were relatively efficient and profitable. Mexico has laid special stress on the need to sell SOEs to strengthen social investment (Devlin, 1992).

It is also perceived that privatisation can raise the private sectors's disposition to save and invest. This is because it is usually less risky to buy existing firms than to invest in a start-up operation. Moreover public firms often provide greater and more accurate information than can be found in other sectors of the economy.

Another consideration is that many SOEs, especially those that provide public services in monopolistic or quasimonopolistic markets, are inherently attractive, low-risk and cash-rich operations in which shareholders can more easily appropriate a significant part of any efficiency gains. Finally, in view of a crisis environment, the investment activity of highly visible privatised firms, even if not additive, could conceivably create positive externalities and help to stimulate private sector expectations (Devlin, 1992).

Privatisation also can broaden and deepen moribund stock markets as well as give rise to windfall profits, new wealth and more optimistic expectations. This, coupled with the externalities of reinvigorated privatised firms and a relaxed external constraint, can contribute to increased economic activity. More growth, in turn, will naturally boost fiscal revenue and provide better conditions for fiscal reforms. Consequently privatisation can be gradually replaced by more stable sources of revenue (Devlin, 1992).

Privatisations are strongly encouraged by the international financial community. A programme of this type therefore enhances external economic relations, especially with the international monetary fund (IMF), the World Bank and commercial lenders. This consideration was probably important in Argentina's decision to initiate privatisation in 1989.

A privatisation programme such as Argentina's, which makes foreign debt paper a legitimate means of payment, creates attractive options for banks, especially the big lenders that make the Advisory Committee. On the one hand the banks gain by the rise in the secondary market price that is the result of the increased demand for the debt paper. (In the case of Argentina, the price rose by some 50 per cent during the finalization of the first round of privatisation). Banks can therefore sell off their bad loans at a smaller loss and can also earn a commission if they are contracted to secure paper for third parties interested in participating in the privatisation. On the other hand a bank can avoid a loss on its own loan portfolio by capitalising it through the purchase of a public enterprise.

Magnitude: How Much Happened?

SOEs have typically had a high profile in the economic activity of the region. Ironically, however, consistent and comprehensive data on the region's SOEs are hard to come by. Their importance can nevertheless be illustrated by reference to a few countries. For instance, just before the 1981–2 crisis the value added of SOEs as a percentage of GDP was about 5 per cent in Brazil, 14 per cent in Chile, 8 per cent in Mexico and 30 per cent in Venezuela. Likewise the region's SOEs were major investors in fixed capital, their activity in this area often being equivalent to a quarter or more of total gross investment (Table 2.4). Each country's story on the origin of its SOEs is different, but in practically all cases one can find a combination of factors that relate to the deliberate promotion of investment and development, nationalisations derived from unexpected political

Table 2.4   Latin America: selected indicators of the participation of public enterprises before the crisis

	Value added as % GDP (1980)	Fixed investment as a (%) of gross investment (1980)	Participation in domestic credit (1978)	Employment (%) (of total) (1980)
Argentina	–	15.4	–	20.0
Brazil	4.7[2]	25.8[1]	11.2	3.0[2]
Chile	14.2	15.8	–	20.4[2]
Colombia	–	12.7	–	–
Costa Rica	–	23.2	12.8	–
Ecuador	–	21.1	–	–
Honduras	–	14.6[3]	–	–
Mexico	8.2	23.1	18.9	–
Paraguay	–	6.5[4]	–	–
Peru	–	10.4	26.4	–
Uruguay	–	18.3[4]	–	–
Venezuela	30.9	35.7	1.6	–

Notes:
1. 1981.
2. 1982.
3. 1978–9.
4. 1978–80.
Source: Nair and Felippides (1988); Floyd *et al.* (1984)

or financial events, the support of macroeconomic stabilisation objectives, and employment and distributional considerations (Devlin, 1992).

Data for a considerable number of the countries in the region indicate that, just before the crisis, the overall financial performance of the region's SOEs was almost uniformally associated with important financing requirements (Table 2.3). The picture improves markedly for a few countries when the SOE balances are adjusted for transfers between the firms and central government. Nevertheless one notices that even after that adjustment, important precrisis financing requirements were registered for the SOEs of Argentina, Brazil, Colombia, Costa Rica, Ecuador (non-oil) and Mexico (non-oil).

During the crisis years SOEs confronted a very complex operational environment as central governments tried to stabilise domestic prices and reduce the public sector's financing requirements. The serious fiscal problems induced adjustments in the region's SOEs and a reduction of their demands for financing. Between 1981–2 and 1986–7 the countries with initial deficits either lowered their negative balances or converted them into surpluses, and, with the exception of Venezuela, those with initial surpluses increased their positive balance.

With the exception of Venezuela and the oil-producing SOEs of Mexico and Ecuador, the total improvement in the SOE balances for the countries in Table 2.2 was equivalent to 2 per cent of GDP. It should be noted that, although significant, the financial balancing nevertheless had an artificial component because it included the effects of sharp and unsustainable cutbacks in investment activity. This is seen in column DH of Table 2.3, which calculates financial balances using precrisis investment levels.

Expenditure cutbacks and tariff adjustments were initially the most important instruments for reforming the financial performance of public enterprises. Sooner or later, however, almost all the countries in the region began to opt for the more drastic reform of outright divestment or liquidation of their SOEs (Table 2.5). The greatest exponents of this were Chile and Mexico, followed by Argentina, Venezuela and Brazil (Devlin, 1992).

Chile was the pioneer of privatisation (Table 2.6). In the period 1975–82 the military government reprivatised more than 200 of the firms (mostly in the tradable goods and finance sectors, worth more than $1.2 billion) that had been nationalised or intervened in by the previous democratic government. Many of these reprivatised firms fell back into the governments's hands in 1982–3 as a consequence of a gigantic systemic collapse of the economy, but they were quickly reprivatised again in 1984–5. Then in 1985 the military government announced the beginning of the privatisation of many of the country's large, traditional SOEs, which before this had been considered untouchable.

Table 2.5   Privatisation in selected Latin American countries during the 1980s and 1990s

	Number of privatised firms	*Amount of sales (millions US$)*	
Argentina	23	3274	Drastic and abrupt privatisation of large public firms started from 1990 onwards.
Bolivia	–	–	No action. There are 67 small public manufacturing firms. Large public mining firms have political and constitutional constraints.
Brazil	20	1470	Slow process and much rhetoric up to 1990. A large steel and an electric-mechanic companies' shares sold at the end of 1991.
Chile	46	3042*	Deep and abrupt privatisation implemented during 1985–9. There remain only a few public firms.
Colombia	–	–	Colombian public firms are not important in the economy; privatisation is not an issue; reprivatisation of large, bankrupt, Grupo Gran Colombiano.
Mexico	615	10 000	Gradual privatisation of small and medium sized firms, during 1982–9. Large-firms' privatisation from 1990 onwards.
Peru	5	39	Only a few cases where plants were transferred to employees. Recent legislation allows privatisation of 23 of the 186 public firms; these 23 firms represent 2 per cent of total public firms' assets.
Venezuela	–	–	No action. Reprivatisation of hotels, sugar mills, cement companies is discussed.

* Corresponds to estimated net worth.
Sources: Cardoso (1991) and *Situación Latinoamericana* (1993).

Table 2.6   Number of public enterprises by legal regime

Sector	1970	1973[1]	1983[2]	1990[3]
CORFO subsidiaries				
Enterprises	46	228	23	27
Banks	0	18	1	0
Seized enterprises	0	259	0	0
Enterprises created by law				
Enterprises[4]	20	23	22	13
Banks[5]	1	1	1	1
Total	67	529	47	41

Notes:
1. Includes banks and enterprises in which CORFO had only a minority share of ownership.
2. Banks and enterprises taken over by the government as a result of the financial crisis are not included.
3. The number of CORFO subsidiaries does not decrease between 1983 and 1990 in spite of the massive sale of enterprises because a number of enterprises were transformed into joint-stock corporations in preparation for divestiture. Notably, 13 regional water and sewage services were incorporated.
4. Including the Corporación del Cobra (CODELCO) from 1973 onwards.
5. Excluding the Central Bank.

Source: Sáez (1992).

Between 1985 and 1989, 30 public enterprises, producing both tradeable goods and major public services, were privatised in whole or in part, generating sales equivalent to US$1.3 billion (see Table 2.8). At its peak in 1987–8 the value of sales were equivalent, on average, to 2 per cent of GDP and 7 per cent of current revenues of the consolidated public sector. At the end of 1989 there were just 45 public enterprises in the country, compared with more than 200 in 1974.

In 1990 the new democratic government of Chile slowed the pace and altered the content of the privatisation programme. Only a limited number of small public firms would be sold to the private sector, whereas a few other firms would sell minority packages. The government also planned to allow private participation in new public infrastructure projects, especially those sponsored by the public water and sewerage companies. In 1991 a small state shipping firm was sold, and minority shares in the Iquique free trade zone were offered on the local stock market. The country's few remaining large SOEs were excluded from the new programme, although in 1992 there was an emerging public debate over their privatisation, including the huge state copper company CODELCO.

Mexico followed Chile in the pioneering of privatisation in the region. The de la Madrid government initiated the process in 1983, and it was intensified in 1989 by the new Salinas administration. The policy of reform led to a reduction in the number of public firms from 1155 in 1982 to 280 in 1990. About a third of this reduction resulted from outright sale and the rest were liquidations, mergers and transfers to local authorities. The process initially focused on relatively small tradeable goods firms, but the size of the firms increased with time (Aeromexico, Mexicana Airlines) and the programme eventually included major public services, of which TELMEX was the most important.

The total value of sales over the period 1983–91 was more than US$15 billion, 90 per cent of this being concentrated in 1990–1 (Table 2.7). This concentration reflects the large size of the privatised firms in this period and the greater importance of outright sales relative to earlier years. In any event, the value of the sales in this latter period was huge, on average equivalent to 2.5 per cent of GDP and 9 per cent of current fiscal revenue. Unless the petroleum and electrical sectors become subject to privatisation (the constitution deems them to be strategic), it appears that the Mexican process of divestment could soon wind down.

Argentina began its programme in late 1989 under the new Menem government. In 1990–1, 17 publicly owned firms involved in tradable goods, including oil production, and major public services were wholly or partially privatised. Moreover the most heavily used highways were transformed into private concessions with the right to charge tolls. The value of sales in the period reached US$4 billion, on average equivalent to almost 3 per cent of GDP and 17 per cent of current fiscal revenue (Table 2.8). The Argentine scheme was probably the most ambitious in all Latin America because the government planned to privatise all its remaining SOEs (as well as many services) by 1994.

Brazil began to privatise under the Collor administration in October 1991. The sales of four firms that year raised $1.7 billion, equivalent to about 0.4 per cent of GDP and 1.6 per cent of current fiscal income. The government initially identified 55 firms for privatisation, with the list expected to expand considerably in the months ahead. Although the initial list focused on tradable goods, some major public services, including roads and telephones, could soon become involved in the privatisation process.

Venezuela has about 370 state entities in a very wide array of sectors. Moreover some of the firms are mixed capital ventures with foreign partners. The government began its privatisation process in late 1990 with a small bank. Then seven firms producing tradable goods and major public services were sold in 1991.The sales produced US$2.3 billion, equivalent to more than 4 per cent of GDP and 15 per cent of fiscal revenue. Twenty-nine

Table 2.7 Latin America: value of privatization transactions for major countries[1]

	Amount[2]	GDP[4] (%)	Fiscal income[4] (%)
Mexico			
1983	40	–	–
1984	5	–	–
1985	115	0.1[3]	0.4
1986	100	0.1	0.4
1987	170	0.1	0.4
1988	520	0.3	1.2
1989	730	0.4	1.6
1990	3 205	1.3	5.2
1991	10 550	3.8	12.7
Chile			
1983	–	–	–
1984	–	–	–
1985	10	0.1	0.3
1986	230	1.4	4.0
1987	310	1.7	5.6
1988	560	2.5	8.1
1989	235	0.9	3.0
1990	–	–	–
1991	–	–	–
Argentina			
1983	–	–	–
1984	–	–	–
1985	–	–	–
1986	–	–	–
1987	–	–	–
1988	–	–	–
1989	–	–	–
1990	2 000[6]	3.3	18.6
1991	2 183[6]	3.4[6]	16.5
Brazil			
1983	–	–	–
1984	–	–	–
1985	–	–	–
1986	–	–	–
1987	–	–	–
1988	–	–	–
1989	–	–	–
1990	–	–	–
1991	1 700[7]	0.4	1.6
Venezuela			
1983	–	–	–
1984	–	–	–
1985	–	–	–
1986	–	–	–
1987	–	–	–
1988	–	–	–
1989	–	–	–
1991	2 300	4.5[6]	15.0

Table 2.7   Continued

	Amount[2]	GDP[4] (%)	Fiscal income[4] (%)
Colombia			
1983	–	–	–
1984	–	–	–
1985	–	–	–
1986	–	–	–
1987	–	–	–
1988	–	–	–
1989	50	–	–
1990	75	–	–
1991	690	0.2[6]	...

Sources: Calculated from the following sources:
Gerchunoff and Castro (1992); Hachette and Luders (1992); Ruprah (1992a); System BNDES, Brasil; Fondo de Inversiones de Venezuela; and CEPAL, Economic Development Division.

1 Reference is made to value of sales and not necessarily cash flow.
2 Millions of dollars.
3 Equivalent, in pesos.
4 Current income of the non-financial public sector.
5 Equivalent, in dollars.
6 Includes foreign public debt paper valued at secondary market rates. Also includes original terms of the sale of Aerolineas Argentinas, which were modified in 1992.
7 Payment was almost exclusively in domestic debt paper.

more firms in tradable goods sectors and tourism services were sold in 1992. The original list, however, is rapidly expanding as 43 additional firms are being prepared for privatisation, including the Caracas water supply. The government is reportedly considering the possibility of privatising its CVG heavy industries. Petroleum, however, is still considered a strategic sector.

Most other countries in the region are much less advanced in the privatisation process than those already mentioned. By 1992, however, virtually every government in the region, except Cuba, had announced a major privatisation programme and most had at least begun some minor sales of public firms.

The exception to generalised privatisation efforts in Latin America is Bolivia. Although Bolivia was one of the first Latin American countries to reform its economy according to the neoliberal model, it is among the last to privatise its companies. The creation of Bolivian parastatals began in the 1940s and 1950s as part of the general trend sweeping Latin America at that time. In 1950 the 18 state-owned corporations in Bolivia included banks and cement factories, as well as railway and airline transport companies. The influence and direct presence of the government in the economy became more pronounced with the nationalisation of the mines following the revolution of 1952, whose goal was the dismantling of the political power of the tin barons.

Table 2.8   Privatisation methods after 1985

Enterprise	Pension Fund	Stock Market	Workers	Public sector employees	Bid	Variation capital	Other
CAP		X	X			Reduction	
COFOMAP					X		
CHILE FILMS					X		AFR
CHILGENER	X	X	X				AFR
CHILMETRO	X	X	X				AFR
CHILQUINTA	X	X	X				AFR
CTC	X	X	X	X	X	Increase	AFR
ECOM					X		
EDELMAG			X				CPR
ELECDA		X					CPR/COR
ELIQSA		X		X			CPR/COR
EMEC		X		X			CPR/COR
EMEL					X		AFR
EMELAR					X		AFR
EMELAT					X		AFR
ENAEX					X		FAMAE
ENDESA	X	X	X	X		Increase	CORA
ENTEL	X	X	X				FAMAE
IANSA		X	X				Agricult

Table 2.8 Continued

Enterprise	Pension Fund	Stock Market	Workers	Public sector employees	Bid	Variation capital	Other
ISE GENERALES		X	X		X		
ISE VIDA					X		
LABOR. CHILE	X	X	X		X		
LAN CHILE		X	X				
PEHUENCHE			X			Increase	
PILMAIQUEN					X		
PULLINQUE					X		
SACRET			X				
SCHWAGER	X	X	X				
SOQUIMICH	X	X	X				CORA
TELEX		X			X		
ZOFRI							

Source: CORFO, Gerencia de Normalizacion a informationes de prensa.

By 1985 the number of state-owned companies had increased to roughly 650. The largest of these produced constant losses because of price-setting policies dictated by political concerns. In 1985 the decision was made to transfer the retail trade of hydrocarbons and their derivatives to the private sector. The same decree decentralised the Bolivian Mining Corporation, dissolved the Bolivian Encouragement Corporation (with more than 15 companies under its administration) and transferred these companies to the Regional Development Corporations. Later the government dissolved its monopoly over the production and sale of dairy products and transferred control of the National Automotive Transport Company to different town jurisdictions. These measures did not constitute actual privatisation but were a first step towards the privatisation of state-owned companies. Nonetheless privatisation in Bolivia is not imminent.

Political parties and the state administration have traditionally used public companies to distribute favours, a scheme that has yet to be overcome. Moreover the government must first turn to Congress to introduce a special law permitting the sale of these companies to the private sector. No such law has yet been presented to Congress, and to make matters worse the government does not enjoy an absolute majority in Congress, making the approval of such a law difficult. Finally, privatisation has been stopped by the opposition of the unions, both in companies likely to be privatised and in national organisations. Recovery contracts entered into by state-owned oil companies have triggered attempts to damage company facilities and equipment (Cardoso, 1991).

How It Was Done: Methods

Worldwide, the most commonly used methods of privatisation are public share offers, the private sale of shares, new private investment in SOEs, the sale of government or SOE assets, reorganisation (or break-up) into component parts, management/employee buy-outs, and lease and management contracts. Several of these methods can bring about total divestiture or can be implemented partially or gradually. Several combinations exist as well. Partial privatisation often takes the form of joint ventures.

The choice of a particular method is dictated by the objectives being sought and other factors. Beyond the above methods of transferring control or ownership of SOEs or government productive assets to the private sector, other actions are sometimes also referred to as privatisation or are linked to it. Examples are contracting out,where private contractors provide services formerly undertaken by the state or municipalities, and full liquidation of an SOE, with the assets ending up in the hands of private purchasers while the SOE's activity is wound up. The Latin American countries used these methods according to their special objectives and conditions.

In Chile the following types of sale have been employed:

- Direct sale to the highest bidder (foreign or domestic). Examples include Empresa Hidroeléctrica Pilmaiquén, SA (purchased by Bankers Trust through debt-equity swap), Telex-Chile, Empresa Hidroeléctrica Pullinque, SA, Empresa Eléctrica de Atacama (EMELAT), Empresa Eléctrica de Coquimbo (EMEC) and Empresa National de Explosivos (ENAEX). This procedure has been used mainly for relatively small firms.
- Partial sale to employees. A factor in practically all cases since 1985, this type of transaction generally offered better conditions to employees than to the other buyers. The goal was to sell at least 12.5 per cent to the employees, thus enabling them to elect at least one employee to a board of seven directors. As of mid-1988 some 14 000 employees had participated.
- Sale of shares on the stock exchange, aimed at both small- and large-scale investors. These transactions, by and large, occurred through ordinary investment banking and stock brokerage firms.
- Popular capitalism. Aimed at the small investor, this procedure offered special deferred-payment programme with subsidized loans. Not all small-package offerings have been equally generous, but all involved significant special inducements that may merit scrutiny by other countries seeking to broaden their capital markets. Examples of this option are banks and the power company ENDESA.
- Partial sale to foreign investors. Examples of this are CTC (the telephone company purchased by Bond Corporation) and SOQUIMICH (the nitrate producer purchased by Kiowa of Japan, Bankers Trust and American Express). Debt equity swaps were used in the latter case but not in CTC.
- Sale to pension funds. Such sales set prices at market value or economic value in all cases. Generally only very small percentages, and sometimes none, of these firms' shares were traded on the stock exchange, making exchange quotations a poor indicator of value. Economic values were inferred through an evaluation procedure. Some special conditions or restrictions on ownership were imposed: no investor, except the government, could own more than 20 per cent; more than 50 per cent of the shares were to be divided among shareholders who owned less than 10 per cent individually; and at least 15 per cent of the shares should be distributed among a minimum of 100 shareholders (Glade, 1991).

As can be seen, all possible methods of selling public enterprises have been used in Chile at one point or other (Table 2.8). In connection with these, several policy issues have been raised (Sáez, 1992). Are there any arguments for preferring one method over another in a specific enterprise? Should the enterprise be sold in one package or in several? Do you want to combine different methods of selling one enterprise? Do you want to impose conditions on the buyers, such as expansion of the enterprise? Is it important who buys the enterprise; for example managers and workers, domestic private investors, foreign investors, pension funds? Does it matter how the buyer pays for the shares?

During the 1970s the methods used were public bids and direct negotiation of the sale, and the enterprises were sold to one investor. The concentration of ownership, high indebtedness and financial fragility that resulted from this process were not a consequence of the method used. The key is to select the buyer and to regulate ownership relationships among the buyers. Most probably, banks and enterprises should not be privatised at the same time.

Sale through bids does not contribute to the development and deepening of the stock market. The Chilean experience in the 1980s, however, shows that divestiture through the stock market to individual investors and pension funds has contributed to the growth of that market. One of the goals in the 1980s was to disseminate property. This was done in large enterprises and in the reprivatisation of two large banks by offering the shares to individual investors or different groups of buyers.

The system of popular capitalism in particular permitted the sale of shares to tens of thousands of buyers, who only had to pay for 50 per cent of the value of the shares purchased. The balance was paid with a loan from CORFO for 15 years with a zero real interest rate and a one-year period of grace, with the shares themselves as collateral. There was also a discount for payment in time and income tax credits. A limit was imposed on how many shares a buyers could purchase with these benefits, which were so large that some taxpayers obtained the shares for free.

In Chile another issue is raised when the choice of buyers includes the managers and workers of the enterprise. Managers have far more information about the enterprise than do other buyers, or even the government. This brings up the problem of inside information that may allow managers and workers to obtain significant capital gains from the privatisation of an enterprise. Besides the obvious distributive consequences that this has, it complicates the political economy of privatisation by showing that specific groups may benefit from the process. In some of the enterprises in which shares were sold to workers, it was the managers that pushed for privatisation and now exercise ownership of the enterprise through investment companies.

Managers and workers paid for the shares they purchased through:

- The anticipated payment of accrued and nonaccrued severance benefits (as an incentive they could choose to receive 20 per cent of the severance pay in cash).
- As part of the settlement in collective bargaining, profit sharing or other bonuses.
- As a loan from CORFO.
- As a loan from a bank (this was usually done to purchase additional shares by creating an investment firm and using shares previously purchased as collateral).
- As a loan from the enterprise itself.
- Their own funds.
- In exchange for paid vacations. Public sector employees were also given the opportunity to buy shares in two enterprises with the anticipated payment of their severance benefits, with the option of purchasing additional shares with a loan from CORFO at a heavily subsidised real interest rate.

Different types of owner may have different goals; for example with regard to dividend policy. It is possible to imagine a situation in which managers of pension funds prefer to reinvesting the dividends. It is also possible to maximise dividends in the short-run; however, in most privatised enterprises two or three shareholders control the board. The exceptions are the two banks privatised through popular capitalism (although in one of them a dominant shareholder is appearing) and ENDESA. In the latter case a minority shareholder has managed to gain control of the enterprise with the support of those members of the board who have been elected by pension funds. This has raised the question of the function of pension funds as shareholders.

In Argentina the means of privatisation include:

- The sale of all or part of the corporation's capital stock.
- The sale of company assets in operation, either as a unit to one buyer or to two or more buyers.
- The sale of all or part of the assets belonging to nonfunctioning firms to one or more buyers.

Privatisation occurs through national or international bidding, according to the terms established in each case. There is broad freedom for disposing of assets, transforming companies and renegotiating contracts with preference given to bidders who already own part of the social capital of the company that is up for sale.

Ministries and other supervisory organisations that preside over public enterprises set the terms of sale, taking into account the value established by official banks or other appropriate public organisations. The executive branch can allow deferred collection of credits that official organisations have extended to establishments to be privatised (Glade, 1991).

In Brazil, the manner of sale has varied according to the case (Tables 2.9 and 2.10). In the transfer of Nova America, a company that had been extensively restructured by BNDES after bankruptcy and is the largest textile firm in the state of Rio de Janeiro, BNDES's controlling shares were auctioned in the Rio de Janeiro stock exchange after a minimum price per share was established.

A different solution was adopted, for example, in the transfer of Máquinas Piratininga do Nordeste, a capital goods producer that had also fallen under the control of BNDES. It was sold by tender after a minimum price had been set. Of the three prequalified bidders, two were asked to present written offers simultaneously. The highest bid, from the Votorantim Group, the largest industrial conglomerate in the country, was 6.1 per cent above the minimum price.

In the first privatisation concluded in 1988, an auction was again used to sell BNDES's controlling shares in Electrosiderúrgica Brasileira (SIBRA), a manganese alloy producer. The shares, making up 57.6 per cent of the voting stocks and 18.4 per cent of the company's equity, were sold at more than four times the minimum price to Companhia Paulista de Ferros Ligas for US$29 million, 20 per cent of which was to be paid in cash. The remaining 80 per cent was financed by BNDES itself. The inflation-indexed debt is to be paid over years at an annual real interest rate of 12 per cent (Glade, 1991).

In Mexico, too, privatisation takes many forms. For example, companies may be sold to the private or the 'social' sectors (such as unions and cooperatives), entities may be transferred to state or local government or be liquidated, and mergers may take place between two or more public entities. In Mexico's steel sector, enterprises merged but remained under government ownership. Likewise enterprises in other sectors that were transferred to state and local governments remain under government control, albeit at a different level (Glade, 1991).

Impact

The privatisations of Latin America are an integral part of the adjustment efforts and their effect on welfare has not been rigorously analysed.

Table 2.9 Concluded privatisations in Brazil, 1980–6

Enterprise	Ministry or public enterprise group	Industry	Date of privatisation	Manner of sale	Operation value in thousands of current US$
Cia. Brasileira de Cimento Portland Perus e Estrada de Ferro penis-Pirapora e Cibrape[1]	Finance Ministry	Cement 20	May 1980	Competitive bid	15 879.4
Cia. Quimica do Reconcavo (CQR)	PETROBRAS	Chemicals	24 Nov. 1981	Direct sale	5061.0
Cia. America Fabril		Textiles	31 Nov. 1981	Competitive bid	28 756.0
Riocell	Banco do Brasil	Paper pulp	10 Mar. 1982	Direct sale	77 542.2
Melodo–Organizacão e Planejamento de Sistemas Empresariais Uda	Caixa Econdmica Federal	Consulting	1 June 1982	Direct sale	11.6
Cia. de Tecidos Dona Isabel[2]		Textiles	July 1982	Competitive bid	16 897.6
Industria Brasileira de Papel (MBRAPEL)	Finance Ministry	Paper	27 Aug. 1982	Competitive bid	3245.3
Cia. Pemambucana de Borracha Sintelica (COPERBO)	PETROBRAS	Synethetic rubber	28 Dec. 1982	Direct sale	24 771.6
Oleos de Palma Agroindustrial (OPALMA)	SOERRBRAS	Vegetable oils	25 Mar. 1983	Competitive bid	3055.5
Cia. Federal de Segeros	Social Security Ministry	Insurance	20 Apr. 1983	Competitive bid	7107.3
Nilriflex–Industria e Comercio	PETROBRAS	Chemicals	27 Aug. 1983	Competitive bid	5871.8
Livraria Jose Olympio Editora, Encine e Didacta	BNDES	Publishing	16 Apr. 1984	Auction	218.2
Cia. Melhoramentos de Biurnenau (Grande Hotel)	Finance Ministry	Hotel	9 June 1986	Competitive bid	420.2

Notes:
1. In the case of this enterprise only fixed assets were sold to the private sector.
2. Reprivatised immediately after falling under state control.
Source: Secretaria de Controle de Empresas Estalas annual reports.

Table 2.10 Concluded privatisations in Brazil, 1987

Enterprise	Public enter-pise group	Industry	Date of privatisation	Manner of sale	Buyer	Operation value in thousands of current US$
Cia. Nacionaf de Tecidos Nova Am!erica S.A.	BNDES	Textiles	9 June 1987	Auction	Multitextile (Cataguazes-Leopoldina Group)	1 5855.7
Máquinas Piratininga do Nordesle S.A.	BNDES	Capital goods	23 July 1987	Competitive bid	Cimento Portland Poly (Votorantim Group)	1 363.2
Maquinas Piratininga S.A.	BNDES	Capital goods	15 Sept. 1987	Competitive bid	Wuppertal-Industria oe Maquinas Uda.	106.6
Ferritas Magneticas S.A. (FERMAG)	CVRO[2]	Magnetic alloys	26 Nov. 1987	Competitive bid	Araldi Participacoes	n.a.[1]

Notes:
1. n.a. – Not available.
2. Compantie Vale do Rio Duce.
Source: Conselho Interministerial de Privatizacão, 'Retarturio de atividades desemolvidas.'

Privatisation affects a government's net worth, employment, enterprise profit and the stock market. However evaluating the effects of privatisation is difficult because of, among other things, the large number of trade-offs that must be considered, the excessively broad nature of relevant counterfactuals, and the difficulty in accounting for the externalities that may be attributed to the process. More importantly the privatisation experience in these countries is still relatively immature, even for pioneers such as Chile. It will be a number of years before we really know all the resulting social benefits and costs of privatisation.

In spite of this the World Bank has attempted to grapple with some of these difficult problems. In a study of nine divestments in three developing countries, it found that eight improved welfare. Thus, to its own question of 'Did divestiture make the world a better place, or not', 'Our case studies answer this question with a resounding yes' (Galel *et al.*, 1992).

As summarised in the right-hand column of Table 2.11, the net world welfare change was positive in eleven of twelve cases, with only Mexicana Airlines showing a net loss. Furthermore the gains were substantial: the annual component of the perpetuity equivalent of the gains averaged 26 per cent of predivesture annual sales and in more than half the cases the gain exceeded 10 per cent, while the single negative case was negative by 19 per cent.

Who are the winners and the losers? As summarised in Table 2.12.

- *Foreigners versus nationals.* When foreigners are involved they generally do quite well. Only in three cases have foreigners lost on balance: British Airways, Mexicana and Aeromexico. In contrast domestic groups have gained on balance in all cases except Aeromexico. In two cases, Malaysian Air Systems and Telmex, domestic groups have gained on balance, but more than three quarters of the benefits go to foreigners. In contrast, with Chile Telecom and Kelang Container Terminal foreigners have gained substantially, but domestic actors have gained several times as much.
- *Consumers versus enterprise profits.* The extreme result at Telmex arose because foreigners were sold a large part of the company and enterprise profits rose dramatically, largely at the expense of domestic consumers because of rising prices. That this is not a necessary result of divestiture is evidenced by the other two telecommunications firms in the sample–British Telecom and Chile Telecom – where consumers gained, in one case by a substantial margin. Overall, consumer welfare showed high variance around zero, rising in four cases, remaining unchanged in five and falling in three.

Table 2.11 Summary of results: winners and losers

	Domestic					Net welfare change	Foreign		
	Government	Buyers	Consumers	Workers	Others		Buyers	Consumers	Others
United Kingdom:									
Telecom	2.7	3.1	4.9	0.2	-0.1	10.8	1.2	0	0
Airways	0.9	1.4	-0.9	0.3	0	1.7	0.4	0.5	0
Freight	-2	0.8	0	3.7	0	4.3	0	0	0
Malaysia:									
Airline	5.2	2.0	-2.9	0.4	0	4.6	0.8	0.8	15.8
Cont. port	37.6	11.5	6.2	7.0	-11.9	50.4	2.9	3.1	-3.0
Lottery	13.6	10.7	0	0	-13.0	10.9	0	0	0
Mexico:									
Telecom	10.6	12.3	-62.0	15.9	28.5	5.3	27.3	0	18.1
Airline Mex	3.5	-1.4	-7.7	0	3.2	-2.4	-1.3	-3.3	0
Airline Aero	62.3	3.9	-14.6	2.4	-2.3	52.9	1.8	-6.2	0
Chile:									
Elct gen	-1.4	2.0	0	0.1	0	0.7	1.4	0	0
Elct dist	-1.6	7.6	2.2	3.9	-7.4	4.6	0.6	0	0
Telecom	8.0	1.0	131	1.0	4.0	145	10.0	0	0

Notes:
1. All figures are the annual component of perpetuity equivalent of the welfare change (ACPE), expressed as a percentage of annual sales in the last predivestiture year.
2. The figure for workers includes both their roles as wage earners and as buyers of shares.

Source: Galel *et al.* (1992).

Table 2.12 Share of book value (%)

	1990	1991	1992
Book value of privatised, corporatised firms	100.00	100.00	100.00
Share of SPA	65.49	86.00	65.61
Share of municipalities	3.42	2.92	1.39
Share of foreign investers	12.90	8.01	0.09
Share of others	18.79	3.17	39.21

Source: Hungarian Finance Ministry.

• *Government versus buyers*. One very general result in the sample is that, in all cases, profits rose. The distribution of these gains between government and domestic and foreign buyers, however, is considerably less uniform. Although both domestic and foreign buyers came out ahead in every case except Mexicana, governments lost in three cases, albeit by small amounts. Overall, however, the immediate fiscal impact was positive in nine of the twelve cases.

• *Workers*. Given widespread union opposition to divestiture, it will surprise some to find that in no case did workers as a whole lose from divestiture, although the gains were substantial in only three cases. Workers benefited substantially from the share appreciation of Mexico's Telecom and Chile's Qod Enersis. A number of individual workers were, of course, made worse off, especially where layoffs or reduced hiring were involved. In the cases analysed, however, there was substantial severance pay and reasonably full employment, so these losses were minimal (Galel *et al.*, 1992).

The privatisation programmes of some countries have generated very large revenues for the government, thereby playing a key role in their economic stabilisation programmes. For example, in Mexico the proceeds from SOE sales in the two years 1990–1 were around $14 billion, which is three to five times various estimates of the benefits to Mexico from the debt-rescheduling operation. Although sales were mostly to Mexicans, the Telmex sale brought in $4.7 billion in foreign capital, and it is safe to say that much of the rest of privatisation revenue derived from the return of flight capital.

Although it is difficult to measure the size of capital inflows, it has been estimated by World Bank staff that there were some $2 billion of new portfolio inflows in 1990 and about $9 billion in 1991. Although the Mexican stock market boom and the related liberalised rules on foreign ownership of shares have encouraged capital inflows, all of the capital inflows of 1990–1 can be implicitly accounted for by the divestiture programme. Thus there is little doubt that revenues from divestiture have played an important role in macrostabilisation. In terms of its short-term revenue impact, it could be argued that privatisation has been even more important than the Brady deal.

Problems

Despite its successes, privatisation in Latin America has not been without some problems. The most crucial relates to the regulation of noncompetitive industries. The signs are that the region's regulatory capacity is lagging far behind the speed of its privatisation. The problem is not so much the lack of formal systems – they are often quite sophisticated and imaginative, as in the case of the Chilean electricity sector – but rather that they are emerging with little or no track record and apparently weak or nonexistent enforcement systems. The problem is aggravated by the fact that to attract buyers and finance their investment commitments, tariffs often underwent prior adjustments that were extremely generous to the privatised firms.

For example the Mexican government has experienced problems in setting up a regulatory environment. In the case of tradable goods reliance has been placed on liberalising imports, and in principle this measure ought to be adequate. The key sectors are steel and fertilisers, which have only just been privatised so it is too early to tell whether trade will do the job. Some experts are warning of serious dislocations in fertilisers supply in the 1995 growing season. The privatisation of sugar mills was a problem case because the complicated regulatory structure and low prices hampered the ability of the newly private sugar mills to make adequate profits. The terms of loans granted to the mills had to be renegotiated. Details of this case are difficult to uncover.

With nontradable goods, a regulatory structure is essential if there is any monopoly power in the market. Two cases have been prominent in Mexico, telecommunications and airlines. In the case of telecommunications, a regulatory structure was put in place before the divestiture of Telmex, and although this mechanism does provide some structure to the market, officials in the Mexican communications secretariat are quick to concede that their regulatory capability at this time is rather limited. As a result the regulations embody quantity targets that were in Telme's own strategic plans and a price regulation patterned after Britain's RPI-X formula but which has already been compromised more than once by agreement between the company and the government.

In the case of the airline industry, no regulatory changes were made for several years after divestiture, causing severe disruption of (or at least uncertainty in) the strategic planning of the firms. Aeromexico was sold in September 1988 and Mexicana in August 1989. Yet it was only in July 1991 that the airline market was largely deregulated. In the meantime the airlines had to live with controlled domestic airfares that were too low, and they had no clear idea of what the entry regulations were going to be. This cost the industry two years of uncertainty at a time when the market was already unsettled by the Gulf War. In some cases, privatisation promoted an unhealthy concentration of assets in the banks of a small financial and business elite. In particular, assets were concentrated in the banks of small groups of financial conglomerates, *los grupos*, such as Vial Crural-Lorrain and Matte in Chile.

In Chile, during the first phase of the privatisation, many of the privatised companies were purchased by highly leveraged domestic conglomerates whose ability to snap up assets was greatly enhanced by their privileged access to the local financial market and by the subsidy provided by the overvalued Chilean currency for borrowing abroad. In effect the conglomerates used their control of commercial banks to tap the lower real interest rates prevailing in overseas capital markets and crowd out other domestic investors.

Conditions favoured those who had access to foreign capital, and, as in the heyday of finance capitalism, speculation on borrowed funds and the pyramiding of debt concentrated ownership and erected unstable corporate conglomerates. The structure of these conglomerates was to prove exceedingly vulnerable to collapse when initial reverses provided the trigger. This led to a concentration of ownership over indebtedness and eventually (during the economic crisis of the early 1980s) the return of several divested firms and banks to the government.

In Mexico this problem relates to the government's policy of selling enterprises to well-identified buyers rather than to diffuse buyers in the stock market. Frequently a particular individual can be identified as 'the buyer'. Thus it may be said that Carlos Slim bought stock (such as in the case of Banamex) or because of innovations that allow them control even with a minority shareholding. This style of sale might be thought desirable in that it gives buyers all the leeway they need to concentrate on maximising long-term shareholder wealth without worrying about corporate raiders or other short-term considerations. At the same time this weakens an important characteristic of the market economy, one that is often cited as one of the key justifications for privatisation.

Private enterprises are said to operate more efficiently than their state-owned cousins because they are forced to face the discipline of the capital market. In part this argument has to do with the fact that private companies must raise the required capital on the capital market, and therefore they have to face the scrutiny of bankers or investors. It also has to do with the assertion that, if the managers of a private company are not performing well, others can take over the company through the stock market. This last kind of check is obviously impossible if the manager–owners control more than 50 per cent of the company, when an important advantage of private enterprise is lost.

There were some transparency problems as well. In Chile it was during this first wave of privatisation that charges arose about the process's lack of transparency. For example, rumours circulated about insider trading and government advisers ending up as shareholders in firms recommended for privatisation. Partly because of the government's inexperience on the pioneering road it was taking, and partly because of sheer haste in restoring legitimacy, these first divestitures were not as transparent as later ones.

The process, however, was never as opaque as it was in Argentina until 1989 or, even more so, in Mexico. Undoubtedly, however, it was the disconcerting spectacle provided by the corporate buccaneers of the late 1970s, together with the perennial and pervasive squabble over asset valuation (a problem in all countries), that accounted for much of the unhappiness with the transparency issue.

In some cases foreign investors, especially multinational companies, have had an unfair advantage. For example, by subsidizing direct foreign investment the debt-for-equity swaps provided an advantage to foreign multinational enterprises and promoted the takeover of Chilean enterprises.

In the case of Telmex in Mexico, it could be argued that, because a large proportion of the stock was sold to foreign investors, too much rent from the sale dissipated abroad. Calculations show that, whereas foreign investors paid the Mexican government a total of US$4.7 billion for about 35 per cent of the stock, they have already gained about $5.5 billion through stock appreciation. In fairness, the government sold at market prices and therefore this argument could be dismissed as 20–20 hindsight. Nevertheless the question remains as to whether government should have anticipated this eventuality because of its intimate knowledge of the case.

2.3 PRIVATISATION IN EASTERN EUROPE

The aim of this section is to provide a background summary of privatisation in Eastern Europe before drawing lessons from the Latin American experience and placing them within the framework of these countries' economic conditions. The privatisation process is still in its initial stage in Eastern Europe so there are many experimental approaches and unsolved problems. All lessons that can be drawn from the Latin American experience, therefore, are of relevance and importance for Eastern Europe. The efficiency of privatisation can be improved by following some of these lessons, for example they can assist in finding the right solutions and allow avoidance of the mistakes made by Latin American countries (for example in the case of debt-led privatisation).

The challenges regarding the radical transformation of overconcentrated state ownership in the economies of Eastern Central Europe are similar in many ways. The major characteristics are:

- Radical cutbacks of state ownership in the respective economies. This requires the privatisation of 50–60 per cent of today's state ownership. At the beginning of transformation it was forecast that this goal would be achieved in 3–5 years. It is now clear that it will take much longer, perhaps a decade or more.
- A change of structure should take place at the same time, transforming today's resource-intensive format into market-oriented, knowledge-intensive structures on the basis of the comparative advantages of each country.
- A fast change of market orientation, from the East to the West, was enforced by the collapse of COMECON.

At the same time this means a radical change of position in the world economy, from a developed periphery of an underdeveloped centre (the former USSR) into an underdeveloped periphery of a developed centre (the EU). This will require the restructuring of the national economies in their entirety.

The necessary transformation processes are also taking place under similar conditions:

- Protected markets and general recession in the world economy.
- A general lack of domestic and foreign capital as the international financial markets are short of hundreds of billions in US dollar terms.

- No clear property rights.
- Inadequate infrastructure and a poor institutional and legal framework.
- High domestic and foreign indebtedness.
- Exhausted population.

Key Objectives

In all the ex-socialist East European countries, privatisation has three key economic objectives: to improve efficiency, to spread ownership widely and fairly (thereby creating a capitalist economy and society), and to raise fiscal revenues. They are following different privatisation paths, however. This is in part because of the difference in their starting points, including the political and social strength of various groups (including workers, the old and new nomenklatura, and former owners), their existing degree of decentralisation and their history of reform efforts.

Privatisation in Hungary has three major and unique characteristics. First, privatisation is closely connected to the 'corporatisation' of state enterprises; that is, state enterprises may convert themselves into joint-stock companies and issue shares that can be bought by individuals. In Hungary corporatisation is considered as a first step to privatisation – as preparation for real privatisation and change of ownership.

Second, privatisation is market and business oriented – that is, Hungary rejects the mass distribution of shares to citizens and relies exclusively on the sale of assets; therefore there is no voucher or coupon system. There is a widely accepted argument that the government has not only the budgetary need but also the duty to the public to sell state-owned assets at the highest price. The compensation of former owners is treated as a separate issue or question. Government provides compensation in money rather than in kind.

Third, the revenue realised from privatisation is to be used mainly to reduce the national debt, due to the huge indebtedness of the Hungarian economy.

In the other Eastern European countries, privatisation is much more politically oriented, especially in former Czechoslovakia, Poland and Russia where the rationale is partly political. With early privatisation there is less risk that the economy will remain state controlled and a greater chance for complementary market-oriented reform.

Techniques and Methods

There are three types or means of privatisation:

- Privatisation where the initiative comes from below, or so-called spontaneous privatisation by managers, workers or outside investors.
- Privatisation where the initiative comes from the above (the state); that is, centralized (controlled) or so-called active privatisation.
- Free mass transfer (various voucher plans).

All are playing a role in Eastern Europe, although with a different mix in each country. Privatisation also relies on such means as the preferential sale of assets (stocks and shares) to employees; local self-government (towns, villages), the transfer of state property to municipalities and social security funds (for example pension funds), instalment and sales (buying, leasing). These means have played a minor part in the privatisation process so far. The stock exchange is also used for privatisation. Small enterprises, mostly in the retail trade and the service industry, are being privatised mainly through local auctions. The possibility of management buy-outs is under consideration.

Rapid privatisation will need to rely on a multitrack approach – no single approach can provide a complete answer. It is clear from recent experience that privatising small firms, particularly in trade and services, is relatively easy. They can be auctioned off by local governments (and in some cases returned to former owners) quite quickly and successfully. About half of Poland's state-owned shops were transferred to private hands in 1990 alone. Hungary and former Czechoslovakia passed laws on 'small privatisation' and have begun to privatise retail trade and service enterprises through auction to the highest bidder.

Large industrial firms present a more complex challenge. The one thing that is clear is that privatisation of these firms is a very complex, imperfect and time-consuming process. Profitable firms are able to privatise 'spontaneously', that is, by issuing their own shares to insiders with access to information and power, as Hungary and Poland have shown. Although sanctioned by law, and still regarded by some as the easiest means to an important end, spontaneous privatisation has suffered prominent cases of abuse.

The two main alternatives to spontaneous privatisation for large firms are sale by the government to the highest bidder and the free distribution of shares to citizens, although the two are not mutually exclusive. Many analysts have argued that sale is preferable to free transfer because it (1) leads to clear corporate control by interested 'real' owners and (2) increases public revenue. Hungary is supplementing spontaneous privatisation with a programme of 'active privatisation', or direct sale by the state. Poland plans to privatise many of its largest enterprises through individual sales. Germany is relying exclusively on public sales to privatise the state enterprises in the east.

In some countries the view is emerging that giving away a large share of state assets to the public may be the fairest and quickest means to widespread privatisation. The most discussed method of giving away assets is issuing citizens with vouchers that can be exchanged for the assets of their choice. Former Czechoslovakia first advocated such a plan in early 1990, and Poland, Russia and Romania later turned in that direction.

Mass transfers have at least three major potential drawbacks. The first is the fiscal cost associated with forgoing sale revenues. This once seemed paramount but now may be somewhat less important, in part because sales appear unlikely to raise as much revenue as initially hoped. The second is the fear that ownership will be so widespread and diluted that owners could not effectively assert control over management. The third is the concern that the public would lack the information to 'invest' vouchers wisely. Various plans attempt to tackle the latter two problems by proposing that intermediaries should hold and 'own' assets in trust for the public. The intermediaries, whether domestic or joint-venture holding companies, mutual funds, or soon-to-be-privatised banks or pension plans, would own relatively large blocks of shares in enterprises and would therefore have a greater ability and incentive than individual citizens to play an active ownership role.

The various voucher plans have many attractive features and could well play a positive role in speeding up and promoting fairness in the privatisation process. The plans, however, are still incomplete in many details. For them to be effective, it is imperative that they are designed and implemented in such a way as to ensure effective corporate governance and facilitate further sales of firms by intermediaries.

Several countries are moving towards the privatization of state-owned or cooperative farms. Both Bulgaria and Romania recently passed land reform laws that provide for the break-up of collective farms and the return of land to private ownership. In each country, claims of previous owners will be honoured, although the land returned will not necessarily be that taken away at collectivisation.

Although the need to restructure collective farms and redefine property rights over land is clearly an important issue, there has not been widespread discussion on how to coordinate land reform and the more general privatisation of state assets. Although the approach to property rights over land should be consistent with property rights over other assets, land should not be owned by widely dispersed absentee shareholders in the way that industrial enterprises would be under the various voucher plans under consideration. Neither state nor collective farms should, therefore, be included in the portfolios of any intermediaries appointed to hold shares on behalf of the public.

Legal and Institutional Framework

The first phase of drafting and implementing new legal status for privatisation has been largely completed in all Eastern European countries. In Hungary the groundwork for privatisation was laid by the October 1988 Law on Economic Association, which allowed state enterprises to 'corporatise' – that is, convert themselves into joint-stock companies. The law also allowed enterprises to issue shares and permitted individuals to buy them.

For self-managed firms (about 70 per cent of all enterprises), the decision to convert rested with enterprise councils. As councils were generally dominated by management, this led to a burst of spontaneous privatisation, often at advantageous terms for managers and the outside investors they brought in. An interesting political coalition supported this process – economic liberals, who viewed spontaneous privatisation as the quickest and easiest way to dismantle the state sector, and the old and new nomenklatura, who saw in the process an opportunity to acquire wealth.

The Transformation Law of 1989 was designed to address some of the previous abuses of spontaneous privatisation and establish a more rigorous monitoring of the process. The State Property Agency was set up with a mandate both to limit undervaluation of assets when the privatisation initiative came from below and to initiate privatisation from above.

Important legislative activity concerning privatisation and regulations characterised 1991. Acts passed included laws on the Central Bank and financial institutions, including the banking sector, state concessions, compensation for formerly nationalised properties, investment funds, the transfer of state property to municipalities, and various tax laws. The new law on cooperatives and a law on the Employee Share Ownership Programme (ESOP) were enacted early in 1992. A privatisation law package, including laws on companies remaining under state control, on the State Property Agency (SPA) and on the amendments required in other laws establishing the crucial legal framework for privatisation (the Act on Transformation, the Companies Act, the Act on the Protection of state Assets and so on), was enacted in June 1992.

Of particular note among the important legal/institutional changes is the State Holding Company, which is to be set up to act as custodian and manager of shareholdings that are to remain under government control.

This company will also have the right to sell off stakes in enterprises that are not wholly state owned.

Poland started its privatisation drive from a difficult position. Previous reforms in the aftermath of martial law had expanded the role of workers' councils. Ownership rights had become ambiguous. Enterprises could enter into any kind of legally permissible contract and could issue their own shares to any investor, including themselves.

The resulting wave of spontaneous privatisation in 1989 provoked a public outcry. In early 1990 the state tried to reclaim legal title to all assets in order to begin privatisation from above, but it did not entirely succeed. After several months of parliamentary debate, the State Enterprises Privatisation Act was adopted in July 1990. It represents a compromise between different viewpoints in that corporatisation, and later privatisation, can take place only with the consent of workers' councils. This law leaves intentionally vague the procedure of privatisation and allows practically all schemes – the sale of entire firms, liquidation and asset sales to private parties, free distribution of shares to citizens and the establishment of share-holding companies.

The latest Polish plan envisages selling off a number of the largest firms and the mass distribution of ownership interests in hundreds more. Whatever the model selected, employees can buy up to 20 per cent of shares at a 50 per cent discount. Foreign investors can acquire up to 10 per cent of shares without explicit government authorisation. A Ministry of Ownership Change has been established to oversee the process and specialised financial institutions have been set up to facilitate it.

Former Czechoslovakia and Romania joined Poland in favouring mass distribution. The Czechoslovakia legislature passed privatisation legislation that calls for widespread distribution of assets via vouchers, as well as the sales of shares of some individual assets (upon liquidation). Romania's law, passed by the legislature in September 1990, proposes to distribute 30 per cent of enterprise assets to the public and to sell off any remaining assets, unless they are specifically designated to remain under state control. Bulgaria has produced five draft privatisation laws, although no clear goals or strategies have emerged.

Former Yugoslavia has had to deal with the most firmly entrenched worker self-management of all the countries. Its strategy has been to try to remove self-management rights while simultaneously providing firms with the legal means to sell their assets, preferably to their work forces (at a discount of up to 70 per cent). The 1988 Enterprise Law and the 1989 Law on Social Capital limit self-management rights and allow workers' councils to transform self-managed firms into joint-stock companies. Initial results have been disappointing – few sales have taken place and the development funds, which are supposed to oversee privatisation and receive a share of the proceeds, are only now being created. The role of these funds differs widely by republic. The Serbian fund, for example, intends to concentrate more on restructuring, whereas the Slovenia fund intends to work exclusively as a privatisation agency, valuing and selling assets as rapidly as possible.

Privatisation in Germany is rather centralised and government controlled, as well as adhering to well-defined policy goals. The German Government set up a specific privatisation institution, the Treuhandanstalt. Its functions include the creation of supervisory boards and the monitoring of management, evaluating the potential viability of enterprises and adjusting balance sheets accordingly (writing off old debts), reorganising and closing firms, finding and evaluating buyers, and increasing employment and investment targets. From the beginning it opted to sell public assets rather than give them away and, generally, to sell for cash rather than enter into credit arrangements. The majority of the East European countries do not have such well-defined objectives and lack similar monitoring and control mechanisms.

Claims of former owners have complicated the privatisation process, particularly in Hungary, former Czechoslovakia and East Germany. The ruling coalition in Hungary agreed in July 1990 to a 'reprivatisation' law for agricultural land, which gave owners dispossessed in 1947 the rights to 100 hectares each. It also gave workers on cooperative or state farms the right to buy land at reduced prices.

The law was approved by parliament but was declared unconstitutional because it discriminated against other former landowners. The current plan is to provide compensation in money rather than in kind. In former Czechoslovakia a law passed in late 1990 provides for the reprivatisation of some 70 000 properties that were nationalised in the late 1950s, although how this will be done is uncertain. The German privatisation programme is being severely complicated by the million or more property restitution claims that have been filed by private individuals, plus 15 000 claims by local governments. In the countries of the former Soviet Union, the creation of the legal and institutional framework of privatisation is at a very early stage.

The governments of Eastern Europe have started to introduce regulations on the operations of surviving natural monopolies and are seeking to prevent the inheritance of monopolistic positions and the emergence of new monopolies in the privatisation process. By doing this, the governments intend to encourage competition and curtail the influence of monopolies. These regulations, however, are at a very early stage and are not yet sufficient.

Achievements: Speed of Privatisation

There are no comprehensive statistics available regarding the speed of privatisation in the region; therefore the timing given here is only an illustration of the privatisation process. Poland began its transition to a market economy with some 8 000 large industrial SOEs. Hungary,Czechoslovakia, Romania and former Yugoslavia each had more than 2500. Before its breakup, the USSR, at a conservative estimate, possessed more than 47 000 very large industrial SOEs (see World Bank, 1992).

In Hungary, privatisation has proceeded relatively rapidly under the influence of some favourably changing macroeconomic conditions; for example the balance-of-payments situation, high but declining inflation and fast export market reorientation, particularly in the second half of 1991. By the end of 1991 some 950 of the 1897 state-owned enterprises belonging to the State Property Agency had been involved in some phases of privatisation, representing about 35–40 per cent of the total book-value of HUF 1900 billion to be privatised. This could also be taken as the rate of privatisation attained so far. (Some 218 of these enterprises were transformed during the privatisation process into normal, share-holding corporations. About 88 per cent of these transformations took place during 1991).

In 126 cases the solution chosen was not transformation, but the creation of completely new corporations, 64 per cent of which were created during 1991. About 45 per cent of the 126 were founded with foreign participation. To arrive at the real rate of privatisation, however, the change in the ownership structure of investors' equity should also be taken into account.

After the transformation of the companies, according to this structure, the State Property Agency remains the main shareholder at 86 per cent, reflecting that in Hungary the idea of issuing coupons to the general public has been rejected. Consequently, 14 per cent of investors' equity of the transformed companies can be seen as a real ownership change, according to which the real rate of privatisation (concerning Hungarian domestic private buyers/investors) is only 3 per cent because the share of local councils is 3 per cent and that of foreign capital is 8 per cent. Although the share of foreign capital is significant, it lags far behind the target figures (25–30 per cent) of the government's privatisation strategy. It is also interesting to note that the share of foreign capital is declining (Table 2.13). It seems as if foreign investors have picked out the best, most profitable options and are waiting for similar opportunities.

The process of privatising the state enterprises of former East Germany relies exclusively on sale to 'qualified buyers'. No firms will be sold through the existing stock exchange or given away to the general public. As of 1 January 1991 the state privatisation agency had concluded about 500 deals, almost all of which had been individually negotiated with West German and foreign buyers. Some deals involved entire firms, whereas others involved spinoffs of the 8000 or so large enterprises to be privatised. In addition about a third of the 11 000 small- and medium-sized enterprises nationalised in 1972 were returned to their previous owners, and some 7000 small shops were leased to private individuals as a step towards privatisation.

In former Czechoslovakia, any citizen over the age of 18 was able to purchase vouchers worth 1000 points with which to bid for a share worth Kcs 1000. Some 8.5 million people have purchased booklets. Most vouchers are concentrated in the hands of a few investment funds (such as Harvard Capital Consulting), and these could play an important role in monitoring the privatised firms.

Table 2.13 Leaders and laggards: regional privatisation, percentage of regional sector

Regional sector	Shops	Restaurants	Other services
Top seven:			
St Petersburg	47.7	30.5	34.3
Moscow	41.9	25.2	35.5
Nizhny Novgorod	39.5	84.0	38.0
Lipetsk	38.1	46.9	30.2
Penza	38.1	76.3	31.5
Stavropol	36.4	70.8	48.4
Kaliningrad	34.6	64.6	14.5
Bottom seven:			
Yakutla	12.8	37.1	4.7
Kalmykia	10.9	4.8	11.0
Marii-El	9.8	9.8	4.2
Ulyanovsk	9.2	27.7	26.1
Komi	7.2	31.8	14.2
Tatarstan	2.2	11.0	0.3
Chechnya & Ingushla	0.5	0.0	2.0

Source: Goskometal, up to 1 July 1992.

In Poland, the sale to the public of five enterprises (compared with an initial target of 150), completed in January 1991, was deemed a moderate success. After a three-week extension of the offer period, 100 000 people had applied to purchase shares, and the issues for four of the five companies to be sold in this manner were announced. In addition, several large companies had been sold to foreign enterprises, and the assets of some 200 others had been sold after liquidation of the enterprises.

In Russia the regions are reforming at different speeds. In the first half of 1992 Moscow and St Petersburg sold nearly half their shops to the private sector, and it was projected that most small businesses would be privately owned by the end of 1993. In contrast the republics had privatised almost nothing (Table 2.13).

In the Baltic states privatisation has only just begun. Latvia launched a voucher scheme in 1993, the first batch of 60 000 privatisation vouchers being valued at 5600 Latvian rubles each (US$43).

Privatisation has resulted in financial scandal in almost every country in this region. For example Latvia's biggest financial scandal broke after the sudden resignation of the director of the Latvian Investment Bank (LIB). The scandal started with a small German company that responded to the LIB's attempt to find foreign investors in the Broken Cement and Roofing Company, which was privatised in February 1993 – the offer involved the apparently fraudulent handling of a US$400 million loan. Such cases draw attention to the importance of transparency.

Constraints

Despite the progress achieved in privatisation in Eastern Europe, it is lagging somewhat behind the pace suggested by the various governments. Beyond the growing political and economic uncertainties in Eastern Europe, some elements of the macroeconomic situation – bankruptcies and, particularly, deteriorating state budgets resulting in high taxes and unusually high social security contributions – have produced an unfavourable effect on both the supply and demand sides of the privatisation process.

Supply-side constraints have impinged on privatisation actions because a significant number of public enterprises are either making a loss or are operating at very low levels of efficiency. The attractiveness of these companies to investors appears to be rather low. In Hungary, for example, investors' greater interest in efficient enterprises might be illustrated by the larger difference between the book value and the contract value of transformed corporations in 1990 (55 per cent in favour of the latter) than in 1991 only 33 per cent in favour of the latter) because of the first choice of efficient companies.

Although several options (decentralisation, sale at a low price and so on) have been tested to find a solution to the privatisation of insolvent and loss-making corporations, no real solution has been found so far. According to the Hungarian experience, a lasting solution can only be reached through radical reorganisation and modernisation of these companies. This task must fall largely on the newly established State Holding Company.

Another supply-side constraint is connected to infrastructural considerations. One problem is that multifaceted practical considerations come into conflict with the rigidity of legal regulations, which are far from perfect (for example concerning the purchase and development of real estate by foreigners). Clarification of ownership is still lacking and laws concerning the protection of the environment have yet to be developed.

Another problem is the lack of an adequately functioning banking system and of other financial institutions, such as investment funds, insurance companies and pension funds. In the absence of a developed capital market, the possibility of sale on the stock market is very limited. Finally, the lack of updated and full information on the economy on both macro and micro levels, particularly on sectoral development policies, is unfavourably affecting the privatisation process.

Record keeping with regard to land and real estate is very complicated, and any environmental damage caused by the firm, which may become the responsibility of the buyer, is often completely unknown. As a result the sale of companies to foreign investors is extremely time consuming and requires extensive and expensive use of expert consultants.

On the demand side, the main constraint is the restricted volume of investment capital, particularly as far as domestic investors are concerned. So far, as we can see in Hungary, most property (8 per cent) has been purchased by foreigners. The share of domestic purchasers is about 3 per cent, of which the share of banks is just 1.3 per cent.

The lack of Hungarian participation in the privatisation process is also a result of limited credit facilities. To overcome this the Hungarian government has introduced various programmes. One of these is E-credit ('E' for Existence, used in Hungarian to mean livelihood), which has provided HUF 1.8 billion in credit facilities for new business; a similar one is the S-credit programme ('S' for Start), which supplied HUF 3.8 billion for almost the same purpose. The government has also decided to create a new guarantee fund to speed up the utilisation of existing credit facilities (for example, the First Hungarian Fund has US$80 million of capital).

Compensation bonds and the Employee Share Ownership Programme will help to strengthen domestic investment capacity and entrepreneuring in the future; large-scale investment activity, however, can only be developed gradually.

There are valuation and equity problems as well. Accurate valuation is virtually impossible given the absence of capital markets (these valuations are carried out mainly by major international accounting and consulting firms and their experiences have shown that the result depends on rather arbitrary assumptions). As far as the equity problem is concerned, the old and new nomenklatura, black marketeers and beneficiaries of current market distortions are seen as likely domestic buyers. Due to the depressed condition of the economy and the high perceived risk, acceptable prices may be low and these buyers may reap windfall gains.

Impacts

In general, the expectations for privatisation were very high – it was (and still is) almost seen as a panacea. The collapse of the former economic systems and the success of developed market economies have clearly demonstrated that the replacement systems should be based on private ownership. Consequently privatisation appears to be a key element in solving the problems inherited from the former economic systems. In the long term this might be so, but in the short term the results are not obvious because of the side effects of privatisation and the time needed for the new behavioural patterns to begin operating.

Only a brief indication, based on the Hungarian experience, can be given here of the possible impacts of privatisation (in other countries there are no proper data). Among the effects of privatisation that could be identified are those on efficiency and exports, at the micro level; and on demand and supply, labour and the state budget, at the macro level.

To illustrate the possible impact of privatisation on efficiency, the economic indicators of 100 transformed companies have been analysed on the basis of their balance sheets. When the economic indicators of these companies are compared with the average values of indicators of five branches of industry, the differences appear to be characteristic only among transformed industries where the share of foreign ownership is high. Here, the efficiency indicators of the transformed companies are above average.

When the wage increase of 25.7 per cent paid by the 100 transformed companies in 1991 is compared with that of the economy as a whole, the difference is negligible. However the amount of personal income tax paid by the employees of the companies increased by 57 per cent, much more than in the economy as a whole, indicating that wage increases were among the high-income brackets during 1991. This is a result of a more efficient labour policy, whereby corporations tend to pay higher wages to workers with higher qualifications and dismiss surplus labour.

Such developments provide evidence that privatisation is contributing to more efficient resource allocation and income distribution. Such a contribution, however, could be seriously jeopardised by the survival of monopoly positions even after privatisation.

The impact of privatisation on export performance is pronounced. In 1991 the total exports of the 100 transformed companies increased by 50 per cent at current prices, with exports to the Western trading area increasing by 73 per cent, faster than the increase of exports of the economy as a whole (24 per cent and 52 per cent, respectively). In the light of these results, it seems that privatisation can be an engine of export-led economic growth.

As regards the impact of privatisation on aggregate demand and supply, it was originally thought that privatisation would reduce excess demand and contribute to supply. The Hungarian economy is essentially characterised by demand constraints, because of the near collapse of the Eastern market, the decline in private consumption and investment, the increase of domestic savings and tight monetary policies.

Privatisation has played only a minor role in the significant increase in domestic savings. Some elements of privatisation – the influx of external capital, preferential credit facilities and compensation vouchers – tended to increase aggregate demand, although this was successfully kept under control. As far as compensation vouchers are concerned, rather than offer restitution the government proposed partial compensation in the form of securities, which can be used to buy new properties. In line with the Compensation Act, the State Property Agency ensures the redeemability of compensation vouchers by creating an adequate privatisation supply.

The positive impact of privatisation on aggregate supply is lagging behind expectations and has not counterbalanced the fall in production. One reason for this is the narrow range of privatisation carried out so far. Another is that some aspects of privatisation appear to work against the growth of production. For example new owners prefer to buy control of a market rather than new capacity, monopoly positions continue to exist after privatisation, rationalisation programmes are set up for the short term only and the rationalisation process, in most cases, starts with a cut in production.

The low-supply effect, of course, has a direct impact on employment by reducing the demand for labour. According to one forecast, the privatisation of some 40 per cent of state assets over a period of three years could result in a 10–15 per cent reduction in the numbers employed.

One should also take into account the job-creating effect of privatisation, because of the growing number of private entrepreneurs and small ventures in particular. Job creation, however, appears to be lagging behind the growth in redundancies, so has not halted the increase in unemployment. To some extent this is because the pace of privatisation has not yet reached the planned speed, the number of real (private) owners is still not large and the share of foreign capital is still small.

An income of HUF 676 million was realised in 1990 from the sale of shares and shareholdings, as well as from the privatisation of the retail, catering and service industries. More than two thirds of this income was in convertible currency, and some 511 million forints, after deducting expenses, was used to reduce the national debt.

As a result of the acceleration of the privatisation process, the State Property Agency realised an income of 40.1 billion forints in 1991. About 72 per cent of this was in convertible currency. The revenues obtained from privatisation have been used to reduce the national debt (HUF 23 billion), covering transfers to the state budget (HUF 13 billion) and local governments (HUF 1.3 billion), and covering privatisation costs and transfers to the corporations (HUF 2.8 billion). In 1992 a revenue of HUF 70 billion was expected, of which 20 billion was to be used to reduce the national debt, 12 billion was to be spent on privatisation costs and 10 billion on the reorganisation of state-owned firms. In 1993 the figures were 70.5 billion, 20 billion, 13 billion and 3.5 billion, respectively. Although Hungarian decision makers have focused on decreasing the national debt, in the light of increasing financial needs for reorganisation processes revenues from privatisation do not seem to be enough for a significant reduction in, or liquidation of, the national debt.

2.4   LESSONS FOR EASTERN EUROPE

Because of the many fundamental differences between the two regions, one must be careful when drawing lessons from privatisation in Latin America for Eastern Europe. Privatisation in the Eastern European ex-socialist countries differs greatly from elsewhere, and privatisation in Latin America has been an easier task compared with the effort required in Eastern Europe. The public sector in Eastern Europe represents 80–90 per cent of GDP. In contrast, even in Mexico, where until the mid-1980s public ownership was widespread, it amounted to just 17 per cent of GDP.

Privatisation in Eastern Europe, therefore, is a more massive and thus a more complex undertaking.

The context is also very different. Latin American countries have mixed economies, where prices bear a relation to scarcity value and concepts of property, ownership, title and contracts. In Latin America there are clearly defined private capital and stock markets and ownership rights, both by states and by private interests. This has not been the case in most of the ex-socialist countries for at least 40 years – longer in the case of the Republics of the Independent States. Drawing lessons from the Latin American experience, therefore, is not an easy task. Bearing all this in mind, and taking into account the experience gained by Eastern Europe so far, the following conclusions and lessons can be drawn from the privatisation experience of Latin America.

Privatisation as an Integral Part of Economic Reform

Privatisation has to be managed and treated as an integral part of the economic reform package, as an element of the transformation of the system. It is not to be undertaken as an end in itself, but as a means to an end: to use resources more efficiently. Removing price distortions and controls as quickly as possible is essential for that purpose. Unless prices are true indicators of costs and consumer demand, the true profitability of an enterprise cannot be known, so its assets cannot be properly valued.

Selling the enterprise at an appropriate price may be impossible, and in the meantime managers will be unable to make informed decisions on investment and production. Letting the price system work as it should means removing distortions such as price controls, distorted transfer prices between enterprises, subsidised loans and preferential access to the budget and credit system. It also means getting macroeconomic policy right. Privatisation has meant much more than merely transferring assets to the private sector. It has been part of a broader exercise aimed at stabilising and liberalising the economy on several fronts, for example regulation, prices, trade and the financial sector.

Governments have consciously set out to redefine the economic role of the state. As part of this shift they have curtailed the SOEs' privileged access to the budget or credit system, tariff or nontariff protection for their products, and regulatory protection from private competitors. The experience of Latin American countries suggests that, in general, one should not aim for short-term government revenue maximisation but rather should take a longer view. Many countries have taken the view that unless privatisation was part of such a broad programme of reform, it would be an empty gesture and would merely transfer the control of rents from the public to the private sector.

Preferred Sequencing

The rationale is that private ownership requires financial institutions, experience and expertise that do not yet exist in the transitional economies. Without this infrastructure, rapid privatisation could lead to widespread corruption and economic and political chaos.

No single reform sequence will fit all the transitional economies. Reform histories vary; for example, unlike other countries, Hungary has had more than two decades of experience with decentralised economic decisions. Macroeconomic conditions range from great instability to relative stability. Preferred sequencing, therefore, would include early steps to stabilise the macroeconomy and deregulate domestic and external-sector prices to give clear, accurate signals for economic activity and for the valuation of enterprises.

These steps would be accompanied and followed by intense efforts to rationalise enterprises, improve economic decision making, reform trade policy, and build managerial skills and a strong, controlled financial sector. Privatisation of large, state enterprises would become the next priority. Some agricultural, retail and residential assets would be privatised early. The primary aim of the privatisation of banks, insurance companies and other financial institutions should be to integrate them into the domestic banking and financial system (through capital involvement, new market contacts, efficient management, expansion of services and technical modernisation). Institution building would be a basic theme from the start at all levels, including the legal contractual system, the structure of ownership and the roles of key organisations in the economy.

As the case of Chile has shown (Sáez, 1992), when the government decided to sell the large public enterprises in the mid-1980s, all structural reforms had been completed and the economy had adjusted to an open trade regime, liberalised domestic goods and capital markets, and the elimination of subsidies. The privatisation process was carried out in a more stable economic environment and the risk of a reversion in divestiture was much lower. It appears that it is more appropriate to advance the reform process first and then privatise public enterprises.

Among enterprises, privatisation should initially focus, as much as possible, on the traded goods sector – where learning by doing can have lower costs – and later concentrate on any large public service firms that may be earmarked for privatisation. Public firms, especially large ones, should be restructured before sale, introducing reforms that are feasible and enhance profitability. A larger portion of privatisation revenue should be spent on modernisation; financing budget flows and current outlays should be avoided or minimised. This will make the value of the firm more visible to the private sector and raise the bargaining power of the seller, because it is easier to hold out for a higher price when a firm is viable.

Also, it should take into consideration that in many cases government is likely to have far less expertise than prospective buyers. The government must decide whether to close a plant or to offer it for sale. Once the decision to sell has been made, there is little logic in trying to improve the price by devoting time and money to a restructuring task that would be better accomplished by the purchaser. Most prospective buyers can imagine what the plant would look like once painted, few would be fooled by a fresh coat of paint.

Timetable

The recent Brazilian experience shows that it is not wise to announce a tight timetable. Privatisation is a prolonged process, which has made it impossible for President Collor to fulfil his promise of privatising one company per month. A supposedly short-term process that is dragged out creates uncertainty and political friction. Thus, before announcing each privatisation, it is essential to prepare the scene by adjusting product prices, eliminating subsidies and solving legal problems such as labour contracts.

Choosing the Right Mode

The Chilean experience illustrates perfectly the importance of choosing the right mode of privatisation as this, together with the quality of its implementation, will determine the effect of privatisation on government revenues, public sector wealth, private sector wealth distribution, the economic industrial structure, capital market development and financial stability, among other things.

There is a need for the flexible use of the various privatisation methods. Much emphasis should be put on the investor-initiated privatisation method and to the so-called spontaneous self-privatisation method to extend the range of participants. This makes possible the transformation and sale of companies without direct involvement from the state, but through independent consulting and property evaluating companies, to be selected by the state by way of competition. In addition, greater attention should be given to such methods as leasing, management contracts, and worker and management buy-outs. Cash payment must be given priority and debt-led privatisation should be avoided because, as the case of Chile has shown, a highly unstable financial system can result from it.

Regulation

The empirical evidence suggests that private ownership has efficiency advantages in competitive conditions, but it does not show that either public or private ownership is generally superior when market power is not present. Policy towards competition and regulation appears to be very important in the latter case. The evidence suggests that, in competitive industries, private ownership is generally (although not universally) preferable on efficiency grounds and that competition may be a more important influence than ownership. In the case of industries with natural monopoly elements, such as water and electricity, the results of the empirical studies are very mixed. Some give the advantage to public ownership, others to private ownership, others can find no significant difference between the two.

The important point to emerge from the evidence is the importance of competitive conditions and regulatory policies, as well as ownership, for incentives and efficiency. A key, therefore, to the future impact of privatisation on social welfare will be the effectiveness of public regulation. Privatisation assumes that firms can be regulated as well or better than they were under public ownership. The regulatory challenge is a major one, especially in public services.

First, effectively regulating powerful monopolies is an inherently difficult and sometimes conflictive task. Second, the speed with which regulatory systems have emerged in Latin America suggest that flaws are likely to be discovered after privatisation. When these are serious, countries will have to find ways of correcting them without disrupting investment or stock markets, where privatised public service firms usually carry a large weight. Third, regulatory systems must be flexible in the face of rapidly changing technological developments in some public service sectors. Fourth, regulators may also have to be international diplomats as many new owners of public service firms are foreign enterprises and many of those are owned by foreign governments.

Rules of the Game

Managers (of both private and public firms) must be granted autonomy from political interference and receive the right incentives. This can only happen if the economic environment is stable and entrepreneurs are able to make long-term investments without fearing that their decisions are liable to be overturned for political reasons. Due to the important role and share of state-owned companies in Eastern Europe in the foreseeable future, creating stable incentives and favourable conditions for their efficient functioning is one of the crucial tasks of national economic management.

Legal rules are a common good allowing coordination of individual actions. Erratic, discretionary rules and privileged access to public officials limit the ability of economic entities to contract, and thus produce economic losses. In the end, erratic rules destroy credibility in economic policy and destroy confidence in the legal process. Resources are wasted on the purchase of influence to pursue an economic transaction. Arbitrary rules also limit the ability of trading agents to commit themselves through contracts, encourage lobbying for privileges and weaken the credibility of transactions.

An impartial enforcement mechanism of explicit legal rules is essential to facilitate private contracting. Neutrally enforced legislation presumes a stable government committed to the existing laws and the strict enforcement of these laws.

Preferential Distribution of Shares to Workers

Many privatisation programme have included schemes to allow enterprise employees to acquire shares in their organisations on particularly favourable terms. The rationale for these policies may be based upon the perceived efficiency-enhancing incentive effects of employee share ownership, but these are questionable in large firms. There may also be a desire to compensate employees for potential loss of rents accrued under public ownership, to achieve political support for privatisation or to influence the longer term probability of renationalisation.

These points, however, are questionable. Pressure from workers for public ownership is likely to be strongest when their firm is in financial difficulty. But share values will tend to be low in that case and, even if employee shareholding exits on a substantial scale, protecting returns to labour may be the overriding priority. Moreover employee share ownership gives workers extra incentives to oppose policies promoting effective competition and regulation. Thus what was initially compensation for loss of privileges may, at a later date, provide stronger incentives for the restoration of those privileges.

The strategy of reducing labour resistance to privatisation through share distribution has tended to work. Awarding shares, however, without the prospect of board representation is similar to a profit-sharing arrangement. Hence it may be more efficient to set up this type of programme directly for the firms' workers and reserve shares for the highest bidders.

This approach would increase the net sale products for the state, as one avoids the lower sale price derived from (1) the subsidy on the shares distributed to workers and (2) the uncertainty that prospective shareholders would face regarding the future role of workers in management of the firm. Moreover a profit-sharing programme could have larger spread effects in the local economy than a special subsidised sale of shares to workers of certain public enterprises. In effect it establishes a precedent that other private firms can more plausibly be encouraged to imitate, which in turn opens up prospects of institutionalising profit sharing for all workers in the productive sector of the economy. Finally, as an incentive for productivity, profit sharing may be better than the free distribution of shares, because it avoids morale problems that can arise from unfavourable fluctuations in the region's still thin domestic stock markets.

Fair Compensation for SOE Employees

As an alternative to a strategy of layoffs followed by new hiring, more effort could be put into retraining and reallocating labour within the firm. Shares with board representation, or profit sharing, could be exchanged for concessions on wages. When layoffs are necessary, indemnification is simply not enough. Cash payments can be easily dissipated; hence distressed workers need counselling, retraining, relocation assistance and follow-up monitoring of their reintegration into the market. As excess employment in the state firms is a 'public problem', it would seem appropriate to finance retraining, counselling and indemnification with special solidarity taxes or loans from international development banks, which have been major creditors of many SOEs.

Debt/Equity Swaps

Swaps can ease financing constraints and help improve a country's investment climate. But it has to be dealt with as a part of general foreign debt management policy; it cannot be a primary goal of privatisation.

Swaps may be a way for heavily indebted countries to bring foreign investors, including commercial banks, into transactions that might not go through without their participation. Nevertheless swaps must be used carefully. Critics of swaps argue, with some justification, that government may be better off selling the enterprise and using the proceeds of the sale to repay or repurchase the debt on the secondary market. In that way it might capture more of the discount and extend the participation of local investors. Countries may be able to increase their access to swaps by creating conversion funds for privatisation, which have been used successfully in Argentina and Chile. They pool eligible debt paper from commercial banks and multinational and individual investors to swap for enterprise assets. Such funds could even be active investors, taking a role in restructuring poorly managed enterprises.

Transparency

Transparency improves social welfare because it reduces the possibility of corruption, collusion and inside information, all of which create privileged gains from the sale of the public's assets. It also can be complementary to many other objectives. Because transparency opens the process to public scrutiny, errors can be checked more easily, and fairer evaluations can be made as to whether the government's stated objectives – regarding the process of privatisation as well as the end product – are being reasonably fulfilled.

The closer results are to objectives, the more likely it is that privatisation will have a happy ending for the firms, the government and the general public, which in turn reduces the risk of policy backlash. Transparency also enhances the efficiency of the 'learning by doing' process, which is an inevitable part of any government's privatisation programme. An improved flow of information will also contribute to overall market efficiency.

Transparency can enhance the government's credibility and have catalytic effects, especially when past governments have had a reputation for corruption or cronyism. In addition, the objective of democratisation and participation in economic matters and society more generally is consistent with greater transparency.

Transparency trades off with the speed of the privatisation. This could be an important consideration if political interests give a priority to this latter objective. Most of the objectives, however, that commonly drive privatisation are not necessarily enhanced by speed. Indeed many of them, such as productive and allocative efficiency, credibility, government revenue and so on, not to mention social equity, can be seriously compromised by a hasty privatisation process.

Which actions improve transparency? The list is long, but a few key policies can be mentioned:

- Information: reserved documentation should be the exception rather than the rule. Although a limited amount of reserved information may be justified during negotiations for the sale, the public should have easy access to all the information following completion of the transaction. This includes preparations for the sale of the firm (debt absorption, labour relations, capital restructuring and so on), firm valuation reports, preselection and selection processes, administrative and promotional costs, and the facts about the buyers and their financing of the purchase.

- If sales require subsidies, they should not be hidden in preferential prices and credit terms. Rather, subsidies should be awarded in such a way that they are explicit and easily accountable to the public. This is an important consideration because a double standard has emerged during the period of privatisation. Proponents of adjustment rankle at hidden subsidies in the social area but turn a blind eye to subsidies hidden in underpriced asset sales and below-market credit terms.

- Earmark sale receipts by putting them in a special account (Mexico has done this). Although earmarking is often frowned upon in public finance, it is justified by the extraordinary nature of the income.

- An independent, official, technical agency should be responsible for ex-post evaluations of individual privatisation, based on ex-ante agreed criteria formulated jointly by parliament and the executive branch.

- Privatised firms should be subject to certain basic disclosure rules that facilitate the types of information that are needed for effective ex-post evaluations of the results of privatisation.

- Government officials and subcontracted technicians associated with the decision to privatise and the process itself should be prohibited from working in privatised firms for a determined period, for example five years.

Role of the State

The transitional period is very long and difficult to manage. Creating a mixed economy and liberalising trade, the domestic goods markets, the financial system and the capital account will take many years. During this period the role of the state is crucial in designing the correct speed and attributes of each stage of reform and transition. The state has to have a privatisation strategy and the duty of the state is to implement this strategy. Due to the very nature of privatisation, it cannot be implemented in a spontaneous manner.

References

Bolton, P. and G. Roland (1992) 'Privatization Policies in Central and Eastern Europe', *Economic Policy*, 15 October.

Cardoso, Eliana (1991) 'La Privatización en América Latina', in J. Vial (ed.), *Adónde Va America Latina: Balance de Las Reformas Economicas* (Santiago: CIEPLAN), pp. 79–100.

Cardoso, E. (1992) 'Privatization in Latin America', paper prepared for the annual meeting of the Red de Centros Latinamericanos de Investigation en Macroeconomia, Cartagena, Colombia, 18–20 April.

Corbo, V. (1992) 'Economic Transformation in Latin America: Lessons for Eastern Europe', *European Economic Review*, no. 36, 407–16.

Devlin, R. (1992) 'Privatization and Social Welfare in Latin America', mimeo, CEPAL, (Santiago, Chile).

Fanelli, J. M. and R. Frenkel (1992) 'On gradualism, shock and sequencing in economic adjustment', paper prepared for the G-24, (Buenos Aires: CEDES).

Floyd, R., Gray, C. and Short, R. (1984) *Public Enterprises in Mixed Economies*, International Monetary Fund, Washington, D.C.

Galel, A., L. Jones, P. Tandom and I. Gogelsang (1992) 'Synthesis of cases and policy summary', paper presented to a conference on the welfare consequences of seedling public enterprises, World Bank, Washington, DC, 11–12 June.

Galgóczi, B. (1992) 'Strategies of Privatization in Hungary', unpublished (Budapest, Hungary).

Gelb, A. H. and C. W. Gray (1991) 'The Transformation of Economics in Central and Eastern Europe', *Policy and Research Service,* no. 17 (Washington, DC: World Bank).

Gerchunoff, P. and Castro, L. (1992) 'La Racionalidad Macroeconomica de las Privatizaciones: El Caso Argentino', mimeo, CEPAL, Santiago, Chile.

Glade, W. (ed.) (1991) *Privatization of Public Enterprises in Latin America,* International Center for Economic Growth, Institute of the Americas and Centre for U. S. A–Mexican Studies (San Francisco: ICS Press).

Government of Brazil (1987) 'Retarturio de Atividades Desemolvidas,' Conselho Interministerial de Privitizacão, Brasilia, Brazil.

Government of Brazil, *Annual Reports*, Secretaria de Controle de Empresus Estalas, 1980–86, Brasilia, Brazil.

Hachette, D. and R. Lüders (1992) *La privatización en Chile* (San Francisco: Centro International para el Desarrollo Económico, CINDE).

Hoós, J. (1992) 'The Main Features of Privatization in Hungary', mimeo, Budapest University (Budapest, Hungary).

Lüders, R. (1991) 'Massive Divesture and Privatization: Lessons from Chile', *Contemporory Policy Issues,* vol. ix (October).

Meller, P. (1992) 'Latin American Adjustment and Economic Reforms: Issues and recent experience', paper presented at the Conference on Economic Reforms in Market and Socialist Economies, Madrid, Spain, 6–8 July, organised by Pensmiento Iberoamericano and the World Bank.

Nair, G. and Filippides, A. (1988) 'How Much Do State-Owned Enterprises Contribute to Public Sector Deficits in Developing Countries – And Why?', World Bank, WP 45, Washington, D.C.

100   *Privatisation in Latin America and Eastern Europe*

Ritter, A. R. M. (1992) 'Development Strategy and Structural Adjustment in Chile', *From the Unidad Popular to the Concretion 1970–92* (Ottawa: The North–South Institute).

Ruprah, I. (1992) 'Divestiture and Reform of Public Enterprises', mimeo, CIDE, Mexico City, Mexico.

Situación Latinoamericana (1993) various issues, (Santiago, Chile).

Sáez, R. (1992) 'An Overview of Privatization in Chile: The episodes, the results and the lessons', unpublished (Santiago, Chile).

Vicker, J. and G. Yorrow, (1991) 'Economic Prospectives on Privatization', *Journal of Economic Perspective*, vol. 5.

Vuylsteke, C. (1988) 'Techniques of Privatization of State-owned Enterprises', volume i, *Methods and Implementation*, World Bank Technical Paper, no. 88 (Washington DC: World Bank).

World Bank (1991) *World Development Report: The challenge of development* (Oxford University Press).

World Bank (1992) *Privatization: The lessons of experience.* (Washington DC: World Bank Country Economic Department).

Interviews and Commentators

Dominique Hachette, Rolf Lüders, Universidad Católica de Chile, Santiago, December 1992.

Robert Devlin, Oscar Altimir Santiago, CEPAL Chile, 7 December 1992.

Ricardo Paredes, José Yánez Santiago, Universidad de Chile, 1 December 1992.

Mario Marcel Santiago, Gobierno, Chile, 10 December 1992.

Raul E. Sáez Santiago, CIEPLAN Chile, 14 December 1992.

3 Fiscal Policy: The Necessary but not Sufficient

Vratislave Izák

3.1 INTRODUCTION

Fiscal policy has obviously played an important role in the Latin American stabilisation and adjustment processes. It will just as obviously play an important role in the transition of Eastern European economies. One school of thought sees fiscal deficits as the prime reason behind the macroeconomic chaos that infected much of Latin America in the 1980s; another sees it as one of several important players; and yet another sees it as being an effect rather than a cause of the disequilibria. This chapter will look at the role that fiscal policy played in the periods of stabilisation, destabilisation and structural adjustment in Latin America to shed some light on its role in the current crisis in Eastern Europe. Although it is clear that there are many differences between the countries of the two regions, it seems equally true that the packages of (proposed) reforms have been very similar in many cases.

Section 3.2 will examine the role that fiscal policy has played in stabilisation packages in Latin America. In particular, it will be interesting to see whether fiscal reform has been a necessary or sufficient condition (or neither) of the stabilisation process. Emphasis will be put on the entire policy package in which the fiscal reforms were placed. In Section 3.3 the changes in the composition of public finances and revenues in Mexico and the Czech Republic[1] are discussed in detail. Particular emphasis is placed upon the different ways of financing the public deficit in the two quite different institutional settings. Section 3.4 analyses the various tax reforms that have taken place in Latin America over the last two decades. It is argued that, although Eastern Europe has much to learn from these reform experiences, one must be careful. In general, tax reforms in Latin America have been a gradual process, whereas in Eastern Europe by necessity it must all happen very quickly. Moreover administrative problems, which were very important in Latin America, are formidable in the context of the transition economies of Eastern Europe. Finally, Section 3.5 summarises the pertinent lessons for Eastern Europe from the Latin American experience of the last 20 years in the areas of tax reform and fiscal policy in general.

3.2 FISCAL POLICY: A SUBSTANTIAL PART OF STABILISATION POLICIES

In designing a comprehensive programme for a change of regime, both Latin American and Eastern European countries face similar problems. Their reform packages entail short-term stabilisation macroeconomic policies on the one hand and long-term structurally oriented policies on the other. The initial conditions for change of regime were of course different. In Eastern European countries there was an urgent need for deep structural changes. Inherited from the command-type economy were:

- The absence of a legal and institutional basis for a market economy.
- An almost nonexistent or negligible private sector.
- Controlled prices for the majority of products and factors.
- Industrial organisation suited to central planning (large enterprises with monopolistic behaviour).
- A state monobank with regional subsidiaries.

This strongly suggests that the transformation in Eastern Europe will take many years, a decade at least, especially as the creation of different market institutions and rules is a time-consuming task. The initial macroeconomic situation was also not the same as in Latin America, although the differences were much larger in the case of the Czech Republic than most other Eastern European countries. At the beginning of transformation in former Czechoslovakia, the absence of serious macroeconomic imbalances was significant because foreign indebtedness was very small, open inflation was negligible, monetary overhang was relatively small and the government budget was in equilibrium.

In other Eastern European economies the macroeconomic situation at the beginning of transformation was less favourable and more similar to Latin American conditions (Russia, Poland). In spite of the differences in the initial conditions, the packages of reform measures have been very similar in the two regions, and almost identical in some areas. The menu of short-term macroeconomic stabilisation policies includes tight fiscal and monetary policies, amended in some countries by different kinds of income policies. Varying degrees of devaluation completed the triangle of Keynesian policies.[2]

Structural policies in reforming economies included, with different degrees of relative importance in reformed economies, price and trade liberalisation, privatisation and deregulation, the fostering of competition, direct government policies in selected fields, and sectoral policies. In Eastern Europe one must add the creation of a market-based financial system.

Broadly conceived fiscal policy has played one of the most important roles in change of regime. Tight fiscal and monetary policies are necessary prerequisites (or 'fundamentals') of a successful stabilisation policy. In the Latin American countries where these fundamentals were not kept in place (Argentina, Brazil), economic stabilisation was not successful. Tight fiscal and monetary policies by themselves, however, are not a sufficient cure.

Additional measures or heterodox features usually had to be added to the fundamentals to stop inflation, the main feature of internal disequilibrium in Latin America. Orthodox programmes have been applied many times in several Latin American countries over more than two decades, usually generating high costs and only a partial and temporary reduction of inflation. Brazil at the beginning of the 1980s is considered a good example of an orthodox programme failure (see Meller, 1992, p. 10; Ortiz, 1991, p. 293).

Loose fiscal policy has been one of the fundamental weaknesses of many Eastern European countries (Russia most of all). On the other hand, in former Czechoslovakia in the 'The Scenario of Economic Reform' (published in *Hospodářské noviny* on 4 September 1990) tight fiscal policy represented the core of the intended stabilisation programme and consisted of the following main objectives:

- To reach a surplus in the three-part government budget (one for the federation and one for each of the two constituent national republics). In 1990 the surplus of the government budget was to have 1–1.5 per cent of total expenditure, in 1991 as much as 2–2.5 per cent.
- To decrease public expenditure as a proportion of GDP, firstly by reducing subsidies for enterprises and households; to separate some expenditure items from the budget; and to create separate funds for social security and environmental protection.
- To postulate rules for the distribution of expenditure among the federal budget, the budget of the Czech Republic, and the budget of the Slovak Republic.
- To prepare, in several steps, a wide-ranging tax reform. The backbone of the system was to be value added tax which would replace consumer taxes and the turnover tax.

The objectives in Eastern Europe have mirrored (with some modifications of course) the planned measures of Latin American stabilisation programmes. Even in the 1970s some Latin American economies based their anti-inflationary policies on major reductions in fiscal deficits and monetary growth. More precisely:

- The substantial chronic fiscal deficit of Chile was eliminated by drastic across-the-board expenditure cuts, together with a later tax reform.
- In Uruguay the fiscal deficit was reduced with the introduction of VAT.
- In Argentina the authorities also tried to solve the problem of the fiscal deficit, although with little success (Corbo, 1992a, p. 31).

But the traditional fiscal–monetary mix proved to be insufficient to combat inflation. In Chile from 1973–5, fiscal policy was reasonably successful in cutting the fiscal deficit by reducing expenditure and raising taxes. On the other hand the money supply increased by 231 per cent and 257 per cent in 1974 and 1975, respectively, so that the rate of inflation remained high – around 350 per cent in each year. Only from 1976–8 did the rate of increase in the money supply begin to decelerate, with consequent consistent reductions in the inflation rate. Summarising the Chilean experiences, Ritter (1992, p. 15) writes: 'Obviously the reduction of the fiscal deficit alone was insufficient as a means of lowering inflation as long as the money supply was increasing rapidly.'

According to Meller (1992, p. 10) some Latin American economists arrived at what seemed to be a rather strange conclusion: 'budget deficits and inflation were unrelated'. Additional heterodox measures therefore had to be added. The most important heterodox view states that Latin American inflation has two components: a fundamental cause such as a fiscal deficit or an external shock that sets off the inflationary process, and an inertial one that sustains the price increases.

The inertial component functions because of indexation and expectations. The economic agents – entrepreneurs and households especially – forecast that future inflation would at least equal current inflation. Heterodox stabilisation programmes have stressed the great importance of dealing with the inertial component of inflation. Heterodox stabilisation programme implemented in Latin America had the following features (Meller, 1992, p. 11):

- A generalised control of prices, wages, exchange rates and public utility prices.
- A tight fiscal programme oriented towards a reduction of the fiscal deficit.

- A monetary reform that had a special financial contract debt conversion to avoid wealth transfers between creditors and debtors when the economy went abruptly from high inflation to low inflation.
- An expansionary monetary policy to avoid sharp increases in the real interest rate and to augment the monetisation of the economy.

From this list it is evident that the fiscal – monetary mix was often supplemented by an incomes policy and a certain degree of government regulation of key prices.

In the Latin American literature the 1987 Mexican stabilisation programme is usually cited as an example of a successful heterodox programme. The scope of this programme was broad, and in addition to macroeconomic (fiscal and monetary) and incomes policies structural policies were vigorously implemented, 'in particular trade liberalisation, deregulation and the privatisation of public enterprises seem to have played an important role in improving expectations and increasing economic efficiency' (Ortiz, 1991, p. 238).[3]

To overcome the impacts of the inertial component of inflation, something like a social accord is often necessary. In Mexico a social accord was formed under the auspices of the Pact of Economic Solidarity (PSE), which was announced on 15 December 1987 and jointly signed by the government, labour, agricultural workers and the private sector. The pact's main features were:

- An increase of the public sector's primary surplus by about 3 per cent of GDP with various revenue measures, but depending heavily on increases in prices and tariffs of public enterprises to yield about 1.5 per cent of GDP.
- A tightening of monetary policy. Tight credit ceilings were announced at the beginning of 1988.
- Trade liberalisation measures were implemented. Maximum tariffs were lowered and practically all import permits were eliminated.
- After an initial depreciation of the controlled exchange rate of about 22 per cent, the exchange rate was to remain stable until the end of February.
- Wages were raised a cumulative 38 per cent in December and on 1 January, remaining fixed until the end of February.

The raison d'être of this social accord was due to a combination of circumstances that were very common in the Latin American experience. Ortiz (1991, p. 293) sums up the situation as follows: 'Inflation in Mexico had an important inertial component that emerged from built-in wage indexation mechanism, which had become more pervasive with the passage of time.... To eliminate inflation in these circumstances, in addition to fiscal and monetary restraint, a change in the indexation mechanism was needed. In the Mexican case, this problem was tackled by reaching social agreements'.

Besides heterodox stabilisation programmes, other programmes labelled as 'neo-orthodox' (Bolivia, Venezuela) and 'neo-orthodox – neo-heterodox' (Argentina in the 1990s) were implemented. These were at least partially successful, although it is too early to pass final judgement (see Meller, 1992, pp. 12–14).

The need to reach a social accord through a package of income policy measures has been felt in the Czech Republic since the beginning of the change of regime. To reduce the burden placed on the fiscal–monetary mix in curbing inflation, the government created the Council for Economic and Social Agreement to allow the social partners to express their views and reach a consensus.

In a tripartite agreement, the government, employers and trade unions have sought to determine *ex ante* the maximum allowable fall in real wages (for details, see OECD, 1991, Annex I). The Council concludes every year with the general agreement on guidelines for minimum and average wages. It is not surprising that an inertial component of inflation because of indexation has been built into the tripartite agreement and the government has tried to put in doubt the raison d'être of the general agreement. At the end of March 1993 the representatives of trade unions accused the Czech government of intending to cancel the general agreement on a nationwide basis in the near future.

The lessons that can be drawn for the design of policy measures in Eastern Europe, and which have been partially supported by the Czech experiences, consist in the assertion that tight fiscal and monetary policies are a necessary prerequisite for success at the beginning of a change of regime, but they are not a sufficient condition. They must be backed by other policy measures that are reflected on both the revenue and the expenditure sides of the government budget and include a package of incomes policies.

3.3 PUBLIC FINANCES

The priority given in Latin America to correcting public finances has been based on the need to provide a necessary margin of action for stabilising the economy and making orderly progress in reform packages. Once balance in public finances is achieved (as well as in the external sector), structural policies can be implemented. The same is largely valid for Eastern European economies.

Fiscal deficits in Latin American countries were the heritage of expansionary policies in the 1960s and 1970s, in particular those related to state intervention and import-substitution policies. A well-known example of public policy interventionism and import-substituting industrialisation was Chile at the beginning of the 1970s. The annual plan for 1971 emphasised economic 'reactivation', to be achieved by the expansion of domestic demand. The reactivation programme consisted of a general real wage raise, a large increase in the minimum wage and ambitious social projects. The macroeconomic impacts of this expansionary policy were positive for 1971 (see Ritter, 1992, pp. 7–8), but in other years this type of policy was unsustainable. The fiscal deficit rose, money creation accelerated, inflation surged and, last but not least, the level of GNP per capita declined.

Some economists have also recommended this Keynesian-type recipe for Eastern European economies suffering from assumed underutilisation of industrial capacity during the transformation process. The deficit financing would start the expansion that would in the future repay the public debt. In a period of deep structural change, especially in property rights, this recipe does not seem to offer much promise.

In Latin America the most successful programmes have been judged to be those which have had sustainable public sector reforms, such as those of Chile and Mexico. In his analysis of Latin American development strategies and policies, Corbo wrote:

> In the 1980s in Latin America there emerged a consensus that included three key components: stabilisation, a restructuring of the public sector and the need to integrate into the world economy. In particular, it has become increasingly accepted that some otherwise desirable reforms could have negative effects if the macroeconomic situation is not brought under control early on. Therefore, a credible and sustainable fiscal, public sector wide reform will be the core of successful reform. In this sense, Chile and Mexico are the countries that have made the most progress in laying the foundation for implementing other efficiency enhancing reforms (Corbo, 1992b, p. 36).

Revenues and Expenditures

During transformation or stabilisation, public finances must undergo a profound adjustment on both sides. Put simply, expenditure must be cut and the structure of revenues must be changed. The action taken between 1983 and 1990 in Mexico to stabilise the economy and redefine the role of state in the economy are reflected in both the level and structure of public sector expenditure and revenues. The Mexican authorities began a serious effort to correct imbalances in public finances in 1983 through the introduction of tax measures and a decrease in government expenditure. The policies implemented led to a reduction in the fiscal deficit,[4] leading to a fall in the public-sector borrowing requirement (PSBR) from 16.9 per cent of GDP in 1982 to only 1.5 per cent in 1991 (see Table 3.1).

The primary balance went from a deficit of 7.3 per cent of GDP in 1982 to a 5.5 per cent surplus in 1991. The operational balance went from a deficit of 5.5 per cent of GDP in 1982 to a surplus of 3.3 per cent in 1991. In its early stages, the adjustment effort fell mainly upon investment expenditure and transfers, subsequently focusing on current expenditure. All measures confirm the drastic tightening of fiscal policy during the 1980s.

In spite of these efforts a substantial reduction of inflation was attained only after the implementation of the Pact of Economic Solidarity (PSE). What was the cause of high inflation before the appearance of PSE? According to Ortiz there was a fiscal dimension of the external debt problem:

> To the extent that external debt obligations represented commitments of the public sectors in debtor countries, governments faced the additional problem of extracting resources from the public to finance the debt service. Clearly the different sectors of society tend to resist the government's attempts to key additional taxes or to gather resources by increasing the real price of goods and services produced by public enterprises. Governments have had to resort to the inflation tax as a

Table 3.1   Overall public finance indicators, Mexico (percentage of GDP)

	1982	1987	1988	1989	1990	1991
PSBR	−16.9	−16.0	−12.4	−5.5	−4.0	−1.5
Operational balance	−5.5	1.8	−3.6	−1.7	2.3	3.3
Primary balance	−7.3	4.7	8.0	7.9	7.8	5.5

Note: Data for 1991 excludes revenues from privatisation.
Source: Banco de Mexico, 1992, p. 102.

means of overcoming the resistance of society to the internal transfer of resources to the public sector (Ortiz, 1991, p. 290).[5]

The foregoing figures show that Mexico was able, in the space of a few years, to reverse a fiscal imbalance. Marked improvements in public sector finances have been instrumental in bringing down inflation, raising government saving, decreasing interest rates and fostering confidence in the economy's prospects.

Public expenditure
In the 1970s the Mexican government sought to use public spending as a means of attaining a higher level of employment. Public expenditure became part of the economic policy aimed at speeding up the pace of economic growth. Its highest level was reached in the period 1980–2, 10 years after the Chilean experience. This therapy was abandoned and between 1983 and 1987 public expenditure was reduced to contribute to the strengthening of public finances. The adjustment was effected mainly by (1) reducing investment expenditure, (2) decreasing current transfers and (3) eliminating subsidies.

Expenditure reductions were strongest for public enterprises. As part of the divestiture process, current spending for all enterprises under budgetary control was reduced by about 0.5 per cent of GDP during the 1980s. Capital expenditures were cut to a similar extent, except in the case of Petroleos de Mexico (PEMEX), where cuts reached 70 per cent (see Table 3.2).

Table 3.2   Consolidated public sector expenditure, Mexico (percentage of GDP)

	1982	*1991*	*1991**
Total noninterest expenditure	38.0	21.6	57
Current noninterest expenditure	27.5	17.2	63
Public enterprises	8.4	4.3	51
General government	19.1	12.9	68
Capital expenditure	10.5	4.4	42
Public enterprises (exclud. PEMEX)	2.5	1.3	52
PEMEX	2.9	0.9	31
Federal government	5.1	2.2	43

* percentage of 1982 expenditure.
Source: OECD (1992), p. 130.

A closer inspection of the change in current transfer payments confirms that, although the overall volume of subsidies declined, the remainder was increasingly focused on health, social security, education and the basic food supply. The share of these items in total transfers rose from 31 per cent in 1983 to 51 per cent by 1990. Transfers to public enterprises declined, however, from 35 per cent to 11 per cent over the same period. Outside the budget, an increasing share of subsidies was provided through input and output price subsidies. Last but not least, credit subsidies and special tax incentives were largely phased out.

The intended adjustment took part in the period of high inflation, therefore 'The targeted reduction in total public sector spending was not attained until 1988, because cuts in programmable expenditures were offset by the effect of higher interest rates on domestic public debt service' (Banco de Mexico, 1992, p. 105).

It was not until fiscal measures were integrated into a coherent overall programme for lowering inflation (the PSE) without causing greater unemployment and without bringing on a recession that the continuous effort that had been made in government spending could be appreciated. The lesson from this development is that it takes a certain time to recover investment activity during the adjustment process. In Mexico, investment expenditure, whose share in GDP fell by 5.3 per cent between 1982 and 1988, began to recover in 1989. Investment in infrastructure was given a further impetus in 1990 and 1991, rising as a proportion of GDP. The possibility of increasing outlays in economic infrastructure and social development was due to resulting saving in interest payments after public debt service, which averaged 15.6 per cent of GDP between 1984 and 1987, began a downward trend in the period 1987–91 because of a combination of favourable elements. These included lower interest rates, the agreement to reschedule the external debt, and the use of resources from privatisation in 1991 to amortise large amounts of domestic debt.

Similar tasks for expenditure policy were formulated in the Czech scenario. Among other things, it was expected that government budgets would benefit from the decrease of subsidies for state-owned enterprises. On the other hand, the costs of creating a new social safety net became significant (see Table 3.3).

Expenditure on social security represents the greatest part of transfers to households. Unemployment benefits were introduced at the beginning of 1990. The biggest drop was made in investment and noninvestment transfers to enterprises, which is an important part of the government strategy to move towards a market economy based on private property.

Table 3.3   Budget expenditure, former Czechoslovakia

	1989	1990	1991	1992*
Total expenditure (bill – CSK)	414.9	455.9	515.9	551.0
Total expenditure (%)	100.0	100.0	100.0	100.0
Transfers to enterprises	20.0	18.4	12.5	9.4
investment	2.6	2.3	2.1	2.3
noninvestment	17.6	16.1	10.4	7.1
Transfers to households	23.4	25.0	30.3	29.4
Public consumption	56.4	56.6	57.2	61.2
investment	8.1	8.0	8.8	8.5
noninvestment	48.3	48.6	48.4	52.7

* Estimate
Source: Mexican Ministry of Finance, *Ekonom*, no. 12 (1993), p. 22.

Public revenue policy
The Mexican stabilisation programme that began in 1983 initially emphasised:

● The search for higher income from tax collection and
● Rationalisation of the operation of state enterprises.

As described in the next section, tax reforms carried out in recent years have been geared towards developing an internationally competitive tax system, with tax rates similar to or lower than those of Mexico's main trading partners, and towards a far larger number of taxpayers than in 1988, without special tax regimes. The reforms introduced in recent years have changed the relative contribution of various taxes to total revenues. For example, between 1987 and 1991 the share of income tax, VAT and nontax revenue in GDP rose about 1.1 per cent, 0.6 per cent and 0.6 per cent respectively.

In addition, public sector prices and tariffs have been substantially adjusted since 1983 to bring them into line with international levels. As a result the revenue of enterprises and agencies under public control (excluding PEMEX) rose from 5.7 per cent of GDP in 1983 to 6.6 per cent in 1986 (public sector revenues are shown in Table 3.4).

From Table 3.4 it is evident that, including public enterprise revenue, total revenue fell during the 1980s by about 3 per cent in relation to GDP,

112   *Fiscal Policy*

Table 3.4   Sources of public sector revenue, Mexico

| | Percentage of GDP | | | Share of total | | |
	1982–84	1985–87	1988–91	1982–84	1985–87	1988–91
PEMEX	12.4	10.1	7.2	39	33	26
Other public enterprises	5.7	6.6	5.1	18	21	18
Federal government	11.0	11.7	13.5	35	38	48
Other	2.7	2.4	2.4	8	8	8
Total	31.8	30.8	28.2	100	100	100

Source: OECD (1992), p. 134.

but remained constant in real terms. The constant revenue share, however, masks significant changes in revenue sources. During the initial phase of adjustment (1982–4) most revenues (57 per cent) originated from public enterprises. Revenue problems provided an impetus to the major tax reform of 1987, which clearly changed the methods and modalities of revenue collection and – together with subsequent reform efforts, particularly in 1989 – helped raise the share of federal taxes in total consolidated revenue to 48 per cent by 1988–91.

The development of Czech budgetary revenues is shown in Table 3.5. What are the most remarkable trends? First, the tax burden of enterprises decreased from 56 per cent of total revenue in 1989 to 45.9 per cent in 1992. Second, the tax burden of individuals remained almost constant.

Table 3.5   Revenues of the budgets, former Czechoslovakia

	1989	1990	1991	1992*
Total revenue (bill – CSK)	415.4	463.1	505.5	540.0
Total revenue (%)	100.0	100.0	100.0	100.0
Tax revenues	91.1	91.3	94.4	86.5
direct taxes	70.6	65.8	67.7	60.2
individuals	14.6	13.6	15.2	14.3
enterprises	56.0	52.2	52.5	45.9
indirect taxes	20.5	25.5	26.7	26.3
Nontax revenues	8.9	8.7	5.6	13.5

* Estimate
Source: Mexican Ministry of Finance, *Ekonom*, no. 12 (1993), p. 22.

Methods of Financing the Public Deficit

In Mexico, after the 1982 crisis measures were introduced to reduce the public deficit sharply:

- Public spending was cut.
- Revenues were increased through adjustments in the price of public enterprise goods and services.
- Measures were taken to modernise the tax system.
- The process of privatisation of government-owned enterprise was begun.

As the above tables indicate, the strengthening of public finances has rested more on the rationalisation of expenditure than on the augmentation of revenue. Currently the results are promising.[6] The public sector makes no demand on funds from financial markets, thus opening up opportunities to channel increased revenues towards productive investment at a lower cost. The Mexican methods of financing the public deficit can be divided into five categories:

- Financing through foreign lending
- Borrowing from the Central Bank
- Forced borrowing from the banking system
- Bond financing
- Use of proceeds from privatisation

During the 1980s, the Mexican government tried to replace foreign borrowing, which was drastically reduced in 1982, by domestic credit, borrowing more than half of the amount involved from the Central Bank. Even prior to this (1978), Mexican treasury bills (CETES) had been created to provide the government with a tradable debt instrument and allow for open-market operations. This contributed to the monetisation of the deficit and allowed the government to maintain expenditure without levying conventional taxes or issuing interest-bearing debt (inflation tax financing).[7]

Inflation tax reached its highest level of over 7 per cent of GDP in 1982, when the monetary base stood at a high of 15.8 per cent of GDP and inflation reached an average of about 60 per cent per annum. The Central Bank money stock increased by 367 per cent between the end of 1981 and 1984.

This way of financing the fiscal deficit has also been practised in Eastern Europe, particularly in Russia. The printing of new roubles by the

Central Bank has been the only way of internally financing the enormous budget deficit approved by the government. According to Russian sources, the preference of the Central Bank is to support industrial production without regard to its price and quality rather than cope with inflation. The fundamental problem is finding a middle way between hyperinflation and a catastrophic fall of industrial production.

To reduce reliance on inflationary Central Bank finance, between 1985 and 1987 the Mexican government switched to forced borrowing from the bank system at below market rates to fund its deficit. Banks were protected from the impact of such borrowing on their earnings through deposit rate controls, which pushed nominal yields on bank deposits below the rate of inflation. The resulting negative real deposit rates led to disintermediation.

Starting in 1987, the government intensified its attempts to reverse financial disintermediation by shifting rapidly from forced bank saving to bond financing at market rates. The strategy succeeded, albeit at the cost of very high *ex post* interest rates, which, because of the very high perceived risks, were required to reduce investors to hold government debt.

The nominal rate of interest promised in the Czech Republic on government bonds seems to be lower than the planned rate of inflation, at least in 1993, with the interest rate for four-year government bonds issued in March 1993 set at 14 per cent while the expected rate of inflation in 1993 was 15–17 per cent. According to the minister of finance, I. Koárník, the rate of inflation should be lower in future, and therefore a positive real rate of interest is being promised. What has been further stressed by the minister is the low risk involved in holding government bonds.

The value of the bonds sold by the Mexican government in 1990 to the public actually exceeded the (much reduced) public sector deficit, allowing it to reduce its debt with the Central Bank. As the government proceeded with the privatisation of public enterprises, it used the proceeds to retire debt owed to the banking system.

In the Czech Republic, in spite of nonfulfillment of the objectives listed earlier, the deficits have remained modest so that covering them is not a major problem. The proposal to reach a surplus to help combat inflation, however, has clearly been unrealistic. The same is valid for the proposal – based on the knowledge of sophisticated economic theory – for a mandatory balancing of the budget over a three to four year period.

The indirect costs of inflation produced by monetisation of the debt have been noted in the Czech Republic, even in government circles.[8] Government economists, mostly with an academic background, are aware of the fact that the net effect of deficits dominating surpluses is secular inflation but – under the pressure of various social groups – they have not been able to reverse the development. The deficit in 1991 was covered through the issue of government bonds, repayable in five years at 14 per cent interest. Bonds were issued in nominal values of CSK 1000, 2000, 5000 and so on to enable households to buy them.

The previous law on state banks did not allow the Central Bank to issue credit to cover government deficits, but according to the Act on the Czech National Bank of January 1993, which is in part devoted to transitional provisions: 'As an exception in 1993, the total position of credits granted to the Czech Republic shall be set forth as a limit of seven per cent of revenues of the state budget of the previous year' (Act of the Czech National Council No. 6, 1993).

This statement evokes a suspicion that the idea of a balanced, never mind a surplus, state budget has been tacitly abolished and the authorities have accepted the necessity of living with a state debt. Furthermore, as mentioned earlier, in 1993 the Ministry of Finance was allowed to issue bonds to cover the 1992 state budget deficit.

Even though the first sale of bonds on 20 February 1992 was successful, because demand by commercial banks and private citizens far exceeded supply, one must be aware of the fact that the deficit has been financed at the cost of crowding out the financing of emerging private sector activities. If one sums up credit sources in the form of treasury bills and government bonds, it is evident that commercial banks and some large enterprises are covering a significant part of the budget deficit. However, this means that:

- There will be a competition for credit sources between government and enterprises. To advance credit to fledging private enterprises has been one of the main tasks of the change of regime.
- There will be pressure to make credit more expensive, and therefore pressure to increase interest rates. Auctionary refinancing credit[9] repayable in seven days with an interest rate of approximately 13 per cent might seem too expensive a credit source for entrepreneurs.
- The government will put pressure on the Central Bank to loosen monetary control and to finance the growing deficits of the state budget via the commercial banks.
- The problem of indebtedness of enterprises will be more complicated.

During any fiscal year, both revenues and expenditures fluctuate. For example, in the Czech Republic during 1991 revenues and expenditures displayed the pattern shown in Table 3.6. The different timing of revenues

Table 3.6   Timing of revenues and expenditures, Czech Republic, 1991

	First quarter	Second quarter	Third quarter	Fourth quarter	1 December
Revenues as percentage of the whole year	24.7	26.9	23.52	4.9	9.4
Expenditures as percentage of the whole year	20.6	25.4	23.93	0.11	2.4

Source: Czechoslovak Ministry of Finance.

and expenditures during the fiscal year and their sometimes unpredictable fluctuations has been the cause of short-term borrowing from the Central Bank. According to the above mentioned Act, the Czech National Bank may purchase from and possibly sell to commercial banks, government bonds or other securities underwritten by the government, which the Czech National Bank may buy and hold for a maximum of one year.

At least one quarter of the issue should be placed with commercial banks in order to widen interest rates. In this way treasury bills have become the first important tool of the money market. Since February 1992 the government has issued treasury bills. The credits ought to be neutral from a monetary point of view, but the problem for future issues consists of the ever increasing block of treasury bills.[10]

The transformation of methods of financing the public deficit in Mexico has been successful: 'By 1992 all government debt was funded through debt instruments issued in the money and bond markets and rates on government treasury bills were low in real terms' (OECD, 1992, p. 48). As the market for government paper developed, the Mexican Central Bank started relying more and more on open market operations as the main tool of monetary management.

The development in the Czech Republic will probably be similar. On 18 March 1993 the Ministry of Finance published the Czech state indebtedness figures. The debt is, according to the official data, approximately CSK 200 billion (see Table 3.7). Debt service in fiscal year 1993 – repayment of both principal and interest – should be CSK 27.2 billion. In the budget, only CSK 13.5 billion are earmarked for this purpose. Of the remaining CSK 13.7 billion, part should be covered from the Fund of National Property (CSK 6.5 billion). The postponement of a CSK 4.3 billion repayment of principal from direct debts has been agreed with

Table 3.7   Composition of the Czech state debt (billion CSK)

Internal indebtedness	91.7
State debt at the Central Bank	58.0
State debt at commercial banks	17.6
Issue of government bonds	16.1
Foreign indebtedness	71.3
Governmental debts	21.7
Debts of the Czechoslovak Commerce Bank	49.6
Foreign indebtedness of the central bank*	37.0

* Stabilisation loan from the IMF, debts from bond issues of previous State Bank.
Source: Ministry of Finance, Czech Republic, 1993.

the Central Bank. The method of payment of the residual CSK 2.9 billion repayment of state debts to commercial banks has not yet been decided on.

We have seen that the proceeds from privatisation concentrated in the Fund of National Property have been partially used to retire debt owed to the banking system, similar to what occurred in Mexico. Once-and-for-all revenues from privatisation[11] had originally been placed in a contingency fund to allow for the cushioning of the economy against unexpected shocks. The government decided in September 1991 to use this fund to repay about one eighth of domestic debt. Domestic public debt was thus reduced from 29.2 per cent to 17.5 per cent of GDP between 1988 and the end of 1991.

All domestic bank debt in Mexico is now redeemed and the government is relying entirely on the capital markets to fund its debt. As inflation and interest rates are coming down, the government is retiring its long-term development bonds, and to reduce funding costs it is using mostly treasury bills with maturities of below a year to meet its financing needs. As a result of the debt management policies, interest payments on consolidated public debt are expected to drop.

3.4   TAX REFORMS

Characteristics

Tax reforms represent an integral part of reform measures in both Latin American and Eastern European countries. In the Czech scenario, the tax reform, along with the stabilization policy and budgetary rules, formed the backbone of the proposed macroeconomic framework of economic reform. The difference is again in initial conditions. The existing tax systems in Eastern Europe were inherited from a command economy. At the beginning of the reforms it was clear that these systems were full of substantial defects from the point of view of a market economy. The systems were discriminatory and intentionally non-neutral. There was an unequal approach to different sorts of economic activities and types of income as well as a lack of transparency. In practice, it was not possible to find efficient tax rates or the real tax burden for individual subjects.

In Latin American countries the prereform tax systems were, in spite of their inadequacies, anchored in market-type economies. They suffered because of a narrow tax base, were eroded by different kinds of exemption, had to cope with a high rate of inflation and were, at least in some countries, vulnerable to external shocks because of excessive dependence on revenue from taxes on foreign trade. Both groups of countries have tried to adopt tax systems patterned after those of advanced market economies in North America or Western Europe. Many observers have doubts about the wiseness of this approach.[12]

In spite of these methodological doubts, the aims of tax reforms are the same or very similar in both Latin America and Eastern Europe and concentrate on improving efficiency and equity on the one hand and on increasing budget revenues on the other. Special features of typical Latin American tax systems are the different corrections for inflation. Other common features are the following:

- The introduction of VAT
- Corporate tax reform
- Expansion of the tax base
- Reduction of top rates in personal income taxes
- Reduction of import tariffs

In Latin American economies the overhaul of the tax systems has been a gradual[13] process with some significant turning points, whilst in the majority of Eastern European economies there have been sudden, profound changes of the systems in a few years.

For example, in Chile the turning points were in 1975 and 1984. In the late 1990s some measures, such as a partial indexation of income taxes, were introduced. Tax reform in 1975 included both temporary tax measures and a major tax reform. The objectives of the former was to increase fiscal revenues, whereas the latter had much broader objectives. The existing tax structure was considered unfair on equity grounds and inefficient in resource allocation. The three main elements of the tax reform were as follows:

- A correction for inflation
- A fundamental change of indirect taxation
- Simplification of the tax system

The emphasis of the tax reform in 1984 was on direct taxes – personal and corporation tax and special treatment of certain investments. Such spreading out of reforms allowed the government to concentrate on problems that were felt to be most urgent at particular times.

In Mexico the significant turning points were in 1980 and 1987. In 1980 VAT replaced the previous sales taxes, and corporate tax rates and personal income taxes were also overhauled. The focus of the subsequent tax reform in 1987 was on unification of corporate and personal tax rates as well as on lowering the highest marginal rates for personal income.

In Bolivia the significant years were 1973 and 1986. In 1973 a general sales tax in the form of VAT was imposed and in 1986 a complete reform of the internal tax system (to reduce the fiscal deficit) was introduced.

A wide-ranging tax reform, representing a restructuring of the whole system, was launched in the Czech Republic in January 1993. The backbone of the new system comprises VAT, social security contributions, a unified corporate income tax and a universal personal income tax. Introducing a whole package of different tax measures in a very limited time period was a rather risky business, as the developments in the first months of 1993 confirm. The main bottleneck was a human factor – the lack of knowledge and qualifications among tax administrators, accompanied and influenced by the problems emanating from the division of the federal republic. A more gradual development would have allowed policy makers to undertake necessary corrections in different parts of the tax system, to react flexibly to emerging problems and to take into account the needs of the budget.

Tax administration is not an easy task for the emerging market economies in Eastern Europe, nor for the majority of Latin American countries. The capability of tax administrators in the Czech Republic to audit all private sector activities and to master the transition from turnover tax to VAT was the main problem of its tax reform, as witnessed in the first weeks of 1993.

In Mexico in recent years, efforts have been focused on improving VAT collection: 'VAT collection was improved by transferring its administration from states to the federal government, which uses banks to collect the tax' (OECD, 1992, p. 128). In Chile, tougher tax administration was part of the package of the new taxation system implemented in January 1975. In Bolivia, poor penalty and enforcement systems resulted in diminishing real collections from direct taxes. Bolivian administrators also complained that VAT, imposed in 1973, was poorly enforced and subject to widespread evasion.[14]

To give an idea of the magnitude of tax evasion, I will illustrate this by referring to one partial market only – cigarettes and tobacco products. According to unofficial estimates, tax evasion in the Czech Republic was estimated to be several tens of billions of Czech crowns, or the amount of budget deficits in the last three reform years.

VAT and Consumer Taxes

VAT, the most modern form of sales tax, has been introduced in the majority of Latin American and Eastern European economies. It is supplemented by consumer taxes on luxuries and 'bads'. In Bolivia VAT was imposed on a broad base that included capital goods at a rate of 5 per cent in 1973. Its introduction was not an easy venture and it produced surprisingly little revenue; later the number of rates and exemptions increased. The traditional excise taxes on beer and tobacco – levied at specific rates per bottle or package, rather than as a percentage of price like VAT – produced more revenue than did VAT in 1973. Bolivia also imposed a wide variety of other consumption taxes that produced little in the way of revenue. Later, in May 1986, within the framework of a complete reform of the internal tax system, a package of taxes on domestic consumption was introduced.

This package included 10 per cent VAT on an extremely broad base, supplemented by taxes on specific consumption items at rates of 30 per cent (alcoholic beverages), rising to 50 per cent (tobacco and jewellery). VAT was also supplemented by a new 1 per cent 'transaction tax' – really a cumulative turnover tax. So in the Bolivian system one finds a special mix of VAT and turnover taxes.

An interesting development was the possibility of offsetting VAT that had been paid out by individuals, as verified by invoices, against the so-called complementary tax. As Bird (1992, p. 13) noted: 'The aim of the complementary tax thus was not just to provide revenue but to encourage consumers to acquire VAT receipts'. Related schemes to encourage consumers to demand VAT receipts have long been tried in other countries, such as Chile, and have proved only marginally useful, at best, in enforcing VAT.

In Argentina, by 1989 the tax system had been heavily eroded by exemptions and incentives, ravaged by inflation and administered in an increasingly ineffective manner. The original intention of the reforms was to make VAT the centrepiece of a revised tax system by substantially broadening its base and improving its administration.

VAT replaced the previous sales tax in Mexico in 1980. In 1987 VAT rates ranged from 0 to 20 per cent. The zero rate applied to basic food-stuffs and at that time a 6 per cent rate applied in regions bordering the USA. The focus in recent years, besides improving VAT collection, has been on equalising VAT rates. The standard rate was reduced from 15 per cent to 10 per cent in 1991 as part of the government's anti-inflationary incomes policy.

Single commodity taxes have accompanied VAT in Mexico. Revenue losses from a cut in the central VAT rate from 15 per cent to 10 per cent have had to be offset by larger revenues from increased petrol taxes and energy prices, as well as increased collection of import duties, other taxes and nontax revenues. These taxes were lowered in 1991–2 after having been raised earlier in the context of fiscal restraint. Excise taxes on tobacco, alcohol and petrol continue to be included in the base for VAT calculation.

In Chile, the new taxation system, implemented on 1 January 1975, included imposition of a single 20 per cent VAT. Although this had a dis-proportionately negative effect on lower income groups, it avoided the cascading effect on prices and eliminated the artificial incentives to inte-grate enterprises vertically to avoid transactions tax. In early 1977 VAT, which had previously been applied to goods only, was extended to ser-vices.

The introduction of VAT in the Czech and Slovak Republics on 1 January 1993 was one of the most challenging tasks for tax administra-tors. The transition from turnover tax to VAT was difficult for tax admin-istrators and entrepreneurs alike. The heritage of the command economy made the switch to this tax very painful and required preparatory steps.

One of the first steps towards price liberalisation was the elimination of negative turnover taxes. In command economies, prices, especially those of foodstuffs, were highly subsidised which distorted the price structure. In July 1990, eight months after the 'velvet revolution', the elimination of negative turnover taxes on food led to an increase in retail prices of about 25 per cent. The government compensated the population for this price increase by transfer payments to all citizens. The payments were financed by savings on subsidies, so there was no net budget effect. Price adjustments for heating fuel, cigarettes and transport followed.

Turnover tax rates were highly individualised. The highest subsidy rates applied to dairy products and heating fuel, whereas industrial consumer goods were highly taxed (for example, the tax on passenger cars was 87 per cent). The redistribution achieved through the turnover tax system could hardly justify the large economic distortions entailed by this system. Household consumption decisions were made on the basis of retail prices that bore virtually no relation to production costs. The large subsidies led to inappropriate consumption patterns and wastage.

Heating subsidies were phased out in May 1991 and replaced by cash payments to pensioners and families with children. Other groups were not compensated.

The highly individualised turnover tax rates were first unified to just four rates (zero, 12 per cent, 22 per cent and 32 per cent) on 1 January 1991, and then in May 1991 these four became zero, 11 per cent, 20 per cent and 29 per cent, respectively. This globalisation of turnover tax rates facilitated changeover to VAT in January 1993. VAT ought to increase fiscal revenues: in 1991 the receipts from turnover tax amounted to CSK 123.4 billion, but the receipts from VAT, including consumer taxes, were expected to reach CSK 190 billion in 1993 in the Czech and Slovak Republics combined. VAT alone was expected to generate CSK 125 billion.

The imposition of VAT has been accompanied by consumer taxes on petroleum and oil products, alcohol, beer, wine and tobacco products. As in Bolivia, the rates are per bottle, package or other natural units.

Direct Taxes

The overall trend in both Latin America and Eastern Europe towards increasing reliance on indirect taxes does not mean that direct taxes have been neglected. Corporate tax is usually an important part of the tax system. The Mexican corporate tax rate was set at 42 per cent in 1978 and became the focus of the subsequent tax reform of 1987. The system of multiple corporate tax rates, ranging from 5 per cent to 42 per cent was replaced by a uniform rate of 35 per cent. The corporate tax base was rationalised through full inflation indexation. The inflation-adjustment of depreciation and inventory valuations was also simplified and made automatic.

In the 1984 Chilean tax reform, retained earnings became subject to a flat rate of 10 per cent and the so-called additional tax on corporations was eliminated. The decrease in the tax on retained earnings was aimed at encouraging enterprises to become self-financing in that retained earning would become a cheaper source of financing than before the reform. The elimination of the additional tax on corporations therefore implied a boost for savings and investment.

In Bolivia, a uniform 'enterprise tax' of 30 per cent was levied on net business income, irrespective of whether the business was organised as a corporation, partnership or sole proprietorship. A lower rate of 20 per cent was levied on state enterprises. Special rules existed for small businesses and natural resource companies. Later, the enterprise income tax was replaced by a 2 per cent tax on the net worth of public and private enterprises alike. A 'simplified' tax was imposed on very small enterprises (in both capital and sales) to replace not only the enterprise net-worth tax but all other taxes payable by such enterprises (for example, VAT). It consisted of a fixed (lump-sum) amount determined according to self-declared revenue from gross sales. Bird (1992, p. 15) has warned, however, that 'the effects of this tax too will depend entirely on administrative success in ensuring that these declarations accord at least roughly with reality'.

In the past, some 70 per cent of all Mexican corporate tax declarations reported no taxable income. Now, all enterprises have to pay a 2 per cent tax on assets, which can be offset against regular corporate tax liability. This effectively establishes a minimum corporate income tax that is independent of profit performance. In Argentina, the corporate income tax rate was cut from 33 per cent to 20 per cent in the 1988–9 reform proposals.

Corporate income tax in the Czech Republic has been lowered by about 10 per cent to 45 per cent, making the tax burden comparable to that in some advanced market economies. The only deductible item is the employment of handicapped persons. In an extreme case, if at least 20 persons are employed and at least 60 per cent are handicapped, the tax rate is lowered by one half (to 22.5 per cent).

With regard to personal income taxes, there was an interesting development in Bolivia. Although personal income tax was in principle fairly comprehensive – for example, all capital gains were supposed to be taxed – in practice it amounted to little more than a tax on labour income in the modern sector. The nominal rate structure was progressive, with the top rate close to 50 per cent, but liberal allowances and exclusions substantially reduced the progressivity.

Since the end of the 1980s, no income taxes have existed in Bolivia, the yield of the taxes that replaced income tax depending on the extent to which the tax administration succeeds in maintaining current market value assessments of real property. These taxes can also be viewed as 'presumptive' taxes on income; for example, a 2 per cent tax on net worth can be considered the same as an income tax of 20 per cent on a presumed income equal to 10 per cent of net worth (in developing countries net worth often means real estate).

In practice the yield of the taxes that have replaced income tax depends on the extent to which the tax administration succeeds in maintaining current market-value assessments of real property. Once again, Bird (1992, p. 18) warns: 'Property taxes are good taxes on the whole but they are difficult to administer well, especially in the face of inflation'.

Income tax rates in Argentina were lowered from the 10–45 per cent range to 6–35 per cent, and in 1988–9 reform proposals flat-rated income tax at 20 per cent. Dividends (now subject to a 10 per cent withholding tax at source) were exempted from personal income tax.

Income tax rates were also lowered in Mexico. The highest marginal rate for personal income, which had been 55 per cent from 1978, was lowered to 35 per cent in 1987, thus equalising marginal corporate and top personal income tax rates: 'One key feature of the personal income tax system remains the extensive list of tax-exempt income components, such as overtime pay, social insurance benefits as well as tax-exempt status of fringe benefits' (OECD, 1992, p. 127).[15] In 1987, the number of tax brackets in Mexico was reduced from 16 to 12. There was a further reduction of brackets to six between 1988 and 1991.

Developments in Chile were not straightforward. During the 1975 tax reform the personal income taxes of those in the top brackets were raised. The highest marginal rate rose to 80 per cent from the previous 65 per cent. The 1984 reform was centred on direct taxes. Personal rates were set so as to decrease gradually over the next two years, to reach a maximum marginal rate of 50 per cent in 1986.

The top personal income tax rates in the Czech Republic of 47 per cent has been practically equalised with corporate income tax. Personal income tax has a construction that needs to be explained. First, there exists a non-taxable part of the tax base, consisting of the following (see also Table 8):

- CSK 20 400 per taxpayer as a minimum
- CSK 9000 per nourished child
- CSK 12 000 per nonemployed wife

Tax rates in six income brackets have been set in the range 15–47 per cent. If we consider the 'progressivity by deduction' we realise that this deduction reduces the rate so that the effective rate is between 7 per cent and 15 per cent for a large number of taxpayers. A taxpayer with an income of CSK 50 000, for example, will pay 15 per cent only on CSK 29 000 (CSK 4350, equal to 8.7 per cent of his or her personal income).

Table 3.8 Czech tax rates and tax base (CSK)

Tax base	Tax rates
0–60 000	15%
60 000–120 000	9 000 + 20% from base exceeding 60 000
120 000–180 000	21 000 + 25% from base exceeding 120 000
180 000–540 000	36 000 + 32% from base exceeding 180 000
540 000–1080 000	151 000 + 40% from base exceeding 540 000
1080 000+	367 200 + 47% from base exceeding 1080 000

Dividend taxation in Mexico was adjusted to increase the neutrality of the tax system between debt and equity finance. Dividends are not taxed at source and are exempt from personal income tax. In cases where taxation at source has not taken place, dividends are subject to the top personal income tax rate of 35 per cent.

Equity market development has suffered from several handicaps. According to experts, the deductibility of nominal interest payments from taxable income strongly favoured debt finance over equity. In the Czech Republic the difference between the tax rate on dividends (25 per cent) and the tax rate on interest earnings (15 per cent) has been the subject of much controversy. Many economists argued that it would deter more risky investment activities. The proposal of the Ministry of Finance to equalise both rates was not approved by the Czech National Council. The reason was allegedly to protect the interests of poorer citizens who do not buy shares but only deposit their money in savings banks.

Tax Systems – Special Problems

One of the most significant features of tax systems in Latin America is taking inflation explicitly into account. The characteristically Latin American saying, 'inflation is more politically acceptable than taxation', confirms that it is not easy to swallow the bitter medicine of tax reform.

Bolivian revenues were hit particularly hard by inflation because of certain structural features of the tax system. Among these one can stress the following:

● Delayed collection of income taxes, together with poor penalty and enforcement systems, result in diminishing real collections from direct taxes.

- Heavy reliance on specific rates of excise taxes ensures that real tax yields will fall as price levels rise unless the rates are constantly increased.
- The effects of the overvalued exchange rate on the real yield of important foreign trade taxes in 1984 reduced real indirect tax collections in a similar manner. Taxes were levied on import prices converted to pesos at the official exchange rate. Because this rate was only about one third of that in the parallel market, the peso price for tax purposes was only about one third of the actual selling price and real tax yields were correspondingly reduced.

The impact of inflation on the tax system was also a big problem in Mexico. Inflation adjustments were introduced into corporate and personal taxes to reduce the distortions caused by inflationary changes in tax bases and to protect revenue from the ravages of inflation by shortening collection time substantially. A key feature of the inflation adjustment package was the introduction of a system of instantaneous depreciation of the present value of fixed assets (discounted at a real interest rate of 7.5 per cent). A 2 per cent tax on the inflation-adjusted assets of enterprises (as in Argentina) can be credited against income tax and obligations and thus functions as a minimum corporate tax.

Indexation of tax arrears was introduced in Chile. In an attempt to avoid tax losses, the reform introduced a correction for inflation of enterprise's assets, liabilities and profits, and individuals' incomes.

In Colombia – where there had been some partial inflation adjustments in the years following the substantial tax reform of 1974 – a major reform in 1986 put the taxation (and deduction) of interest on a real rather than a nominal basis. Then reforms in 1988 began a gradual process of moving towards a fully indexed tax base for business and capital income.

In Latin American countries, there has been a significant Olivera–Tanzi effect, discussed briefly earlier. According to this hypothesis, a money-financed deficit fuels inflation and inflation then feeds back into the fiscal deficit. The lags in tax collection account for a significant decline in fiscal revenue in the presence of inflation. The magnitude of the Olivera–Tanzi effect is closely connected to the existing tax structure.

Indeed certain tax systems are better equipped to cope with inflation than others. For example, the tax legislation in Chile in the early 1970s was not suited to an inflationary environment, even though partial indexation of income taxes had been introduced in the late 1960s. Delay in collection has been estimated at about one year. The idea embedded in the Chilean tax reform of 1975 was to tax real rather than nominal profits.

The reform therefore institutionalised the correction of enterprise's assets, liabilities and profits to reflect inflation. Individuals' income brackets were indexed to inflation. In general, all obligations and credits began to be expressed in a new unit (*unidad tributaria*) of constant purchasing power.

Tax measures adopted between 1983 and 1986 in Mexico increased revenue from direct taxes, but income tax revenue was eroded considerably by high inflation. This was a result of the erosion in the value of taxes in real terms between the time when tax liabilities arose and the time of payment.

In addition, up to 1986 interest paid on debt contracted by companies was tax deductible. Later, the inflationary amortisation component of interest payments on company debts was included in the taxable income base. Therefore the high inflationary component that was implicit in interest payments eroded tax revenue. As a result the share of revenue from income tax in GDP dropped from 5.5 per cent in 1980 to 4.0 per cent in 1987: 'Under the previous system, the full deduction of nominal interest payments was allowed. In practice, with growing inflation, this significantly reduced the taxable base and encouraged firms to seek financing through debt instead of the issue of stocks' (Banco de Mexico, 1992, p. 112).[16]

A further specific feature of small, open, low-income countries is the extreme vulnerability of revenue systems to external shocks due to excessive dependence on revenue from taxes on foreign trade. When the world recession hit in the early 1980s, both current revenues and Bolivian access to foreign capital fell sharply. One must remember that the tax system depended heavily on taxes on imports and exports, with each category accounting for about a third of tax revenues in the mid-1970s. The only way out was to borrow from the Central Bank – to print money, with the predictable consequences of rising inflation, further declines in revenue and still more inflation.

Broadening of the tax base, simplification of the tax systems and the prevention of evasion have been further directions of tax reforms in Latin America. A broadening of the tax base was taken into account in the imposition of VAT in 1973 in Bolivia (the inclusion of capital goods at a rate of 5 per cent). The reform undertaken in the 1980s was surprisingly successful in its registration campaign for new taxpayers. The number of registered business taxpayers doubled.

The base for collecting VAT receipts was also broadened in the 1980s in Argentina. This country was able to reduce the number of nonpayers among 'hard-to-tax' groups (farmers, professionals, small business owners). In Mexico in 1980 the base for collecting VAT receipts was broadened by including some capital gains and dividends. The 'special' tax regimes that favoured farmers and transportation and construction companies, among others, were abolished in 1990. This measure increased equity and raised revenues. In 1977 in Chile, VAT, which had previously been applied to goods only, was extended to services.

Mexico in particular seems to have been successful. The measures implemented over the previous years to broaden the income tax base yielded favourable results in 1991. Tax revenue rose from 4.9 per cent of GDP in 1990 to 5.1 per cent in 1991. This was a significant increase, considering that the maximum tax rate applied to enterprises had been lowered from 36 per cent to 35 per cent, a tax exemption had been given to low salary earners, and the tax rate on interest earnings had been reduced. The increase in tax revenue resulted from an increase in the number of taxpayers, stricter supervision and the growth of economic activity. Since 1987 measures have been introduced to improve tax administration by making the tax system more equitable and efficient and by broadening the tax base. Recently the number of registered taxpayers increased by more than 60 per cent (OECD, 1992, p. 125).

In Bolivia, a 'simplified' tax was imposed on very small enterprises (in both capital and sales) to replace not only the enterprise net-worth tax but all other taxes payable by such enterprises (for example VAT). It consists of a fixed (lump-sum) amount determined according to self-declared revenue from gross sales. Bird (1992, p. 15) cautions once again that 'the effects of this tax too will depend entirely on administrative success in ensuring that these declarations accord at least roughly with reality'.

The strong emphasis on simplification seems to be one of the reasons why the Bolivian reform was successful. The simplification further consisted of eliminating minor taxes, investment incentives and other exemptions from direct and indirect taxes alike, of withdrawing from the complex task of taxing personal and corporate income and adopting a uniform tariff. Bolivia made the remarkable achievement of increasing taxation to 13 per cent of GDP by 1986 and 17 per cent by 1987, from a low of 3 per cent in 1984.

In Chile the tax system was simplified with the reduction of most special treatment clauses. According to Larrain (1991, p. 104) the significant evasion that previously existed was the result of many factors:

- Insufficient and inefficient policing by the Internal Revenue Services.
- The proliferation of groups receiving special treatment, which helped to produce a highly complicated tax system and induced the disguising of one source of income as another to qualify for a lower tax rate.

- The existence of an indirect sales tax applied to the total value of every transaction (rather than VAT), a provision that significantly encouraged evasion.

3.5 SUMMARY

Tight fiscal and monetary policies are a necessary prerequisite of a successful stabilisation policy. The experiences in Latin America show that in countries where these fundamentals were not kept in place, economic stabilisation was unsuccessful. But it is only a necessary condition, which must be complemented with a sufficient condition; that is, by additional heterodox measures. The content of these additional measures depends on the particular situation in certain periods in different countries, but structural policies such as liberalisation, deregulation and privatisation must form part of the package. In certain situations incomes policies are also needed. The ability to reach a social accord among major social groups in order to break inflationary expectations seems to have been very important in a number of cases.

Structural policies can be implemented after the correction of both public finances and external economic balances have been achieved. Part of the heritage of expansionary, import-substitution policies in the past has been fiscal deficits. During the stabilisation period public finances must undergo a profound adjustment on both sides. Expenditure must be cut and the structure of revenues must be changed.

Different groups inside society tend to resist the government's attempts to levy additional taxes or to gather revenues by increasing the real price of goods and services produced by public enterprises. The government often has to resort to inflation tax as a means of overcoming the resistance of society to the internal transfer of resources to the public sector. Marked improvements in public sector finances are instrumental in bringing down inflation.

Adjusting public expenditure has been affected mainly by reducing investment expenditure, decreasing current transfers and eliminating subsidies. It is advantageous to integrate expenditure cuts into a coherent programme or 'social accord', such as the Mexican Economic Solidarity Pact.

Revenue problems provide an impetus to tax reforms that have tried to change the methods and modalities of revenue collection. The methods of financing the public deficit are similar to those used in Eastern European economies – through foreign lending, borrowing from the Central Bank, forced borrowing from the banking system, bond financing and the use of privatisation proceeds.

In an inflationary environment, which is typical for Latin American countries, conventional deficit figures should be corrected for inflationary influences. The monetisation of the deficit, also common to a majority of Eastern European economies, imposes an inflation tax on the public.

It is often preferable to move on forced borrowing from the banking system in order to reduce reliance on inflationary Central Bank finance, as happened in Mexico. The corollary of this method of financing the public debt, however, is negative real deposit rates that weaken the propensity to save, which has been a problem for both Mexico and Czechoslovakia.

Necessary and logical is the shift from forced bank saving to bond financing at market rates. The desired task is to fund the debt through debt instruments issued in the money and bond markets. As the markets develop, the Central Bank can start relying more and more on open market operations as the main tool of monetary management. The proceeds from privatisation can also be used in both Latin American and Eastern European countries to ease the pressure on the banking system.

Tax reforms represent an integral and very important part of reform measures. Latin American countries have had a certain advantage in this area because their prereform tax systems, in spite of significant insufficiencies, were anchored in the market system. Both groups of countries are trying to adopt tax systems similar to those of advanced market economies, with the emphasis on an improvement in (horizontal) equity and efficiency. Experiences of Latin American countries confirm that improving the tax system takes time, that it is a gradual process with some significant turning points.

Tougher tax administration, simplification of the system and broadening of the tax base are the general features of Latin American tax reforms. Value added tax has replaced old-fashioned turnover taxes in many countries, with a tendency to reduce the number of tax rates. VAT is usually accompanied by consumer taxes on luxuries and bads. A reduction in the number of tax rates has also been a significant feature of corporate taxation. There has been a great deal of discussion (and some positive movement) towards replacing corporate income tax by a tax on net or gross worth.

Income tax rates have been lowered in recent years in many Latin American economies. In addition the number of tax brackets has been reduced. The neutrality of the tax system between debt and equity finance (nonexistent in Czechoslovakia) is another new feature of most Latin American countries.

Eastern European countries could also benefit from the Latin American experience with tax systems in the presence of high inflation. Inflation adjustments must be introduced into corporate and personal taxes in order to reduce distortions and protect revenue. Further interesting developments are indexation of tax arrears, a system of instantaneous depreciation of the present value of fixed assets, and shortening of the lags in tax collection.

In summary, despite some quite different initial conditions, the reform effort undertaken in Latin America in the area of fiscal policy is very similar to the ones being undertaken or proposed in Eastern Europe. Although the different underlying structures suggest that at times the responses of the economies may be quite ·different, it does seem that Eastern Europe can learn a great deal from the successes and failures of different fiscal reform efforts in Latin America.

In particular, attention should be paid to the various problems with the introduction of VAT, the administrative problems that different reforms entail (which will usually be magnified in Eastern Europe) and the need to incorporate inflation into the tax system. Finally, the Latin American experience shows us that fiscal reform is an ongoing process, which never really comes to an end as fiscal systems have to be able to adjust to changing times and circumstances.

Acknowledgements

The author of this chapter would like to express his thanks to all participants of the workshop on Eastern European and Latin American economic reforms, organised by the International Development Research Centre, Ottawa, Canada and held in Santiago in December 1992 and Prague in April 1993, for their critical remarks and suggestions. Last but not least the author must thank Carlos Urzúa from El Colegio de Mexico for fruitful discussions on Mexican fiscal policy.

Notes

1. Although 'Czech Republic' is used throughout this chapter, events and data prior to 1 January 1993 refer to former Czechoslovakia; that is, the Czech and Slovak Republics combined.
2. This does not mean that traditional orthodox stabilisation was used in all cases. For a variety of Latin American experiences see Meller (1992).
3. In a very comprehensive analysis Ortiz divides the adjustment process in Mexico into three stages: (1) the initial phase, 1983–5; (2) from the oil shock of 1986 until October 1987; and (3) since the end of 1987. For the Mexican adjustment process, the adoption of structural policies from the

outset has been typical. The prevention or at least the postponement of the large-scale bankruptcies in the initial phase and the avoidance of them in the second resembles the attitude of the Czech/Slovak government during the 1990–3 period.

The tight fiscal and monetary policies after the shocks – the decrease in oil prices and the stock market crash in October 1987 – also have a counterpart in our policies. The tight fiscal and monetary policies practised in the former Czechoslovakia in the 1990–2 period were because of another shock – the collapse of COMECON and therefore the loss of a substantial part of export markets.

4. In Mexican terminology, one distinguishes three alternative measures of the public sector fiscal position. Each indicator measures a different aspect of fiscal policy. The financial balance gauges the difference between total revenue and expenditure and thus the effect the budget has on financial markets by either adding (in case of a deficit) or subtracting (in case of a surplus) financial assets to/from the economy.

The operational balance, by eliminating the inflation component from nominal interest payments, measures the government claim on resources not financed by regular revenue. The primary balance attempts to measure discretionary government effort to balance its accounts. It is the difference between revenue and expenditure excluding interest payments on both domestic and external public debt (see OECD, 1992, p. 39; Banco de Mexico, 1992, p. 101).

5. Tanzi (1992, p. 642) summarises: 'Inflation and external payments problems are almost always accompanied by fiscal imbalances. Thus, fiscal adjustment is a prerequisite to economic stability'.

6. Public debt has been a big problem for Mexico in the past. After reaching an average of almost 80 per cent of GDP in 1986, the net public debt increased to 36.6 per cent in 1991. This reduction was observed in both domestic and external components. Public debt is held by the private sector, commercial banks, local governments and external creditors, although in general the fall in the latter has been more remarkable because of the rescheduling agreement with foreign creditor banks and the substantial accumulation of international reserves in 1990 and 1991.

Concerning the domestic component: 'The net domestic public debt in the consolidated version with the Banco de Mexico decreased by 3.7 percentage points of GDP from its highest level over the period 1987–91. If the broad economic debt version is considered, the decline amounts to 4.4 percentage points of GDP from 1989 to 1991. Simultaneously, the average maturity of domestic public debt instruments was extended from 110 days in January 1989 to nearly 420 days in December 1991' (Banco de Mexico, 1992, pp. 121–2).

7. The role of inflation in Mexican public finance has been important 'in assessing the impact of fiscal policy on aggregate demand, conventional deficit figures should be corrected, for the real debt amortisation resulting from inflation' (Diaz and Tercero, 1988, p. 371). The authors present the figures for a full-inflation-corrected budget deficit: that is, the adjusted operational deficit. This concept takes into account five effects: the Olivera–Tanzi effect, the effect of inflation in financial subsidies, the effect of

inflation on the composition of the peso public debt, the inflation tax on noninterest-bearing public debt, and the inflation tax on the peso-denominated interest-bearing public debt.

In all the years under consideration (1965–86), inflation made a positive net contribution to public revenues. Thus, had a price freeze been implemented in any given year, an increase in explicit taxation or a reduction in spending would have been necessary to maintain the without-freeze rate of growth of public debt.

8.   Václav Klaus, former minister of finance and current Prime Minister, has stressed 'the admission of whatever kind of small budgetary deficit would mean the abolition of budgetary discipline and the start of an uncheckable process of deepening this deficit without an end' (*Finance a úvěr*, [Finance and credit], no. 1, 1992, p. 3).

9.   In September 1992 credit allocated by the Central Bank was equivalent to 18.4 per cent of the total volume of credits that commercial banks loaned to clients (CSK 136.6 billion). This indicates that the Central Bank has been able to influence directly only a small segment of the credit market.

In the Czech Republic two kinds of credit are extended to commercial banks: redistributive credits and refinancing credits. Redistributive credits have been extended to three commercial banks only: those banks created on 1 January 1990 because of the dissolution of the Unitary State Bank. Refinancing credits have been granted to all commercial banks. They consist of several kinds of credit: rediscount of bills of exchange, lombard of securities, auctionary refinancing credits, and daily refinancing credits.

10. In the first half of 1992, 15 issues were realised with a total value of CSK 66 billion, with repayment within a month.

11. The funds stemming from privatisation are being used to finance the sunken cost of the reform: '... the financing of the fiscal deficit by means of privatisation crowds out investment in physical assets in general. As is well known, privatisation as a means of financing the deficit is not different from issuing governments bonds' (Fanelli and Frenkel, 1992, p. 45).

12. McLure has mentioned the lack of administrative capacity of Eastern European countries to implement, for example, a Western style income tax (McLure, 1992, p.5).

13. With regard to Mexico, Bird (1992, p.25) says: 'Taken as a whole, the Mexican tax reform of the last decade has been substantial. But in fact, it never was taken as a whole but rather in small, more digestible pieces'. One speaks about a gradual adaptation to changing circumstances, not a sharp break with the past stimulated by extreme external pressure.

14. Tax evasion, because of weak tax administration, has become prevalent in most Latin American countries. In Bolivia, only about 20 per cent of capital income ended up in the personal income tax net compared with 75 per cent of labour income (Thirsk, in Khalilzadeh-Shirazi and Shah, 1991, p. 62). But tax evasion is also present in developed market economies. For example, in the United States, the Internal Revenue Service has estimated that in 1987 noncompliance with corporation and income tax cost the Treasury over 20 per cent of tax liability (Slemrod, 1990, p. 171).

15. The resource cost of operating the income tax system alone is high. In the United States this cost, including the administrative cost borne by the gov-

ernment and the compliance cost borne by taxpayers, has been estimated to
be about 7 per cent of revenue (Slemrod, 1990, p. 168). In the United
Kingdom the operating costs – public (administrative) and private (compliance) – of the tax system come to about 4 per cent of revenues, or 1.5 per
cent of GDP (Bird, in Khalilzadeh-Shirazi and Shah, 1991, p. 41).
16.   Tanzi (1992, p. 655) remarks: 'Inflation, especially if accompanied by price
controls, almost always increases the tendency to evade taxes'.

References

Banco de Mexico (1992) *The Mexican Economy* (Mexico City: Banco de Mexico).
Bird, R. (1992) 'Tax Reform in Latin America', *Latin American Research Review*,
vol. 27, no. 1, pp. 7–36.
Corbo, V. (1992a) 'Development Strategies and Policies in Latin America',
Occasional Papers, No. 22 (San Francisco: International Centre for Economic
Growth).
Corbo, V. (1992b) 'Economic Transformation in Latin America: Lessons for Latin
America, *European Economic Review*, vol. 36, pp. 407–16.
Diaz, F. G. and R. R. Tercero (1988) 'Lessons from Mexico', in M. Bruno *et al.*,
Inflation, stabilization (Cambridge, MA: MIT Press).
Fanelli, J. and R. Frenkel (1992) 'On Gradualism, Shock and Sequencing in Econ-
omic Adjustment' (Buenos Aires: CEDES).
Khalilzadeh-Shirazi, J. and Anwar Shah (eds)(1991) *Tax Policy in Developing
Countries* (Washington, DC: World Bank).
Larrain, F. (1991) 'Public sector behaviour in a highly indebted country', in
F. Larrain and M. Selovsky (eds), *The Contrasting Chilean Experience: The
public sector and the Latin American crisis* (San Francisco: International Centre
for Economic Growth).
McLure, C. E., Jr (1992), 'Tax Policy Lessons for LDCs and Eastern Europe',
Occasional Papers, No. 28 (San Francisco: International Centre for Economic
Growth).
Meller, P. (1992) *Latin American Adjustment and Economic Reforms: Issues and
recent experience* (Santiago: CIEPLAN).
OECD (1991) *OECD Economic Survey* Czech and Slovak republic (Paris: OECD).
OECD (1992) *OECD Economic Survey* (Paris and Mexico: OECD).
Ortiz, G. (1991) 'Mexico Beyond the Debt Crisis: Toward sustainable growth with
price stability', in M. Bruno, *et al.*, *Lessons of Economic Stabilization and its
Aftermath* (Cambridge, MA: MIT Press).
Ritter, A. R. M. (1992) 'Development Strategy and Structural Adjustment in
Chile' (Ottawa: The North–South Institute).
Slemrod, J. (1990) 'Optimal Taxation and Optimal Tax-systems', *Journal of
Economic Perspectives*, vol. 1.
Tanzi, V. (1992) 'Fiscal Policy and Economic Reconstruction in Latin America',
World Development, no 5.

4 Privatisation and Fiscal Reform in Eastern Europe: Some Lessons from Latin America

Raúl E. Sáez and Carlos M. Urzúa

4.1 INTRODUCTION

During the last two decades, for a plethora of reasons, all Latin American countries have introduced economic reforms, attempting, with varying degrees of success, to stabilise and liberalise their economies. More recently, and in much more dramatic fashion, the former socialist countries of Eastern Europe have turned the wheel 180 degrees and have embarked on drastic reforms to transform their systems into capitalist economies.

Although the initial conditions in both regions were radically different, it is natural to ask how the Latin American experience can be of use to Eastern European reformers. That such a question is worth consideration is well illustrated by the chapters in this volume. This chapter is intended to complement, in particular, the excellent analysis made by Janos Hoós (Chapter 2) and Vratislav Izák (Chapter 3) of the Latin American and Eastern European experiences of, respectively, privatisation and fiscal reforms.

The privatisation of state-owned enterprises is an essential component of the transformation of the Eastern European economies. Private ownership is crucial for providing efficiency incentives to firms in market economies. It is also likely to be one of the most difficult aspects of the institutional and policy reforms underway in those countries. In Section 4.2 we address some of the privatisation issues that we think are relevant in the light of the Latin American experience. In Section 4.3 we focus on another essential component of any economic programme: the fiscal side. Although fiscal reform commonly signifies only a tax reform, we also take the opportunity to comment, albeit briefly, on other fiscal issues. We conclude in Section 4.4 with some qualifications, and further comments, on the Eastern European economies and their transition from socialism.

4.2   PRIVATISATION

Drawing relevant lessons for Eastern Europe from the Latin American experience of privatisation is not an easy task. In spite of the large and increasing role played by the state in the production of goods and services since the great depression of the 1930s, Latin American countries have always had a private sector and well-defined property rights. Moreover capital and stock markets, although imperfect and shallow, were already operating prior to the privatisation programmes initiated in the second half of the 1980s, and despite several policy shifts there was a long experience of dealing with foreign investors. Furthermore none of the Latin American economies (with the exception of Cuba, of course) was ever structured on the basis of large vertically and horizontally integrated state-owned monopolies.

For one thing, those differences imply that the privatisation effort in Eastern Europe will take longer than the programmes carried out in Latin America. In particular the divestiture of medium to large enterprises in manufacturing will have to be done at a much slower pace, and the transfer of public utilities will probably have to wait until the first round of privatisation and reforms is consolidated and an institutional framework for their regulation is in place.

These differences notwithstanding, one can find several commonalities in the Latin American and Eastern European privatisation processes. Janos Hoós has pointed out most of these, and here we try to complement his exposition.

The Sequencing of Privatisation

The complexity of choosing a sequence of reforms is stressed in Chapter 2. We agree with the idea put forward by Hoós to start with small enterprises and residential assets, and then move on to large industrial enterprises, in the latter case, starting with the tradeable sectors, rather than with the sectors that are more isolated from foreign competition due to natural or trade policy barriers. Nevertheless, given the magnitude of the changes that are currently being introduced in the Eastern European economies, the reforms will have to move simultaneously on several fronts. It has become apparent during the last few years that there will not always be enough time in those countries to wait for the consolidation of a specific policy change, or for progress in the divestiture of certain types of productive assets, before moving to the next step.

Who Really Owns the State-Owned Enterprises?

One important privatisation issue that tends to be forgotten is, as emphasised by Tirole (1991), whether the state is the sole owner of the enterprises. As a rule, Latin American governments were in full control of the
enterprises prior to their divestiture. For instance, when the government of
Chile initiated a privatisation effort in the 1970s, one of its first actions
was to reinforce control over the state-owned firms, and then to proceed
towards reducing difficulties of having the agents (the managers) follow
the goals of the principal (the government). Opposition to divestiture
comes not only from workers, who feel they have a claim to ownership,
but also from interest groups that obtain benefits from the state-owned
enterprise or use it to provide favours.

Industrial Regulation

It is likely that public utilities will not be privatised in Eastern European
countries in the first or perhaps even the second phase of divestitures. A
possible exception could be telecommunications, although this sector may
be privatised through the expansion of private investment rather than
divestiture. Therefore regulatory issues involving natural monopolies are
not yet as relevant as in Latin America.

In the case of the other monopolies for sale, however, there is a strong
need to break them up prior to their privatisation, for several reasons. To start
with, as happened in some Latin American countries, it is not enough to rely
on trade liberalisation alone to put pressure on monopolies or oligopolies
because in a traditionally protected economy it will take time for importers to
set up distribution chains, and in some cases local producers will end up
becoming importers as well. Thus the desired effect is far from immediate.

Another reason is that once property rights have been allocated it is very
difficult to undo things. This is clearly shown by the Chilean experience
with the privatisation of regulated natural monopolies, which resulted in
problems such as the lack of separation into different companies for electricity generation and transmission, or the restitution by the hydro-electric
generator companies of the water rights they were given. The breaking up
of monopolies has to include the abolition of any rights or privileges that
the enterprise may have been granted when owned by the state because, in
the end, they become barriers to entry.

It is interesting to note that most Latin American countries have tended
to overlook entirely the issue of industrial regulation and its relationship

with privatisation. For instance a fully-fledged antitrust commission was created in Mexico only after the privatisation process had, for all intents and purposes, already been completed (1993). This behaviour can be perhaps explained by the fact that monopolies can be sold at a higher price as complete entities, a fact that can make politicians reluctant to break them up before selling them. This reasoning, however, obviously neglects the future social welfare losses that will arise from monopoly practices.

The Emergence of Conglomerates

The Latin American experience shows that the divestiture method used has consequences for market and ownership structures as well as corporate governance. The privatisation processes of the 1970s in Chile, and of the 1980s and 1990s in Mexico and Argentina, led to the formation of highly leveraged conglomerates: through public bids domestic investors acquired banks and enterprises simultaneously.

In the case of Chile this proved to be disastrous in the early 1980s. Since the conglomerates were using the banks to provide credit to their own enterprises, when the economy entered a recession in 1981 the conglomerates collapsed and the enterprises reverted to state ownership (see Bitran and Sáez, 1994). Certainly the issue is not the simultaneous ownership of banks and enterprises *per se*, but rather that their emergence as a result of privatisation has consequences for economic stability and financial regulation, an issue to which we will return. But the question remains: do you want to facilitate the formulation of conglomerates by choosing a determinate method of sale, as was the case in several Latin American countries?

To avoid concentration of ownership as an outcome of privatisation, the use of retail sales of shares has been suggested, but this may have implications for corporate governance. Insufficient empirical research has been done in Latin America regarding the consequences of having either a large number of small shareholders, through popular or people's capitalism, as opposed to one dominant owner, or having only one type of shareholder, as opposed to a combination of shareholders such as large domestic investors, foreign investors, institutional investors and small shareholders. In general, the vast majority of enterprises in Latin America were awarded to one dominant owner, or stable core to use Lipton and Sachs's (1990) expression. This had the advantage of alleviating the agency problem that would result by the lack of incentives to monitor managers in the case of a very disseminated structure of shareholding.

Financial Regulation

A private financial system is now being developed in Eastern Europe, and, as is well known, the implicit government insurance on bank deposits creates a moral hazard and adverse selection problem that requires appropriate regulation. As noted earlier, the Chilean experience in the 1970s can be used as a lesson on this matter. The existence of conglomerates and of joint ownership of banks and enterprises was not the sole reason for the financial collapse of the early 1980s. The problem was that transactions between related parties was not regulated, which led to self-lending. The lesson that can be drawn here is that appropriate prudential regulation mechanisms must be in place before starting to privatise. Again, once property rights have been allocated and interest groups have developed, it is very difficult to regulate properly.

Investment Funds

In a related fashion, the government also has to provide the right incentives for the managers of investment funds to represent truly the goals of the ultimate owners of the firm. This may become an important issue in Eastern Europe considering that some countries are relying on these funds for the privatisation of large enterprises. Investment fund managers should have in mind the maximisation of long-run profits and not short-run profitability.

Furthermore, in the countries choosing voucher systems for the distribution of shares and investment funds for corporate control, policy makers should also consider the possible consequences of having fund managers (or board members elected by them) sitting, simultaneously, on several enterprise boards, because of the potential for indirect horizontal or vertical collusion between these enterprises.

Transparency

In Chapter 2, Janos Hoós devotes some space to the issue of transparency. We agree that this is important for equity, fairness and political economy reasons. The impression that a privatisation programme is benefiting specific and clearly identified groups linked to the administration in power, or past administrations, reduces support for the reform. As shown in Latin America, the political economy of privatisation is complex, and lack of transparency or legitimacy (real or perceived) makes it even more

difficult. In a plebiscite, voters in Uruguay rejected a privatisation programme precisely because they had the impression that the sales would
only benefit investors tied to the government. The rejection in Eastern
Europe of 'spontaneous' privatisation by the managers of state-owned
enterprises and the former nomenklatura, as described in Chapter 2, shows
that transparency is also an important issue in those countries.

To conclude this section, there are no simple guidelines for an optimal
privatisation programme. The specific features of the divestiture efforts
have to differ from country to country on the basis of the initial conditions
of the enterprises, national idiosyncrasies, political constraints and the
macroeconomic environment. Nevertheless, judging by the Latin
American experience, a necessary condition for the success of any privatisation programme in Eastern Europe is that the rules of the game be
clearly defined and respected, so that the high degree of uncertainty and
noise already existing in their economies is not increased.

4.3   FISCAL REFORM

The most pressing fiscal task that the Eastern European countries had to face
from the beginning of their economic reforms was reshaping their tax
systems. From the beginning of the socialist period, and especially until the
1970s, taxes tended to be quite rudimentary (see Gray, 1991, for a review).
This reform has been, and will continue to be for some time, one of the most
important items on the agenda. In the following subsections we will remark
on this and other fiscal issues, following the lead taken in Chapter 3.

Novel Tax Systems

Given that the tax systems in the Western world are themselves hardly
optimal, one could ask whether the former socialist countries should not
take the opportunity to adopt a novel system. In particular, one could
wonder, following McLure (1992), if the time for a system based on cash
flow taxation has not come.

The Eastern European countries apparently do not think so, for two very
good reasons: since several of them are looking forward to economic integration with the rest of Europe (Hungary and Poland have already applied to
become members of the European Union), a cash-flow tax would be a
headache to administer across borders, because it would not qualify as an
income tax on the rest of the continent. Furthermore, a cash-flow tax that
exempts returns to savings and investment would yield less than an income

tax (see Tait, 1992). Those two reasons are quite similar to the ones heard in Latin America when the adoption of such a system was suggested.

Value Added Tax

Most countries in Eastern Europe have already introduced value added tax (and a host of excise taxes). As described in Chapter 3, VAT allows for multiple rates and exempts some services. Furthermore VAT is, wisely enough, in the main tailored after the ideal value added tax advocated by the European Commission. It will be interesting to see how much revenue will be collected through these indirect taxes. Our own conjecture is that, in the short run, the most open and administratively centralised countries will have the greatest success. There is, nevertheless, another point that deserves even more attention: the welfare impact of all those indirect taxes across the population. The analysis of this impact seems to us an important and urgent research topic. On this, by the way, Eastern Europe would do well not to look for advice from Latin America, where there have been very few serious studies at the household level of the impact of taxes. Rather it should concentrate on Western Europe.

Progressive Income Tax

In all capitalist countries, the majority of economists (and most other people, for that matter) continue to endorse progressive personal income tax rates. Curiously enough, some important economists and policy makers in former socialist countries are, in contrast, not so enthusiastic about progressivity (the most illustrious case is Kornai, 1990). One possible reason for their dislike could be the belief that there is no need to be concerned about income distribution, since their societies are relatively more egalitarian than the rest of the world. To qualify this view, however, one can note that the redistribution of income in favour of the rich can be quite large during sustained periods of high inflation and/or stabilisation, such as the ones that their countries are currently enduring. Moreover the privatisation process itself will lead to a redistribution of assets. On this, Latin America can provide many sobering examples.

Asset Tax

Chapter 3 has drawn attention to the gross asset tax on firms implemented in Mexico in 1989, whose main purpose is to decrease evasion by taxing visible assets. Leaving aside the issue of whether or not this tax has been truly successful (see Urzúa, 1994, for a sceptical view), it is worth nothing that similar taxes have been tried and abandoned in other Latin American countries: in Colombia, where a tax on wealth for both individuals and enterprises was implemented in the 1970s (and has been recently abolished); and in Bolivia, where a tax on net assets was tried in 1988 without much success (the main problem seems to have been that firms were able to decrease tax payments by exaggerating their liabilities). It is also interesting to note that most Eastern European countries used to have, during their socialist period, a tax on fixed assets, with the purpose of encouraging the efficient use of capital. Curiously enough, as described by Gray (1991), Poland has recently reintroduced a tax along that line.

Tax Compliance

Under socialist regimes, the shortage of goods and the abundance of bureaucrats made citizens distrustful of any government policy. Thus, Izák's remarks in Chapter 3 on the extent of tax evasion that currently prevails in former socialist countries should come as no surprise. He mentioned some traditional medicines that will help to control the disease of tax evasion, but we would like to add one that should be as good as penicillin: honesty on the part of the government. The authorities should try to gain the confidence of the citizens by being seen as trustworthy. Regarding this, Latin America can provide several examples of countries where widespread corruption by government officials is a big factor that discredits, *a priori*, any campaign against tax evasion.

Social Security

In most economies of Eastern Europe the burden of social security is sufficiently large to be quite worrisome. Among possible reasons for its magnitude are an increasing share of old people, too generous benefits, bad administration and, for some countries, the simultaneous use of social security contributions for both the pension system and the health care system.

Except for some platitudes, such as improving the administration of the funds and increasing the age of retirement, it is hard to suggest what to do to solve the problem. However, one point seems clear: given the current state of their economies, the Eastern European countries should not try to follow the road taken by some Latin American countries and privatise their pension systems. Given the lack of suitable financial institutions in Eastern Europe, this policy would seem to be too adventurous in the short- and medium-terms. Furthermore, in the case of the intertwining of the pension and health systems, any drastic reform of the social security system will have to wait until the mature development of a private market for health services (perhaps together with an independent public health system).

The Need for New Institutions

Tanzi (1993) has called attention to the very strong links between fiscal and monetary policies in the Eastern European countries. Often fiscal goals have to be pursued through monetary policy (for example, the monetisation of the public deficit), because of the lack of fiscal and financial institutions such as bond markets. Tanzi (1993, p. 26) in fact dares to say that 'To a large extent the success or failure of the transformation process will depend on how quickly modern fiscal institutions can be created'. We strongly agree, but to these fiscal institutions we would add the counterparts that are also much needed by the private sector: commercial banks and other financial intermediaries. Regarding the financial markets, of which the most cosmopolitan and glorified is the stock market, we think they are less important in the short and medium terms – although there are, of course, exceptions, such as the voucher market developed in the Czech and Slovak Republics during their privatisation processes.

The Debt Burden

It almost goes without saying that most Eastern European countries suffer from 'debt overhang', the same problem that has afflicted most of Latin America since the 1980s. The very high burden of foreign debt in the case of countries such as Hungary and Poland clearly leaves very little room for fiscal manoeuvring, even during this period of relatively low international interest rates. The industrialised countries in the West are fully aware of that, and some minor help has been provided, but we are afraid that there will never be the political will to go beyond that (except, of course, in the case of Russia). What can be done? Here we believe that several Latin American countries have a good lesson to offer: bargain, and bargain hard, with the private banks.

4.4 SOME QUALIFICATIONS AND FINAL REMARKS

Before concluding, it is perhaps worth making two qualifications. The first is obvious, but important: the Eastern European countries are a very heterogeneous group, much more heterogeneous than the Latin American ones.

Furthermore, the initial conditions under which each of the Eastern European countries initiated its own economic transformation process differ markedly from each other (which, again, was not quite so in the case of Latin America). Thus, care has to be taken when drawing lessons, even in a cross-sectional fashion. To give an example, the Czech and Slovak Republics started their transformation with a very low level of foreign debt, with fiscal balance, low inflation and an insignificant private sector; Hungary started with exactly the opposite initial conditions on all four counts.

The other qualifications concerns the fact that some pressing issues in Eastern Europe are foreign to Latin America. An obvious case is the inter-enterprise debt problem, particularly in the states of the former Soviet Union (see, for example, Rostowski, 1993), which constitutes a serious issue to be considered during the privatisation process. Other cases are the fiscal coordination problems that are already arising in several Eastern European countries after their partition into different states (see Kopits and Mihaljek, 1993), and the large proportion of their firms that were artificially surviving through public subsidies during the socialist period (see, for example, Richet, 1993).

Instead of concluding by summarising our views, we make two final remarks that lie outside the economic sphere. The first concerns the importance of social and cultural institutions. After reading about the stabilisation processes undertaken by most countries in Central Europe after the First World War, we were struck by the similarity of the initial conditions then and now for some of the countries (even though they were then capitalist!) For instance, the foreign debt owed by Czechoslovakia and its level of inflation were then, just as now, quite small compared with neighbouring Hungary and Poland. What caused then, and what causes now, these differences? It is certainly not financial expertise – Hungary, for instance, has always had a stronger financial sector than Czechoslovakia.

In a remarkably prescient conference in 1990, which described most of the issues that would become relevant during the later economic transformation of Eastern Europe, Arrow (1991) chose to conclude by drawing attention to the economic consequences of the fading importance of the nation state in our times. The recent fragmentation of several countries in Eastern Europe makes Arrow's message worth remembering. Countries can ignore international economic integration only at their own peril.

References

Arrow, K. (1991) 'Transition from Socialism', *Estudios Económicos*, vol. 6, pp. 5–22.

Bitran, E. and R. E. Sáez (1994) 'Privatisation and Regulation in Chile', in B. Bosworth, R. Dornbusch and R. Labán (eds.), *The Chilean Economy: Policy Lessons and Challenges* (Washington DC: The Brookings Institution).

Gray, C.W. (1991) 'Tax Systems in the Reforming Socialist Economies of Europe', *Communist Economies and Economic Transformation*, vol. 3, pp. 63–79.

Kopits, G. and D. Mihaljek (1993) 'Fiscal Federalism and the New Independent States', in V. Tanzi (ed.), *Transition to Market: Studies in Fiscal Reform* (Washington DC: International Monetary Fund).

Kornai, J. (1990) *The Road to a Free Economy* (New York: W. W. Norton).

Lipton, D. and J. Sachs (1990) 'Privatisation in Eastern Europe: The Case of Poland', *Brookings Papers on Economic Activity*, vol. 2, pp. 293–341.

McLure, C. E. (1992) 'A Simpler Consumption-Based Alternative to the Income Tax for Socialist Economies in Transition', *World Bank Research Observer*, vol. 7, pp. 221–37.

Richet, X. (1993) 'Transition Towards the Market in Eastern Europe: Privatisation, Industrial Restructuring and Entrepreneurship', *Communist Economies and Economic Transformation*, vol. 4, pp. 229–43.

Rostowski, J. (1993) 'The Inter-enterprise Debt Explosion in the former Soviet Union: Causes, Consequences, Cures', *Communist Economies and Economic Transformation*, vol. 5, pp. 131–53.

Tait, A. A. (1992) 'A Not-So-Simple Alternative to the Income Tax for Socialist Economies in Transition: A Comment on McLure', *World Bank Research Observer*, vol. 7, pp. 239–48.

Tanzi, V. (1993) 'Financial Markets and Public Finance in the Transformation Process', in V. Tanzi (ed.), *Transition to Market: Studies in Fiscal Reform*, (Washington DC: International Monetary Fund).

Tirole, J. (1991) 'Privatisation in Eastern Europe: Incentives and the Economics of Transition', in O. J. Blanchard and S. Fischer (eds.), *NBER Macroeconomics Annual 1991* (Cambridge, MA: MIT Press).

Urzúa, C. M. (1994) 'An Appraisal of Recent Tax Reforms in Mexico', in G. McMahon and G. Perry (eds.) *Tax Reform and Structural Change* (London: MacMillan).

5 Lessons of Monetary Policy in Latin America

Nikolay Karagodin

5.1 INTRODUCTION

This chapter examines the strategies and results of monetary policy in Latin American countries during the last two decades. These decades were a crucial period for the economies of the region as many of them suffered from diverse external shocks and a deep economic crisis. A steep increase in net transfers abroad caused by the external debt problems of the 1980s (in a number of cases combined with a legacy of overexpansionary financial policies in previous periods) produced, in many countries, serious financial disruption.

In the 1980s, to the outside world the Latin American economy became associated with chronic high inflation, crippling foreign indebtedness, massive capital flight and failed attempts at stabilisation. In order to overcome this crisis, many Latin American nations undertook a comprehensive revision of their previous development strategies. Anti-inflation programmes were often combined with thorough structural reforms aimed at opening the economy to the world market and diminishing state regulation.

The Latin American experience in the monetary policy field is highly relevant for Eastern Europe. The post-socialist countries of the region are now plagued by many of the financial problems that were so typical of Latin America. This is especially true with respect to inflation. In almost every Eastern European country, the breakdown of state control over the economy in the course of the market transition has triggered high inflation. As in Latin America, the primary causes are those of the price of tradables and the fiscal crisis.

In attempting to cope with these problems, all post-socialist states have undertaken stabilisation programmes. The programmes were significantly different in design: some relied on orthodox monetary instruments (such as the Gaidar stabilisation attempt of 1992); others included elements of income policy and control over exchange rates (for example, the Polish stabilisation programme). The results of the programme ranged from relative success in curbing rapid price growth (for example, in the Czech Republic and Poland) to complete failure (as in Russia in 1992). The situation in Russia is especially grim as the country is currently on the verge of hyperinflation.

Even among the more successful East European 'stabilisers', however, inflation is far from under control. The relative stabilisation reached is very fragile, because it has been secured at the expense of a substantial fall in production and consumption by the major part of the population. The problem of combining relative price stability with sustained growth of GNP and incomes has yet to be solved.

Many questions about the optimal anti-inflation strategy in Eastern Europe are still unanswered. The search for the right answers could begin by turning to the results achieved in the course of a long series of experiments in the Latin American economic 'laboratory'. These experiment were carried out by diverse political regimes and were often inspired by conflicting ideologies. The region has acquired a vast wealth of experience in different types of stabilisation programmes, ranging from classical, orthodox-based monetary recipes to innovative varieties combining monetary measures with administrative control over some very important economic parameters.

In particular, the history of monetary policy in Latin America may teach much about the use of price, wage and exchange rate controls, which are currently provoking so much debate in the postsocialist world. Latin American experience is also instructive about 'life after stabilisation' and the ways of resuming investment and economic growth.

There is also much to be learned from the Latin American experience on the issue of sequencing economic reforms. The issue is very topical for Eastern Europe, where the order of economic reforms has proved to be far from optimal. Liberalisation of prices, banking activity and foreign trade typically preceded privatisation and restructuring of the state sector as well as the formation of mature institutional structures. This has engendered serious distortions and hampered the revival of growth.

Thus marketisation of the banking system in an unstable economic situation has had a number of negative effects. It has seriously contributed to the general economic crisis through raising the price of credit beyond the reach of the bulk of enterprises and channelling financial resources from production to trade and other 'quick profit' activities. By the same token, a problem of moral hazard and adverse risk selection in newly created commercial banks has surfaced strongly. There is a clear need to create a developed system of state supervision and regulation in the financial sphere. Latin American (especially the South Cone) countries passed through their own experiments with deregulation of the financial sphere in the 1970s and the beginning of the 1980s. They learned some very important lessons about the dangers of the process.

Another area where East Europeans could gain from the study of the economic history of Latin America is the relation between stabilisation and liberalisation of the external sector. All postsocialist countries have liberalised their import and export trade substantially and made serious steps towards deregulation of capital flows. The results have often been dubious. In particular, indiscriminate liberalisation of foreign trade heavily burdens the balance of payments, hampers industrial revival and facilitates a large-scale loss of national income through capital flight (for example, in Russia). These effects conflict with the goals for the exchange rate and price stabilisation.

The negative effects mentioned are more than familiar to students of the Latin American economic reforms. The region provides ample material on the pitfalls of import and capital account deregulation and on possible ways of escaping them. Furthermore, the Latin American experience allows one to make interesting deductions about the connection between a successful stabilisation and state control over the main export industries.

The relevance of the Latin American experience for the European post-socialist countries is also connected to the similarities of the political setting in the two regions. In the majority of Latin American states, as in Eastern Europe, stabilisation and structural adjustment programmes have to be undertaken by relatively fragile democracies coping with the legacy of deeply ingrained populist and egalitarian traditions.

Thus, the Latin American experience should provide useful inferences about possible ways of making painful reforms both socially and politically sustainable. Especially important is the experience of securing the collaboration of the main social groups with the reform efforts and of building strong political coalitions in favour of the economic changes. A careful examination of the sequence of mainly failed stabilisation attempts that have been undertaken by different Latin American democracies may also be very useful for forecasting future sociopolitical developments in some parts of Eastern Europe.

The Latin American experience should also contribute to the debate about comparative strengths and weaknesses of representative and authoritarian regimes in carrying out stabilisation and structural reforms. Currently the debate has much more than purely academic significance in some of the least successfully adjusting countries of Eastern Europe (including, first and foremost, Russia).

The main focus of this chapter is on issues relating to anti-inflation strategy. This focus is prompted by the high priority of the stabilisation task in the anticrisis agenda of Eastern Europe. (It is in fact the task of Russia, which still faces a long and agonising fight to suppress inflation.)

Other aspects of monetary reform are viewed predominantly through the prism of the inflation issue.

The chapter is organised as follows. Sections 5.2 to 5.5 describe the results of the three alternative stabilisation and liberalisation strategies (orthodox, heterodox and mixed types). The discussion is built around concrete country experiences, which are 'models' for each type of strategy. Section 5.6 deals with the social, economic and political sustainability of monetary reforms. At the end of each section or subsection some general lessons are listed. Finally, section 5.7 presents a sketch of the principal financial problems of Russia and some recommendations are given, based on the Latin American experience.

5.2 ORTHODOX STABILISATION PROGRAMMES

In the long string of anti-inflation programmes undertaken by Latin American countries in recent decades, the major portion belongs to the orthodox type. 'Orthodox' relates to those programmes that do not include incomes policy (control over prices and wages) in their arsenal. In some cases, the programmes may use a fixed or predetermined exchange rate as a nominal anchor for prices.

Is Austerity Enough?

One type of orthodox stabilisation programme is a money-based programme. To arrest inflation, it relies on 'austerity' measures (fiscal cuts and monetary restrictions) aimed at curtailing demand. There are a number of examples of money-based stabilisation attempts in the recent history of Latin America. One such is the Chilean programme of 1974–5, which featured a major effort to cut the budget deficit in combination with a drastic monetary crunch. Despite exemplary success in cutting money supply, the rate of inflation fell only marginally (from 505 per cent in 1973 to 375 per cent in 1975) (Kiguel and Liviatan, 1991).

A tight fiscal and monetary programme was undertaken by Brazil in 1983–4. The operational fiscal deficit was reduced from 7.3 per cent of GDP in 1982 to 2.7 per cent in 1984, whereas the primary deficit (excluding interest payments) was transformed into a surplus of 4.1 per cent of GDP. In spite of these achievements, the annual inflation rate increased from 100 per cent in 1980–2 to 200 per cent in 1983–4 (Damill *et al.*, 1991).

A stabilisation programme of a similar type was launched by the Fujimori government in Peru in 1990 in a hyperinflationary setting. The main components of the orthodox shock were an increase in the price of petrol and a cut in public sector real wages (to obtain the fiscal adjustment), as well as strict control over credit supply. After the initial post-shock jump, prices stopped rising for about a month. Then inflation regained momentum and in the following quarter reached a monthly rate of about 10 per cent. This happened despite the fact that fiscal and monetary targets were successfully attained. The new rounds of public sector price increments and credit curbs in 1991 produced monthly rates of inflation that oscillated between 3 per cent and 10 per cent.

Similar policies undertaken by the government of Argentina in the year between March 1990 and March 1991 were even less effective. Although hyperinflation was quickly halted, inflation remained at 10–15 per cent per month for most of the period of the programme and significantly accelerated at the beginning of 1991 (Frenkel, 1992).

The lacklustre results of the orthodox policy in the abovementioned cases (as well as in many others) are explained by a number of factors. In the first place, programmes of the orthodox type tend to ignore the problem of inflation inertia. The stubborn downward rigidity of inflation in chronic high-inflation countries may be largely attributed to the existence of formal and informal indexation. The indexation mechanisms, which may cover wage and price setting, taxes, interest rates and so on, allow high-inflation economies to survive, averting disruptive redistribution conflicts. The indexed system is very sensitive to price changes in any part of the economy. Supply shocks (for example, decreased food supply because of drought), devaluations and other changes produce immediate inflation repercussions throughout the economy.

The indexation mechanisms do not stop working automatically after the fundamental causes of price increases are eliminated. Unless an economy has converged virtually to a daily adjustment of prices, many contracts will have a maturity of at least a few months. After the start of a stabilisation programme, the contracts will still be valid for some time, driving up prices and wages.

There is also the problem of credibility. If at least some economic agents lack confidence in government policy, they continue to set prices or wages on the expectation that the programme will fail. Trying to preserve their relative shares of national income, other agents adjust their prices correspondingly.

Besides the credibility issue there is the problem of coordinating the behaviour of individual agents. For inflation to start subsiding some agents must abstain from raising their prices. In the absence of reliable information about the attitudes and future behaviour of other actors, however, individual agents are very reluctant to make the first move as it may result in a sizeable loss of real income (see Dornbusch and Simonsen, 1987). In this situation many firms prefer to cut their production as much as possible, but not to lower their prices. All of this produces an inflation momentum that is almost independent of demand.

Lack of credibility about the outcome of stabilisation policy is more characteristic of chronic high-inflation countries with a long experience of coexisting with inflation (Kiguel and Liviatan, 1991). Economic agents in these countries have good reason to suspect that once government efforts have brought inflation down to a level that is 'normal' for the country (although quite high by others' standards), the monetary and fiscal stringency is likely to be relaxed. These expectations of failure often become self-fulfilling.

In the presence of inertia phenomena, to lower inflation significantly through contraction of demand is typically achieved at the expense of a substantial drop in production and employment (the effect is the result of cuts in public spending and high real interest rates). In the absence of coordinating measures, such a drop is in fact necessary to send all agents a clear signal about the change of situation. For example, in Chile the costs of the 1974–5 stabilisation programme were a 14 per cent fall in GDP and a 17 per cent fall in employment. In Brazil in 1983, GDP fell by 3.4 per cent whereas Argentinean manufacturing output contracted by 5.6 per cent in 1990 (Fanelli *et al.*, 1990; Kiguel and Liviatan, 1991; O'Connel, 1992).

A very serious weak point of a number of money-based programmes was adherence to a floating exchange rate regime. The Argentinean programme mentioned earlier is a good case in point. In March 1990 a fiscal adjustment coupled with a strict monetary constraint on private banks proved to be sufficient to stop the run on the local currency and to arrest the rise in the price of the dollar, which had been the main motor of the hyperinflation process. In the highly dollarised Argentinean economy, stabilisation of the exchange rate initially helped to stop the rise in domestic prices. Inflation, however, reaccelerated a few weeks later for inertial and other reasons. At the same time the monetary constraint and a fall in production activity produced an excess supply of dollars in the market.

This situation persisted throughout 1990 and presented the authorities with a difficult choice between allowing the exchange rate to appreciate in nominal terms and intervening to stabilise the nominal dollar price. In the first case, export performance would suffer; in the second, progress in stabilisation was put at risk because of additional money creation through government dollar purchases. As a result of some central bank interventions, the local currency (the austral) remained *ex post* stable in nominal terms while appreciating significantly in real terms. The appreciation produced a strong negative effect on the balance of payments, creating a new and dangerous disequilibrium in the economy. This disequilibrium finally blew up with a burst of speculation in the foreign exchange market, renewed flight to foreign currency, abrupt devaluation and acceleration of inflation.

On the one hand, the floating exchange rate behaved in a basically similar way in the course of the Peruvian stabilisation of 1990–91. The tendency towards real appreciation with a negative effect on trade balance was also observed in other cases of orthodox stabilisations with a floating exchange rate regime (Frenkel, 1992). On the other hand, attempts to keep the exchange rate at a depreciated level in real terms with the help of periodic devaluations may also prove to be damaging for an orthodox stabilisation. This can be illustrated by the case of Brazil in 1983–4. To cover an external gap created by an abrupt deterioration of external financing conditions, the country had to undertake a number of sizeable devaluations. The measures were aimed at reallocating resources in favour of tradeables and increasing exports.

Such measures may succeed without activating general inflation if some sectors of the economy and social groups are willing to tolerate the reduction in their incomes caused by the higher price of tradables, higher private payments on foreign debt and so on. In a country with a long and institutionalised tradition, however, such a redistribution is bound to run into formidable obstacles and trigger an immediate escalation of inflation. Indexation was the main cause of failure of the Brazilian, fiscal-based stabilisation. Nevertheless, the depreciated exchange rate plus the internal demand contraction were instrumental in bringing about a significant export expansion. The export drive in Brazil helped to improve the trade balance and facilitated the resumption of GNP growth in 1984.

It should be mentioned that, in many cases, an important mechanism for transmitting inflation impulses caused by devaluation to the economy at large is the increase in state budget outlays for servicing external debt (as a result of an exchange rate depreciation, the government has to buy foreign currency at higher prices). The budget may also be indirectly affected because of growing payments on internal debt de facto indexed to general inflation. In such situations, attempts to use monetary 'brakes' to support the real value of the exchange rate are usually insufficient to stop inflation. At the same time, high interest rates hamper production activity and significantly add to the burden of the public sector internal debt service.

The lessons

- In countries with an established tradition and institutions of formal and informal indexation, stabilisation programmes relying solely on demand contraction can suppress hyperinflation but, as a rule, are not very effective in fighting a moderate inflation.

- Money-based stabilisation packages have high costs in terms of output and employment.
- A floating exchange rate is not very compatible with price stabilisation. In the case of a 'permissive' monetary and fiscal regime, it is likely to produce extreme volatility of the exchange rate, speculative runs on the local currency and damaging devaluations. This could become a direct route to hyperinflation. Speculative foreign exchange bubbles giving a boost to inflation are highly probable under a stringent monetary regime as well. Some form of Central Bank direct control over the evolution of the exchange rate therefore seems to be a must in any stabilisation package.
- In an indexed economy, attempting to restore external equilibrium via a devaluation is highly inflationary. Hence external shocks may drive up inflation even in a situation where the budget deficit and level of seigniorage are relatively stable.
- Money-based stabilisation with a depreciated exchange rate is less recessionary than the variety with a floating exchange rate regime (the former is conducive to export expansion whereas the latter tends to produce an exchange rate appreciation that hinders exports).

Exchange Rate-Based Orthodox Stabilisations

An exchange rate-based orthodox stabilisation programme combines a package of fiscal adjustment with an exchange rate regulation that is designed to suppress inflation. The addition of an exchange rate anchor to orthodox programmes was often a reaction to the abovementioned low effectiveness of purely money-based programmes. The exchange rate rule may take the form of a fixed exchange rate or a preannounced rate of devaluation. The idea is to influence the behaviour of prices through stabilising the exchange rate, which is one of the key parameters determining the rate of inflation. The measure may be particularly effective in economies that are highly dollarised and dependent on imports.

Among the countries that used the preannounced rates of devaluation was Chile. It used the instrument from 1978–82 after the failure of the money-based programme. A schedule of future values of the exchange rate (the *tablita*) was introduced. In 1980 it was replaced by a fixed exchange rate. The combination of the schedule with a tight fiscal stance proved to be more effective in bringing down inflation than was the previous monetarist phase. Inflation fell from 92 per cent in 1977 to 35 per cent in 1980 and 10 per cent in 1982 (Kiguel and Liviatan, 1991). This was achieved, however, at the expense of a serious, real appreciation of the currency, which caused significant difficulties in the external sector, a threat of a balance of payments crisis and, finally, a massive devaluation that gave a new boost to inflation.

Real appreciation in the Chilean case (as well as in the similar circumstances in Argentina and Uruguay in the late 1970s) was caused by devaluations systemically lagging behind inflation. The stickiness of inflation in Chile, despite the fact that the budget was in surplus, may be largely attributed to backward-looking indexation of wages and lack of full confidence in the outcome of the stabilisation programme.

In a high-inflation country, overvaluation of the currency seems to be an unavoidable price of any programme using the exchange rate as a nominal anchor. As the overvaluation cannot be sustained for long, however some strategy for depreciating the real value of the currency must be devised. Chile solved this problem by replacing the exchange rate anchor with money targets in 1982–3, when the currency was finally devalued.

Exchange-rate-based orthodox stabilisations differ significantly from the money-based varieties in terms of their impact on output, wages and current account. The former are typically characterised by a specific cycle of expansion and recession in GDP growth. In the initial phase of an exchange-rate-based programme there is usually a boom in output and an increase in real wages, which are followed later by a recession. In some cases the collapse of the exchange rate regime may be accompanied by a severe crisis (for example Argentina in 1980–1 after the collapse of the *tablita*).

One possible explanation has to do with a lack of confidence in the programme that makes agents anticipate a balance of payments crisis, tight credit conditions and renewed restrictions in the future. These expectations cause them to shift their expenditure, especially on imported goods, to the current period. In such circumstances a consumption boom is often observed. Some segments of the local economy, benefiting from the import increase and slower inflation, may also start growing vigorously. All this complicates the balance of payments situation and makes the expected collapse of the foreign exchange regime more and more likely.

The expansionary tendency is also partly responsible for a rise in real wages and real appreciation. In addition, growth of wages is stimulated by lack of credibility in the persistence of the official exchange rate policy and expectations of eventual devaluations in excess of the current ones. This process results in an increase in real wages (or their downward rigidity) even after the expenditure boom is over. Such wage behaviour worsens the ensuing recession.

The relatively greater effectiveness of exchange rate targets as nominal anchors compared with monetary targets (at least in the initial period) may be largely attributed to the fact that the former may be more clearly defined and easier to control. The money supply is much more difficult to target as there exist different money aggregates, information on which is not readily available to the general public. Establishing money targets is further complicated by the difficulty of predicting the demand for money at the disinflation phase. Larger than planned increases in the money supply may be necessary and not inflationary provided the money demand rises correspondingly. Under an exchange rate rule the problem does not arise as the money supply is determined exogenously by the balance of payments situation (see Kiguel and Liviatan, 1991).

It is also noteworthy that costs resulting from lack of credibility are more easily absorbed in the short run in the case of an exchange rate rule than under a monetary rule. In exchange-rate-based programmes they usually lead to overvaluation and gradual depletion of foreign exchange reserves while the interest rates may be kept relatively low and recession postponed. In money-based programmes persistent inflation obliges the government to impose ever stricter credit limits, with highly recessionary consequences. The defence of any given exchange rate regime, however, if taken too far, may lead to an accumulation of foreign debt.

The lessons

- An exchange rate rule as a nominal anchor in stabilisation programmes is helpful in coordinating price expectations of the agents and price setting, and may greatly facilitate transition to a low-inflation situation.
- An exchange-rate-based stabilisation in its initial phase is not recessionary and may even lead to a boom in consumption and output.
- In countries with considerable inflation inertia, an exchange rate rule inevitably leads to a growing real appreciation of the exchange rate, with corresponding export and balance of payments problems. The instrument cannot be used for too long, therefore, and must be replaced fairly soon by some other instruments (for example a switch to a crawling peg can be made with more weight shifted to the budget or monetary policy as a central stabilising force).

Two Successful Orthodox Stabilisations

There are two examples of relatively successful orthodox stabilisation in Latin America in the 1980s. One is the Bolivian stabilisation of 1985–6. In the 1960s and 1970s the country had moderate rates of inflation by Latin American standards. Inflation accelerated strongly after 1981 because of a sharp reduction in the financial inflows from abroad that had been used to cover budget deficits. The government turned to financing the deficit through monetary expansion. Seigniorage increased sharply from 1.6 per cent of GDP in 1981 to 15.9 per cent in 1984. Inflation rose from 29 per cent in 1981 to 11 750 per cent in 1985. The accelerating inflation further eroded real tax revenue and by 1983 had practically eliminated them (the Olivera–Tanzi effect) (see Kiguel and Liviatan, 1988).

The stabilisation programme, launched in 1985, quite rapidly brought down inflation to low levels (from 276 per cent in 1986 to about 15 per cent in the following years). Although the programme favourably differed from the majority of other stabilisation attempts, the design of the Bolivian programme was standard orthodoxy. It featured strict monetary discipline and reduction of the budget deficit (from 20 per cent of GDP in 1984 to 3 per cent in 1986). The fiscal and public firms' budget was balanced in a special account at the Central Bank, and the minister of finance had to approve the use of these resources to finance current public firm expenditures. Public employment and wages were cut drastically and public investment frozen for a full year. There was a sharp increase in public tariffs and petrol prices (incorporating a high tax). The programme started with a floating exchange rate, but it led to an acceleration of inflation. Prices were stabilised only after the rate of exchange was fixed in February–March 1986 and kept at that level for a year (see Frenkel, 1992).

The fact that Bolivian inflation was stopped comparatively easily can be largely attributed to the absence of 'indexation inertia'. The inertia was practically eradicated by the very process of hyperinflation. Progressive shortening of the nominal contract periods, which accompanied the rise in inflation, finally put all contracts on a daily adjustment basis. By 1985 practically all prices were fully indexed to the daily changes in the price of the dollar. This eliminated the lags in the price setting system that were typical of high-inflation (but not hyperinflation) countries. The situation in that sense resembled a system of fully flexible prices and wages with no nominal rigidities and it was able to respond very quickly to disinflation (see Kiguel and Liviatan, 1988). Fixing the dollar price in such circumstances was very effective in stopping inflation.

Another key to the success of the Bolivian programme was suspension of external debt service payments. This move substantially reduced the budget burden and helped to limit cuts in noninterest budget expenses. Moreover, Bolivia was able to obtain additional foreign resources, mostly in the form of aid, which financed the residual budget deficit. In 1985–8 these resources amounted to 5 per cent of GDP (Meller, 1992). The improvement of the budget position was also greatly facilitated by the growth of real tax revenues after disinflation (threefold within a year and fourfold between 1984 and 1989 – Dornbusch *et al.*, 1990).

One should not overlook the fact that in 1985 Bolivia was not a country that was accustomed to high inflation. As the hyperinflation developed rather quickly, the country did not have enough time to develop a sophisticated system of defences against inflation. The presence of such a system in many other Latin American countries allowed them to coexist with inflation for a long period without slipping into hyperinflation. This ability to adapt undermines the determination to fight inflation and reduces the credibility of stabilisation programmes in the eyes of the public once they are undertaken.

Unsustainability of the hyperinflationary situation in Bolivia contributed to the credibility of the disinflation programme. By the same token, the main cause of inflation (the seigniorage) was clear and visible. The resolute end to money financing of the fiscal deficit was a credible signal for all agents about the change of regime. This signal was supported by radical structural changes, such as denationalisation and liberalisation of both foreign trade and the domestic financial system.

Another example of inflation being successfully brought down to low levels through orthodox means was the Chilean stabilisation after the collapse of the *tablita* system in 1982. The measures undertaken included new efforts to increase budget revenues and cut spending, the abolition of wage indexation and periodic devaluations. Inflation subsided only slowly, from 27 per cent in 1983 to 19 per cent in 1986, 17 per cent in 1989 and 12 per cent in 1992. It now appears as if Chile has largely managed to break the inflation inertia and establish new, low-inflation attitudes on the part of agents. This was only achieved, however, after a deep recession in 1982–3 and a long period of monetary stringency. The Chilean stabilisation also received sizeable external financial support. In 1983–7 multilateral organisations provided credits amounting to 3 per cent of GDP, which were complemented by the equivalent sums supplied by commercial banks (Meller, 1992).

A significant feature of the Chilean case is the important role that the public copper enterprise, CODELCO, played in its stabilisation. From 1982–4 and 1985–90 it provided 8 per cent and 15 per cent, respectively, of all fiscal revenues (Meller 1992). Being the country's leading exporter, CODELCO (and the state budget) greatly benefited from the real depreciation of the exchange rate. In this case, a real devaluation helped simultaneously to reduce the external imbalance and the fiscal deficit.

The lessons

- Stabilisation is much more likely to bring quick results in countries without a strong tradition of high inflation.
- In a chronic high-inflation country, money-based stabilisation may finally succeed if the government can afford politically to stick to austere monetary and fiscal policy for a long time and is able to eliminate wage indexation by noneconomic means.
- Fixing the exchange rate is especially helpful for stabilising hyperinflation.
- Significant external aid in the form of financial inflows or the rescheduling of debt payments is a necessary prerequisite for a successful stabilisation in highly indebted countries.
- Public control over the revenues from raw material exports is very helpful in the process of financial normalisation.

5.3   HETERODOX STABILISATIONS

This section discusses three examples of heterodox stabilisation attempts that failed. The intellectual foundations of the heterodox approach were laid by the academic critics of the orthodox 'excess demand' explanations of inflation. They belonged predominantly to the structuralist school. These critics provided an alternative set of explanations stressing inflation inertia as the main driving force. They indicated the need to replace or supplement conventional fiscal and monetary restraint with more direct measures to break the inertial cycles. Later the idea of a structural fiscal crisis was added. The proponents of the idea maintained that a reduction of public debt payments had to be an essential element of any stabilisation in Latin America (see Bresser Pereira, 1993).

The Austral Plan in Argentina (which started in 1985) and the Cruzado Plan in Brazil (which began in 1986) were among the first attempts in Latin America to combine conventional fiscal and monetary policies with a price/wage freeze. The programmes were undertaken by the newly elected democratic administrations at a time when inflation stood at over 800 per cent in Argentina and about 400 per cent in Brazil. They shared the following features:

- A generalised control over prices, wages, the exchange rate, and public utility prices.
- A special financial contract for debt conversion to avoid wealth transfers between creditors and debtors as the economy went abruptly from a high to a low inflation regime.

• The introduction of a new currency, which removed a few zeroes from the old one (see Meller, 1992). In addition Argentina implemented a number of demand-management measures with budget cuts and a restrictive monetary policy in 1985–6. The Brazilian policy was much more expansionist.

The programmes were highly successful in the initial period. Within a few weeks inflation dropped to close to zero. The policy was immensely popular in both countries, with thousands of people taking part in enforcing price controls. The results were achieved without contraction of production. Moreover, in both cases the fall in inflation was followed by a rise in real wages and a significant upswing in economic activity. Inflation is, in fact, a highly regressive tax, so stopping it may actually raise demand (the so-called wealth effect). In Brazil, the consumption boom was additionally spurred by a 33 per cent increase in the minimum wage, decreed simultaneously with the introduction of the plan.

The honeymoon, however, did not last long and quite soon problems began to surface. After several months of the freeze, signs of overheating appeared. For example, in Brazil shortages and illegal surcharges became widespread by mid-1986, with speculation and long queues for some consumer goods, especially cars and meat. The price freeze and wage increases squeezed profit margins in many sectors and hampered investment. In Brazil, the problem was complicated by many prices being frozen at relatively low real levels (see Kaufman, 1987). In 1986–7 Argentina experienced a progressive deterioration in the external account as the trade surplus started to shrink. This produced pressure on the peso and forced the government to devalue it significantly in real terms.

Due to the growing pressure on prices, the governments were obliged to allow selective price increases, which finally totally undermined the price control system. Inflation reappeared and reached 131 per cent in Argentina in 1987 and 343 per cent in 1988. In Brazil it rose to 230 per cent in 1987 and 682 per cent in 1988.

The most important reason for the collapse was an inability to keep budget deficits and monetary expansion under proper control. In Argentina, the budget deficit grew to about 8 per cent in 1987–8 and in Brazil it grew to 5.9 per cent in 1987. The initial success and the huge rise in popularity were not used to solve the fiscal crisis that lay at the core of the inflation problem in Latin America.

There were other reasons for the failure. In Argentina, the Austral Plan coincided with bad harvests and a fall in export prices that dealt a serious blow to exports, government revenues and the balance of payments. Furthermore, the government's task was greatly complicated by a chronic dollarisation of the Argentine economy. The traditional emphasis of Argentine business and the public on liquid assets and the ease with which funds are moved abroad severely limit any stabilising government's room to manoeuvre.

A somewhat fresh approach to tackling the stabilisation problem was demonstrated in March 1990 by the newly elected President Collor of Brazil. He launched a radical plan featuring an 18-month blockage of 80 per cent of private savings and a substantial reduction of internal debt through a capital levy. The levy took several forms and resulted in effectively cancelling about 50 per cent of the internal public debt, worth over 110 billion. A 45-day price freeze and a firm fiscal adjustment were also implemented, transforming the 1990 federal public deficit into a surplus of 1.2 per cent in operational terms (see Bresser Pereira, 1993).

The plan, however, failed to secure price stability. After an initial fall, inflation rose again and by December 1990 it had reached 20 per cent on a monthly basis. One of the main causes of the failure was the unsettled problem of distributing financial rights and responsibilities between the federal government and the states under a democratic regime. The federal government had to shoulder most of the expenditure while it lost a lot of revenue in favour of the states. This contributed greatly to the growth of the federal budget deficit.

Nor did the saving blockage attain its goals. The shock produced by the measure was too big for the economy and the population to swallow. (GDP in 1990 fell by 4.2 per cent and industrial production by about 9 per cent.) The government quickly had to abandon its tight position on the issue and make concessions to different groups of depositors. After three or four months about 80 per cent of all blocked savings were back in circulation.

At the same time, the seizure of savings did a lot to destroy confidence in financial assets and the government's word. This further aggravated the problem of financing the public-sector deficit through borrowing in the local market. By the end of 1991 the government had trouble selling even seven-day debt papers, and almost the entire public debt was being rolled over daily.

Likewise, the room for an inflation tax became extremely narrow because of the unwillingness of the public to hold currency. M1 (cash plus demand deposits) fell to less than 3 per cent of GDP compared with 15–20 per cent in the middle of the 1970s (see 'Brazil survey', *The Economist*, 7 December 1991, p. 15). Such a demonetisation is fraught with danger as even a relatively small additional supply of money may cause great surges in inflation. In fact that was the outcome in Brazil, where inflation rose to about 1000 per cent in 1992.

The lessons

- An incomes policy may be extremely useful in quickly bringing down inflation. It must not, however, become a substitute for eliminating the fundamental causes of inflation.
- The price and wage freeze must not last long as it is bound to exacerbate distortions in relative prices and produce shortages. The larger these accumulated distortions, the more difficult the subsequent liberalisation phase becomes.
- A blockage of financial assets as a means of relieving inflation pressure is self-defeating. It is practically impossible to keep to the measure for a long period as it undermines the creditworthiness of the state and exacerbates the demonetisation problem.

5.4 LOOKING FOR A PRAGMATIC COMBINATION

There are two anti-inflation programmes in Latin America that, up to now, have been relatively successful, representing, as it were, a state of the art in the stabilisation technology of the region. These are the Mexican programme, which started in 1987, and the Argentinian Cavallo Plan of March 1991. The design of the programmes benefited greatly from the knowledge gained in the agonising process of experimenting with different stabilisation tools in the region.

The Cavallo Plan had the following components (see Fanelli *et al.*, 1990; Canavese, 1991; Meller, 1992; O'Connel, 1992; CEDES databank):

- A resolute fiscal adjustment. Public tariffs were raised and various subsidies were cut. Public domestic debt payments were also reduced through the forced rescheduling of public internal debt maturity and the interest rate changes that had been undertaken in 1990. Government liabilities of seven days or more were reprogrammed to 10-year bonds linked to the dollar with an interest rate equal to LIBOR. This helped to cut interest payments on the public debt by 4.8 per cent of GDP in 1990, implying capital losses for bond holders of over 50 per cent.

    On the other hand, budget revenues were increased because of a tax reform. Numerous loopholes were closed and the tax-collecting mechanism strengthened. In particular, competent and honest people enjoying the full support of the president were put in charge of the tax-collecting body. Harsh penalties for evasion were employed.

Very significant additional tax revenues were received because of an abrupt fall in inflation (a reverse of the Olivera–Tanzi effect) and resumed growth (in real terms, taxes increased by about 55 per cent in 1991 compared with 1990). The residual part of the budget deficit was covered by the proceeds from the privatisation of public enterprises. To stress the radical break with the past, any public deficit was declared illegal by law.

- A convertibility law was adopted that established a fixed nominal exchange rate (1 peso per US dollar). The monetary base has to be fully backed by liquid international reserves. Thus, the money supply can be increased only through the purchase of foreign currency by the Central Bank.
- An explicit prohibition of indexation clauses in wages and financial contracts was introduced, as was an implicit incomes policy with industrial and trade union leaders, who were persuaded not to pursue price and wages rises.
- Structural reforms, such as liberalisation of imports and privatisation.

Thus the Argentinean programme represents a complex mixture of orthodox and heterodox components. It succeeded in quickly reducing inflation from 27 per cent a month in 1991 to 1.5–2 per cent a month. The abrupt fall in inflation increased real incomes and brought about the resumption of growth. GDP in 1991–2 rose by more than 5 per cent per year.

There was a reversal of capital flight. Capital inflows attracted by high real interest rates amounted to 8 billion in 1991. Remonetisation of the economy allowed a significant increase in consumption and production credit, which helped to finance the economic growth.

Nevertheless the stabilisation that has been achieved is very fragile. The Achilles heel of Argentina's spectacular recovery is the weakness of the external accounts. The fixed exchange rate has been constantly appreciating in real terms because of residual inflation. This growing overvaluation combined with the opening of the economy to imports and strong domestic demand have produced an import explosion (from 4 billion in 1991 to 13–14 billion in 1992). In addition, the external debt service, which was previously only partially paid, increased significantly in 1993 in accordance with the agreements struck with foreign creditors.

To date the inflow of capital has been sufficient to cover the balance of payments deficit. There is no guarantee, however, that the inflow will continue to grow as fast as the financing requirement itself. Incoming capital is predominantly short-term in nature and is dangerously 'footloose'.

The government's room for manoeuvre is very limited. The badly needed devaluation is extremely risky as it would revive mistrust in the currency and rekindle inflationary expectations. In fact, President Menem has bound himself politically by his solemn promise not to devalue (besides this, the devaluation is made more difficult by a strong inflow of capital).

Another weak point of the programme is the reluctance of national entrepreneurs to commit themselves to significant investment in new plants. Memories of recent crises are still vivid and the lack of confidence in the sustainability of stabilisation has not been overcome. These expectations are worsened, of course, by the growing external trade problem. In 1991–2 the boom in output was mainly supported by utilisation of the existing facilities, whereas new investments were concentrated predominantly in internal trade and housing construction. Unless a vigorous expansion in export industries materialises, the external equilibrium and the current relative price stability cannot be sustained for long.

In many respects the design of the Mexican programme is similar to that of the Cavallo Plan – there are important differences, however. The Mexican incomes policy is based on the 'Economic Solidarity Pact' between the government, trade unions and entrepreneurs with respect to limiting and coordinating key prices, wages, public tariffs and the exchange rate. The agreement is supported by all the powers of a quasi-authoritarian state with a longstanding tradition of control over trade union activity. This allows the government to be more flexible (compared with Argentina) while using stabilisation tools. In particular, control over wages permits the Mexican authorities to adjust the exchange rate without dangerously activating inflation. For this a creeping, preannounced devaluation is used (for example devaluation by one peso per day). The pace of the correction is periodically changed in accordance with the balance of payments and inflation dynamics.

The stabilisation package also includes far-reaching tax reforms and drastic cuts in the budget deficit. The primary budget deficit of 8.3 per cent of GDP in 1981 was turned into a sizeable surplus. Large-scale privatisation and radical liberalisation of trade have also been carried out.

The stabilisation effort has been considerably aided by the agreement with foreign creditors (1989), which allowed Mexico to reduce its external debt substantially. Debt service was cut by 2 per cent of GDP per year (4 billion from 1989–94).

The programme has been effective in reducing inflation from 159 per cent in 1987 to about 12 per cent in 1992. The country managed to restore growth (3.8 per cent in 1989–91 and 2.3 per cent in 1992). The Mexican stabilisation (like the Argentinean one), however, is insecure because of a balance of payments problem. The government was not able to avoid the overvaluation of the peso. Coupled with an import boom, this led to a sharp deterioration in the balance of trade. In 1992 the trade deficit reached about $15 billion. As in Argentina, the deficit is currently being financed by a vast inflow of private capital, a large proportion of which is represented by 'hot' money.

The lessons

- To be successful, a stabilisation programme must pragmatically utilise all disposable tools, including nontraditional ones. A stabilisation policy should avoid stubborn adherence to standard recipes and must be tailored to fit the specific economic, political and ideological setting of a particular country. In this sense, designing a stabilisation policy is an art as much as a science.
- Price, wage and exchange rate controls, although essential for coordinating decisions and expectations, should be flexible enough to prevent the formation of significant distortions. Periodic adjustments to prices, especially the exchange rate, must be allowed.
- A social pact is a useful device for rationally distributing stabilisation costs between different sectors of the economy and social groups, inhibiting a distributional conflict, with all the inflationary consequences that implies.
- Drastic import liberalization has important drawbacks as an anti-inflation tool. Although its impact on internal prices is often limited, the measure tends to produce an import boom that may seriously threaten the external equilibrium and the stabilisation programme at large.

5.5 FINANCIAL LIBERALISATION: THE SOUTHERN CONE EXPERIENCE

Latin American reform experience includes a number of cases of very far-reaching experiments with financial decontrol that illustrate well the dangers of premature liberalisation in the financial field. The most important are the cases of Chile and Argentina in the late 1970s. In these countries, interest ceilings on deposits and loans were removed, bank supervision relaxed and restrictions on capital inflows and outflows loosened. Only Chile, however, managed to achieve a significant improvement in its fiscal situation. The Chilean experience therefore provides a clearer idea of liberalisation consequences.

An outstanding feature of the postliberalisation situation in Chile was very high interest rates. Average real annual rates on peso loans were about 39 per cent in 1977–9 and about 27 per cent in 1980–2, although lending was typically much less than a year in duration (see McKinnon, 1991). The situation was partly caused by high and variable inflation rates that made the banks 'overshoot' to protect themselves from the risk of possible losses.

Another reason was the proliferation of bad loans within the banking system. The borrowed money was widely used for speculative operations. In particular the large economic groups used their control over domestic banks for self-finance, bidding up the prices of their own companies' equity. After deregulation Chile witnessed a stock market boom financed by the bank loans. In all cases speculation was accompanied by the deterioration of enterprise balance sheets. The necessity to roll over the outstanding debts created an artificially high demand for credit at any cost, which contributed greatly to real interest rates being forced to abnormally high levels (see Fanelli *et al.*, 1992). In turn, the stock market boom created excessive optimism on the part of the public and many Chilean firms regarding future asset values and their rates of return.

Another characteristic of the Chilean situation was the large spread between the interest cost of borrowing in pesos compared with borrowing in dollars. This was mainly because of the *tablita*. Gradual appreciation of the peso diminished the real cost of borrowing abroad. The cost was often low or even negative. This stimulated a massive inflow of funds, largely used for consumption and speculation on domestic assets (see Fanelli and Frenkel, 1992). The inflow greatly increased foreign debt and contributed to the overvaluation of the peso.

In 1981–2, the inflow of foreign credit subsided abruptly as a result of the deterioration of the balance of payments situation. This pushed real interest rates on peso loans from 15 per cent in the first quarter of 1981 to 46 per cent in the second quarter of 1982 (Meller, 1991). The position of many debtors was further worsened by a sizeable devaluation and a swift contraction of GDP in 1982. Under the weight of all these pressures, the financial bubble burst. A series of defaults on outstanding bank loans forced bankruptcy on virtually all of Chile's financial intermediaries. The government had to renationalise private banks in order to protect domestic depositors and foreign creditors. The operation resulted in the state budget assuming a huge amount of bad internal and external debt, amounting to about 30 per cent of GDP (see Fanelli *et al.*, 1992).

Similar developments were observed in Argentina, where an experiment with financial deregulation, coupled with a *tablita*, finally led to bank defaults and massive capital flight. As in Chile, the state had to shoulder the costs by saving the banking system at a very high price.

The Chilean and Argentinean experiments also give a good idea of the consequences of prematurely relaxing controls on international capital movement. One negative result was the dollarisation of the economy and the increased probability of capital flight. Dollarisation and capital flight led to the shrinking of the domestic financial system. This development usually hampers the ability of the government to extract inflation tax and increases the probability of a violent price explosion, even in the case of moderate budget deficits.

A similar effect is produced when the private sector borrows abroad. In fact this is a way to escape the high price of local loans, which include the implicit inflation tax extracted by the government. Allowing untaxed dollar bank accounts may be expedient in the short run as it may encourage remittance of foreign exchange earnings and the return of flight capital. However, once in place, a large foreign currency component in the domestic financial system puts the latter on a potentially explosive path (see McKinnon, 1991). It is important to note that once the business community and public at large have acquired a taste for dollar assets, it is very difficult to eradicate.

The lessons

- Full liberalisation of banking activity during times of high and variable inflation is not warranted. To prevent unduly high real interest rates, interest ceilings may be imposed that allow for moderately positive real rates.
- A tight official supervision of the commercial banks is necessary to curb undue risk taking.
- Before allowing the private sector to borrow freely from and deposit in international capital markets, the domestic price level must be stabilised and domestic capital markets fully liberalised. Otherwise capital flight and unwarranted build-up of foreign indebtedness may follow. Free foreign exchange convertibility on the capital account should be the last stage in the optimal order of economic liberalisation.
- Allowing foreign currency to circulate freely in parallel with a 'soft' domestic currency is a recipe for inflation acceleration.
- The combination of national currency overvaluation and free capital flows is especially explosive.

5.6   SUSTAINABILITY OF STABILISATION

To be sustainable, a stabilisation programme must be able to endure the social and political tensions that it generates. This section discusses the prerequisites for such sustainability.

Social Aspects

In high-inflation countries, sustainable stabilisation is usually a socially costly and long endeavour. For instance, reducing the fiscal deficit to a financeable level in Chile took three years in the 1970s and four years in the 1980s; in Mexico it took two to three years; in Bolivia it took more than five years; and in Argentina it took about six years. Social costs were especially high in cases of orthodox stabilisations. For example, in Chile a contractionary shock adjustment applied in 1982–3 led to a GDP fall of 14.2 per cent in 1982 and 0.6 per cent in 1983, and an increase in unemployment of more than 30 per cent. Unemployment was above 24 per cent for four years (1982–5), real wages were cut by more than 20 per cent for at least five years and per capita social expenditure fell by 10 per cent (Meller, 1991).

In Mexico, in the stabilisation period (1986–8) there was a large reduction of real wages (around 30 per cent); however this wage flexibility helped to avoid a rise in unemployment, which remained below 5 per cent from 1985 onwards. Social expenditure per capita fell by 40 per cent from 1986 to 1990. In Argentina, average wages in 1986–90 fell by 28 per cent (Meller, 1992). Stabilisations usually also demand large cuts in subsidies to industry as well as in public investment, both of which hurt many sectors of the economy.

Economic sacrifices in the course of a stabilisation programme inevitably produce serious social and political tensions that are difficult to tolerate for long. A resumption of production and income growth is therefore a crucial prerequisite for the stabilisation's long-term sustainability. The Latin American experience shows that even successful stabilisations do not bring automatic economic growth. A country can be stabilised and structurally adjusted but remain stagnant. The Bolivian situation after 1985 may serve as an example. Average annual gross investment in 1986–90 was as low as 13.4 per cent of GDP. Average GDP growth in 1986–8 was 0.7 per cent, in 1989–91 only 3.1 per cent and in 1992 about 3.5 per cent.

The key issue is overcoming the lack of confidence on the part of the private sector. Private investors are apt to adopt 'a wait and see' attitude after stabilisation, fearing that the government will not be able to resist political pressures to change the policy of austerity. This attitude can easily become the cause of failure as it makes the government unable to show positive results soon enough.

The waiting period of private investors can be reduced through an increase in public investment, which traditionally has served as a prime mover of economic growth in Latin America. For example, a high level of public investment helped to keep the Chilean economy away from the stagnant equilibrium of self-fulfilling prophecies in the 1980s. The investments were largely financed by revenues from the state copper industry and the increased supply of external financing. That example was difficult to follow in many other Latin American countries where the state did not have direct access to export revenues and faced tight rationing abroad (see Fanelli *et al.*, 1990).

Sustained external financing after stabilisation is very important, not only economically but also psychologically as it enhances local investors' confidence. In the Chilean case, domestic entrepreneurs started investing only after the state and foreign firms had begun, when they realised that foreigners were taking the most lucrative investment opportunities (Meller, 1992).

Growth resumption can be greatly supported by export expansion, which was the case in Chile and Mexico. Mexico in particular managed to obtain a powerful anchor for its stabilisation efforts by linking its market to the huge markets of the USA and Canada through the North American Free Trade Agreement. This move greatly stimulated an increase in investments in tradeables and export growth in the country (the average growth of Mexican exports of manufactured goods has been more than 10 per cent during the last years).

The lessons

- A critical 'push' from public-sector investments may be a necessary prerequisite for overcoming a lack of growth optimism and stagnation inertia after stabilisation.
- Resumption of growth after stabilisation may not come about without a significant injection of external capital, creating a powerful 'umbrella' for expectations.
- Export expansion is one of the critical ingredients of the stabilisation-with-growth scenario.

Political Aspects

The political sustainability of stabilisation depends on the ability of a government to overcome resistance on the part of social groups to make the necessary sacrifices. The governments that adopted far-reaching stabilisation programmes share a common feature of a strong and autonomous central executive authority. The strength of the executive power can be built on very different political bases. Latin American experience shows that among successful stabilisers one can find authoritarian, quasi-authoritarian and democratic governments.

Comparisons of the stabilisation performance of different types of political regimes in the region do not reveal a clear superiority of authoritarianism compared with democracy. The failure rate of military dictatorships is no lower than in other cases.

The studies offer evidence, however, that countries in transition to democracy (as distinct from established democracies) do have special difficulties in controlling fiscal and monetary policy. They have to contend with high levels of political participation and distributive expectations as well as with discontinuities in policy-making authorities and institutions (see Remmer, 1986; Nelson, 1989).

Clearly the experience of democratic regimes is of most interest to East European countries. A few generalisations stand out among the factors explaining the ability of representative regimes to carry through their stabilisation programmes. Stabilisation programmes are typically undertaken by a new administration taking power after a decisive electoral victory when opposition forces are in disarray (for example Menem in Argentina in 1990, Seaga in Jamaica in 1980, Estensorro in Bolivia in 1985).

A crucial prerequisite for success is neutralising opposition on the part of the popular sector, especially powerful trade unions and populist parties. From this point of view, the ideal situation exists when socially painful measures are carried out by leaders with established populist reputations and backing (Menem, Estensorro). For example, Menem's ability to control the powerful Peronist party allowed him to neutralise traditional opposition to attempts at financial adjustment and structural change. Lack of this ability was one of the prime reasons for the failure of the Alfonsin government. At the time of his presidency, the Peronist party and the unions remained opposed to liberalising reforms, and in fact blocked the structural measures necessary for consolidating stabilisation – in particular privatisation of loss-making public enterprises (see Nelson, 1989).

It is interesting that Menem also proved to be much more shrewd in mobilising the support of the business community. This was partly due to the fact that top government figures were chosen because of the respect they enjoyed in business circles. This was distinct from the Alfonsin government, which mainly comprised bright academics without connections in the business world.

In Bolivia, President Estensorro's political capital, accumulated in the period when he headed the workers' movement, allowed him to enforce harsh measures against the trade unions. At one point he even had to impose a state of siege in order to break a strike declared by trade unions.

Other governments relied more on negotiations and compromises to contain union pressure. Thus, in Colombia, the Betankur government (1984–6) gained the unions' consent to austerity measures through a combination of discussion and persuasion. The unions were partly compensated by the introduction of a sliding-scale wage increase (weighted strongly in favour of the lowest paid workers) and by the appointment of a top labour leader as minister of labour (see Nelson, 1989).

Politically, stabilisation is an exercise in coalition building. A leader undertaking it must display a talent for choosing the right mix and phasing of policies. A conclusion that can be drawn from the experience of Latin American and other countries is to try not to alienate too many important social groups simultaneously and keep potential opposition groups isolated from each other (see Waterbury, 1989). For instance, such painful measures as devaluation, investment reduction, deindexing of wages, privatisation and elimination of consumer subsidies should not be undertaken all at once, if possible.

A stabilisation programme is more viable if the costs of adjustment are distributed between different social groups. Real wage and social spending cuts meet less opposition if accompanied by a progressive tax reform. For example, in the Menem case the propertied classes shared the burden through improved tax collection and internal public debt restructuring.

Efforts should be made to compensate those interests that may represent the highest political danger (these may, for instance, include the military, the most powerful trade unions and so on). For this purpose one can use periodic, but noncomprehensive, wage increases, temporary subsidies for specific goods, investment in strategically targeted infrastructure and public housing, tax rebates and so on. Such a policy may at times conflict with economic efficiency in a narrow sense. The compensation should be differentiated and its distribution should preferably not be transparent to the general public (see Nelson, 1989). At the same time, the government should provide a clear set of incentives to those economic actors who are to lead the adjustment and constitute its support base.

Carefully designed and tightly targeted programmes aiding the poorest groups of society can diminish their opposition. Experience shows, however, that the poorest and most vulnerable groups do not represent the main political threat to adjustment. The most aggrieved (and potentially aggressive) victims are usually the lower middle class and near-poor groups, particularly in large cities. Hence, the strategies that are most likely to succeed are those that reorient public funds to benefit both the poor and the more politically active middle deciles (see Nelson, 1989).

It is also important to set realistic goals. A credible disinflation goal should not be absolute price stability in the near future but a progressively more stable price system over a period of years (see Whitehead, 1989). Solid and durable disinflation demands a remoulding of expectations and very serious structural changes that may take a long time. The Latin American experience shows that even in the most successful cases stabilisation was not able to keep inflation below double-digit level for many years.

Stabilisation programmes, incorporating income policy elements and control over the exchange rate cannot only quickly suppress inflation but also raise real incomes and revive production activity. The political popularity produced by these effects can be used by a democratic government to press forward with structural reforms. The period is dangerous, however, in the sense that the determination of the government to go on with reform measures may slacken once the signs of immediate economic crisis disappear.

A serious threat to stabilisation reforms is presented by the electoral cycle, as fiscal expenditure typically increases in the run-up to an election. For example, in Brazil the congressional elections of 1986 played an important role in delaying badly needed adjustments to the Cruzado package (see Kaufman, 1990).

Acceptance of a stabilisation package in a democratic setting crucially depends on society's attitude to the inflation problem. A government can undertake serious stabilisation measures only if the economic situation is perceived by the majority of the population as intolerable. This was the case in Bolivia in the mid-1980s after the traumatic hyperinflation experience, in Argentina when Menem took power, and in Fujimori's Peru in the 1990s. There seems to be a point in the process of progressive economic destruction after which the political price of attacking the roots of the financial disorder is smaller than the cost of muddling through the crisis (it seems that this point has not yet been reached in Brazil).

The lessons

Besides the inferences already formulated in the text, one general lesson is worth mentioning:

● Political backing for a stabilisation effort in a high-inflation country cannot be imported. It can only be a product of a national process of learning, debate, conflict and compromise that may be agonising and protracted but unavoidable.

5.7   MONETARY REFORM IN RUSSIA AND WHY IT IS FAILING

This section briefly discusses the main design and results of the monetary reform in Russia that began in January 1992. The experience of Russia is important because the country's economy is by far the largest in Eastern Europe and its development, to a great measure, will determine the economic and political situation in the whole region. By the same token, the problems that Russia is encountering are, in many respects, characteristic of other postsocialist economies.

The Russian reform programme, started by the new democratic government, features the following main elements: liberalisation of prices, deregulation of imports and relaxation of import controls, the introduction of partial currency convertibility with a floating exchange rate, deregulation of banking activity, attempts to limit the money supply through credit restrictions, and budget cuts. The policy has two principal goals: (1) to change the structure of production through realigning relative prices and shifting resources into the most internationally competitive sectors of the economy – in this way the government is seeking to increase exports and create growth industries aimed at stopping the general decline in production; and (2) the gradual stabilisation of prices.

In its design the programme is similar to many orthodox programmes in Latin America. It is no surprise that the results are in many respects similar as well. As in the majority of the Latin American cases, the social and economic costs of the package have proven to be very high. Gross domestic product in October 1993 was 26 per cent lower and industrial production about 30 per cent lower than at the beginning of 1992. About 30 per cent of the population was brought below the poverty line (*Kommersant*, 4–10 October 1993; *Finansovie Izvestia*, 8–14 October 1993; *Izvestia*, 2 November 1993).

The results, in terms of curbing inflation, also very much resemble the results of many Latin American stabilisation episodes. After some initial success in slowing price increases, the Russian programme (like numerous failed Latin American projects) ran into serious structural obstacles. By the second half of 1992 the money supply had already run out of control and stabilisation had been practically derailed. The budget deficit in 1992 and in the first quarter of 1993 exceeded 105 per cent of GDP and was almost totally monetised by the Central Bank. The prices of consumer goods rose by 2500 per cent in 1992 and grew at a rate of 20–25 per cent per month in 1993 (*Finansovie Izvestia*, 30 April–7 May 1993; *Kommersant*, 25–31 October 1993).

In order to understand the reasons for the programme's failure to stabilise production and prices one has to proceed from the two fundamental characteristics of the Russian economy. First, it is a very highly monopolised economy. For instance, about 60 per cent of all engineering plants individually monopolise more than 75 per cent of the total national production of some kind or kinds of equipment (*Voprosi economiki*, Moscow, no. 2, 1992, p. 23). Second, in world terms the prices of energy, raw materials and semifinished products in the USSR were traditionally kept at low levels relative to the prices of manufactured goods. This policy has strongly influenced the choice of technology in consuming industries. For example, manufacturing is 1.5–3 times more energy and raw-material intensive than in Western countries. Calculated in world market prices, the profits of all the main branches of the Russian economy (besides oil, gas and metallurgy) would be negative. Many industries would even have a negative value added (for example the petrochemical, chemical and food industries) (see *Kommersant*, Moscow, no. 1, 1993, p. 18).

Liberalisation of prices and foreign trade under these circumstances had the following effects: (1) the monopoly sector quite predictably chose to maximise profits by reducing production and raising prices; and (2) the prices of exportable commodities (which in Russia are represented mainly by raw materials and semi-finished products) started moving quickly towards world market levels, outpacing the prices of industries supplying the internal market (which are constrained by national demand). As a result the structure of relative prices has drastically swung against the non-monopolised (or less-monopolised) sectors catering to the national needs. The double price shock produced a powerful cost-push effect, which has been the prime mover of the current Russian inflation.

The difficulties of the weak sectors have been further aggravated by serious budget cuts and the extremely stringent credit policy of the Central Bank in the first phase of the reform. (In the first half of 1992 the money supply increased by 9–14 per cent a month while prices rose by more than 100 per cent a month on average. The real money supply in that period fell by 75 per cent (see Ross, 1993).)

Coupled with liberalisation of banking activity and drastic cuts in public investment, monetary policy led to an abrupt rise in the commercial banks' lending rates, which remain well above the real return on capital for most producers. Hence, financial liberalisation has been instrumental in channelling credit resources from the production sphere to trade (especially the import trade) and private services, which are the only sectors able to afford the expensive credit.

In fact, the policy is aggravating the inflation problem as it is undermining investment and the productive capacity of the economy. The country is facing an unprecedented investment crisis. Total investment in 1992 fell by 50 per cent compared with 1991 (*Delovoi Mir*, Moscow, 5 January 1993). Most enterprises are unable to finance their restructuring.

Large sectors of the economy, including the engineering industry, light industry and agriculture, have found themselves squeezed between rapidly rising input and credit costs and shrinking internal demand. Especially grave is the situation in military industries, which make up the core of heavy industry (for example, in 1991 about 80 per cent of engineering production was directly or indirectly catering to military needs) (*Komsomolskaja Pravda*, 17 January 1991). Drastic cuts in military orders and the lack of financial support for conversion led many enterprises to the brink of collapse.

In fact, the idea of squeezing inefficient producers and making them either restructure or perish was a very important rationale behind the government's policy. Inefficient producers, however, were able to bypass the monetary restrictions by accumulating arrears to their suppliers. By the summer of 1992 interfirm debts had snowballed, and the process had involved practically the entire economy.

The payments crisis severely hit even those 'competitive' enterprises that, theoretically, were to benefit most from the relative price changes (for example, primary materials producers.) Often the authorities do not allow them to stop supplying bankrupt customers. This is especially true for producers of strategic inputs such as oil and gas – about one half of all payment arrears are owed to them. Raw material producers also suffer from the monopolistic practices of their suppliers and chaotic growth of input costs, which precludes any rational investment planning.

In the face of the imminent stoppage of industry under the burden of debts, in mid-1992 the government and the Central Bank had to relax their monetary stance and bail out producers by a massive injection of money. In this way the initial cost – push impulse was transformed into a demand – pull inflation wave. The wave drove up all costs and prices again, hitting weak industries the hardest and bringing back the problem of arrears on an even more dangerous scale. New money inflows followed in December of 1992 and later.

A democratic government (especially one as unstable as the current Russian one) cannot afford, for social and political reasons, to force bankruptcy on a major part of the economy. By the same token, the collapse of many inefficient industries would create voids that cannot be filled with imports. So it is not difficult to foresee that, given the current state of industry and agriculture, new and uncompromising steps to cut the money supply would simply worsen the vicious circle of growing payment arrears and new waves of emergency financing of failing enterprises.

Latin American countries have amply demonstrated that large-scale structural fiscal and quasi-fiscal deficits cannot be eliminated rapidly. The goal can be reached only through determined effort over a number of years. In Russia, as in Latin America, the essential prerequisites for balancing the budget include privatisation and increasing the efficiency of public enterprises. This is bound to take quite a long time and a lot of investment. It looks as if, under the current circumstances, too stringent monetary targets aimed at curbing money supply 'at any cost' could be quite harmful and aggravate the main cause of inflation by perpetuating the inefficiency of large sectors of the economy.

In a crisis situation the distribution of financial resources cannot be entrusted solely to the market. The government cannot escape a very important role in organising the finance needed for the restructuring of weak sectors. Therefore, to overcome the current acute investment crisis, economic and administrative instruments must be used to channel banking resources to long-term investment needs. For example, special investment banks should be created and quantitative limits on credit to specific sectors should be introduced (like those that exist in some Latin American countries). The Latin American experience also testifies in favour of creating a system of state supervision over private financial intermediaries to prevent their imprudent behaviour.

One more lesson from Latin America is that it is very difficult to stabilise a complex economy by relying on monetary instruments alone. A very important inference for Russia, in particular from the practice of Argentina and Mexico, is the necessity to use controls over some key prices. These are especially needed in monopoly industries.

Among the main causes of the current financial difficulties in Russia are problems with tax administration. Although the state budget has to shoulder the heavy burden of supporting those sectors of the economy and social groups that are suffering most from liberalisation and interindustry resource shifts, the government is unable to obtain a fair share of the increased incomes of those sectors that have gained from the reforms. The existing tax collection mechanism, which is geared to the needs of the tightly controlled planned economy, is utterly inadequate in a market situation. In particular, tax evasion is rampant in private trade, banking and other services. These sectors have benefited most from liberalisation and often reap abnormally high profits – according to some estimates, about 70 per cent of all profits in the economy are currently made by these sectors (*Delovoi Mir*, Moscow, 10 January 1993).

Illegal operations in primary commodity exports are resulting in huge tax losses. Estimates of capital flight in 1992 range from $15–30 billion (*Izvestia*, 13 January 1993). Up to now, state controlling bodies have been unable to change the situation. This may be attributed not only to their lack of technical expertise but also to the political clout of the Mafia-type organisations that are active in the export field. Tax collection is also hampered by opposition on the part of regional authorities, which are demanding tax concessions. In its attempt to placate separatists, the central government often has to give in to those pressures, weakening the federal budget.

The foregoing shows that in Russia, as in Latin America a serious attempt to improve tax collection must form an essential part of any stabilisation package. In strengthening its tax base Russia could learn a lot from the practices of Argentina, Chile and Mexico, where improved tax collection was crucial in balancing the budget. Another indication from the Latin America experience (especially the Brazilian one) is that lasting financial stabilisation is not feasible without a clear-cut division of financial responsibilities between the different entities of a federation.

An important element of the inflation mechanism in Russia is the floating exchange rate. The rate is set at the Moscow Interbank Foreign Currency Exchange, where no more than 15 per cent of the total foreign currency inflow is traded (exporters try to keep as much of their foreign currency as possible for their own needs). When supply is very limited, the exchange rate is strongly influenced by the demands of importers of luxury goods and of the owners of extensive rouble assets wishing to protect them from inflation. The exchange rate formed in this way is inevitably artificially depreciated compared with the real parity of internal and world market prices, and this drives up the domestic prices of exportable commodities, which are, in many cases, still lower than the world market prices.

The exchange rate situation is directly connected to the dramatic increase in income differentiation that has taken place in the country. Recently a quite sizeable high-income social stratum has appeared. It consists mainly of private entrepreneurs, corrupt civil servants, managers of state enterprises and the employees of some 'privileged' industries (oil and coal production, metallurgy, private trade, banking and so on). The demands of this stratum have pushed up the prices of imported consumer goods and hard currency. Thus income differentiation has become a separate and strong factor of the rouble's undervaluation.

The Central Bank has been trying to influence the exchange rate by using its foreign currency reserves to intervene in the market. In fact, this policy allowed for a decrease in the gap between the nominal exchange rate and the purchasing power parity exchange rate from about 700 per cent in October 1992 to about 25 per cent in November 1993 (according to the estimates of A.S. Lushin, Institute of World Economy and International Relations, Moscow). This produced a certain moderating impact on inflation through lagged import prices. In a situation of a great macroeconomic imbalance and lack of sufficient foreign currency reserves, however, the potential of Central Bank interventions is limited.

In the area of exchange rate regulation, Russia could learn a lot from Latin America, where it has been proved that stabilising the exchange rate is an essential prerequisite to stopping inflation. It also indicates, however, that such a stabilisation cannot be reached without first cutting the fiscal and quasifiscal deficits and accumulating sufficient foreign exchange reserves. As has already been pointed out, the first condition will require substantial time to be satisfied in Russia. To satisfy the second will require, first of all, severely limiting capital flight. To reach this goal, the reintroduction of some form of effective state control over the export of principal primary materials (especially oil and metals) seems to be absolutely necessary. (In this respect, the practices of public-sector raw material corporations in Chile and Mexico are quite instructive.)

After (and if) these two conditions have been met, the fixed exchange rate could be used as one of the key anchors in the stabilisation package (as it was used in the hybrid-type stabilisation in Mexico and Argentina). The current real undervaluation of the rouble could then become an advantage as it allows substantial room for positively influencing prices through a gradual real appreciation of the national currency.

The foreign exchange market could also be stabilised through imposing higher import barriers for nonstaple consumer goods and through better control over illegal capital transfers covered by fictitious import contracts. As indicated by the Latin American experience, complete import liberalisation is too costly to be implemented in extremely unbalanced economies.

Another important cause of inflation is related to developments at the enterprise level. The self-management regime introduced at the state enterprises has led to increased outlay on wages and social needs at the expense of tax payments and investment funds. In the absence of a real advocate for the interests of capital, state property is in many cases being rapidly decapitalised. This process is stimulating inflation whilst diminishing state budget receipts, artificially augmenting the demand in the consumer market and drastically reducing the demand for investment goods, thus necessitating state financing of the losses in investment-goods-producing industries.

It is clear that unwarranted wage growth cannot be curbed without privatisation. In Russia, however, the privatisation process is giving ownership rights predominantly to worker–management alliances. In many cases this does not augur well for the prospects of limiting wage claims. Therefore, some additional measures must be taken. In particular, a tripartite national social pact along the Mexican lines of establishing guidelines for wage increases (especially in more affluent industries) should be tried.

Financial disequilibrium in Russia is also being seriously affected by trade relations with the former Soviet republics, almost all of which have strong negative trade balances with Russia. This is presenting the Russian government with a dilemma: should it cut supplies to the republics, causing economic disruption and political chaos there, or go on crediting them at the expense of a deteriorating market situation and accelerating inflation in Russia. Up to now a middle road between these two positions has been taken, with financial flows to the republics continuing, although on a somewhat smaller scale.

Lack of space does not permit more than the very sketchy picture given above. Even this brief analysis, however, shows that the deep structural roots of Russian inflation preclude any one-sided and dogmatic approach to stabilisation. In particular, purely orthodox remedies based on the 'lack of financial discipline and excess demand' diagnosis are unable to bring positive results. Very relevant to the situation is the main conclusion from the Latin American experience: stopping inflation without incurring prohibitively large economic and social losses requires a very pragmatic and imaginative approach to stabilisation. It is also essential to take into account the specific situation of the particular country.

Another lesson from the Latin American experience that is worth stressing is the importance of adequate and timely external aid during a stabilisation programme. In view of the dramatic external debt situation of Russia, such aid (especially in the form of debt relief) is absolutely essential to economic progress.

Finally, one last but probably the most important conclusion. The Latin American experience demonstrates that a sufficiently strong executive power is a *sine qua non* of successful stabilisation, as well as for successful transformation to a market economy. This crucial condition is currently absent in Russia. The process of building strong and effective democratic institutions has only just begun. In fact, the country is facing huge problems with nation building, including the problem of finding a working formula for federalism. Until these political problems are solved, the prospect of suppressing inflation looks very bleak.

Acknowledgments

The author is grateful to Jose Fanelli, Roberto Frenkel and Mario Damill of the Centro de Estudios de Estado y Sociedad in Buenos Aires, whose highly valuable instructions were very helpful for analysing the situation in Latin America.

References

Bresser Pereira, Luiz Carlos (1993) 'Economic Reforms and Economic Growth: Efficiency and Politics in Latin America', in L. C. Bresser Pereira, J. M. Maravall and A. Przeworski (eds), *Economic Reforms in New Democracies* (New York: Cambridge University Press).

Canavese, A. (1991) 'Hyperinflation and Convertibility-based Stabilisation in Argentina', mimeo (Buenos Aires: Instituto Torcuato di Tella).

Damill, M., J. M. Fanelli and R. Frenkel (1991) 'Shock externo y desequilibrio fiscal: Brazil', mimeo (Buenos Aires: CEDES, December).

Dornbusch, R. and M. Simonsen (1987) *Inflation Stabilisation with Income Policy Support: A review of the experience in Argentina, Brazil, and Israel* (New York: Group of Thirty).

Dornbusch, R., F. Sturzenegger, F. and H. Wolf (1989) 'Extreme inflation: Dynamics and stabilisation', *Brookings Paper on Economic Activity*, no. 1.

Fanelli, J. M. and R. Frenkel (1992) 'On gradualism, shock and sequencing in economic adjustment', CEDES document no. 81 (Buenos Aires: CEDES).

Fanelli, J. M., R. Frenkel and G. Rozenwurcel (1990) 'Growth and structural reform in Latin America. Where do we stand?', CEDES document no. 57 (Buenos Aires: CEDES).

Fanelli, J. M., R. Frenkel and L. Taylor (1992) 'The World Development Report 1991: A critical assessment', CEDES document no. 78 (Buenos Aires: CEDES).

Frenkel, R. (1992) 'Comment on "Latin American adjustment and economic reforms: Issues and recent experience" by Patricio Meller', mimeo (Brunswick, NJ: Rutgers University).

Kaufman, R. (1987) 'Politics and Inflation in Argentina and Brazil: The Austral and Cruzado packages in historical perspective', mimeo (Santiago: CIEPLAN).

Kaufman, R. (1990) 'Stabilization and adjustment in Argentina, Brazil and Mexico', in J. Nelson (ed.), *Economic Crisis and Policy Choice: The politics of adjustment in the Third World* (Princeton, NJ: Princeton University Press).

Kiguel, M. and N. Liviatan (1988) 'Inflationary Rigidities and Orthodox Stabilisation Policies: Lessons from Latin America', *The World Bank Economic Review*, vol. 2 (September).

Kiguel, M. and N. Liviatan (1991) 'Stopping Inflation: The experience of Latin America and Israel and the implications for Central and Eastern Europe', in V. Corbo, F. Coricelli and J. Bossak (eds), *Reforming Central and Eastern European economies* (Washington, DC: World Bank).

McKinnon, R. (1991) *The Order of Economic Liberalisation: Financial control in the transition to a market economy* (Baltimore, MD, and London: Johns Hopkins University Press).

Meller, P. (1991) 'Adjustment and Social Costs in Chile during the 1980s', *World Development*, vol. 19, no. 11.

Meller, P. (1992) 'Latin American adjustment and economic reforms: Issues and recent experience', paper presented at the conference on Economic Reforms in Market and Socialist Economies, Madrid, Spain (mimeo).

Nelson, J. (ed) (1989) *Fragile Coalitions: The politics of economic adjustment in the Third World* (New Brunswick, CA, and Oxford: ODC).

O'Connel, A. (1992) 'The Argentina economy: Short-and-middle-run prospects', mimeo (Buenos Aires: Centro de Economía Internacional).

Remmer, K. (1986) 'The Politics of Economic Stabilisation: IMF standby programs in Latin America, 1954–1984', *Comparative Politics*, vol. 19, no. 1.

Ross, J. (1993) 'The fundamental errors in principle of Mr. Fyodorov's economic package', mimeo (Moscow).

Waterbury, J. (1989) 'The Political Management of Economic Adjustment and Reform', in J. Nelson (ed.), *Fragile coalitions: The politics of economic adjustment* (New Brunswick, CA, and Oxford: ODC).

Whitehead, L. (1989) 'Democratization and Disinflation: A comparative approach', in J. Nelson (ed.), *Fragile Coalitions: The politics of economic adjustment* (New Brunswick, CA and Oxford: ODC).

6 External Liberalisation Through Stabilisation[1]

Andrzej Slawinski

6.1 INTRODUCTION

In 1990, Poland launched a radical adjustment policy to stabilise the economy and rectify the balance of payments. The strategic goal of Poland's adjustment policies was to pave the way for external liberalisation of the economy in order to put it on the path of stable economic growth.

It will probably take years for economists to provide a full and statistically verifiable explanation of what really happened in the Polish economy in early 1990. Accordingly, this chapter does not provide a detailed analysis of adjustment policies in Poland. Rather it offers some explanations of the sequence in which events unfolded. What is helpful in arranging the facts in a proper order are Latin American experiences. Accordingly, the main objective of this chapter is to review these experiences and use the relevant lessons as a tool with which to analyse the adjustment policies in Poland.

There are many differences between the economies of Latin America and Eastern Europe. Latin American countries already lived under a controlled market system and had a large number of fundamental, market-oriented institutions. Eastern European countries had to create a market mechanism and the corresponding institutions from scratch. Nevertheless, there are some important similarities that make the lessons from the Latin American experience helpful in understanding the policy options available to the former socialist countries. The main lesson for Eastern Europe is that external liberalisation requires a long period of stabilisation.

Section 6.2 concentrates on adjustment policies in Latin America. It reviews experiments with the monetary approach to the balance of payments in Chile and Argentina, adjustment policies in Brazil and Mexico in the 1980s, and the recent phenomenon of the return of capital flows to Latin American countries. Section 6.3 is dedicated to adjustment policies in Poland, analysed in the light of the Latin American experience. Finally, Section 6.4 focuses on current challenges.

181

6.2   ADJUSTMENT POLICIES IN LATIN AMERICA

Southern Cone Experiments

In the late 1970s, the countries of the Southern Cone of Latin America decided to implement stabilisation polices that followed the prescriptions of the monetary approach to the balance of payments. The distinct feature of the Southern Cone experiment was that the countries of the region intended to establish a positive feedback between stabilisation policies and external liberalisation.

Chile

The Chilean adjustment policies had two stages. From 1973–7 Chilean economic policy followed that of a closed economy. From 1978–82, after liberalisation of the capital account of the balance of payments, the Chilean government adopted a monetary approach to the balance of payments.

The adjustment policies started in 1973 after the military coup d'état. In the initial stages the main problem was the necessity to combat the 1000 per cent hyperinflation resulting from the huge budget deficit of 25 per cent of GDP. Beginning in 1974, the Chilean government adopted an economic policy that aimed at balancing the budget and improving the mobility of resources (through liberalisation of the financial system). The government was aware that it would take time to open up the economy. Thus, in the beginning, monetary and fiscal policies were the main tools to combat inflation.

The government's adjustment policies followed the prescription of the absorption approach to the balance of payments; that is, a combination of real devaluation and financial restrictions. The need for the devaluation was strengthened by an adverse external shock: a 50 per cent drop in copper prices in 1974. The devaluation brought about an improvement in the trade account. Its inflationary impact, however, had to be neutralised by highly restrictive fiscal policies. In 1975, GDP fell by 13 per cent and unemployment rose to 16 per cent. Nevertheless, in 1976 there was spectacular improvement in the Chilean economy as inflation fell from 431 per cent to 174 per cent.

Despite the continuation of strict fiscal policies, GDP grew by 3.2 per cent. This was made possible by a substantial reduction of the budget deficit. Due to cuts in budgetary spending and the massive privatisation of state firms, the government managed to reduce the budget deficit to 2.3

per cent of GDP. This allowed resources to be released to the private sector without expanding domestic credit. By reducing the budget deficit the public sector averted demands for funds from the financial markets, thus opening up opportunities for channelling increased resources towards productive investment.

In 1977 there was a further improvement in the economy. National income grew by 9.8 per cent and the unemployment rate was reduced from 16 per cent to 13 per cent. On the negative side, the rate of inflation remained stubbornly at 60 per cent. Although this was substantially less than in 1975 and 1976, the authorities thought that this inflationary momentum was unwarranted. Inflation was recognised as inertial; that is, caused by inflationary expectations. Thus there was the danger that if the government continued to combat inflation with monetary policy, this would cause a fall in production because rigidities of expectations would produce a difference between the expected inflation and that consistent with monetary policy. The resulting deceleration in nominal aggregate demand would reduce production.

The Chilean government decided to stabilise the economy by following the prescriptions of the monetary approach to the balance of payments. According to this a government has to have effective control over fiscal policy in order to be able to adjust credit policy to changes in international reserves. The other precondition is opening up the economy in order to facilitate arbitrage in goods and financial markets. In the late 1970s the Chilean economy seemed to fulfil both conditions. The balanced state budget made it possible to adjust credit policy to changes in international reserves. The government counted on the assistance of the 'law of one price' – from 1973 to 1977 import tariffs were progressively reduced from 90 per cent to 15 per cent.

In January 1978 Chile started its famous experiment with managing inflationary expectations. The main tool was a preannounced timetable of devaluations. The goal was to provide a clear signal to the general public that the government was determined to push down the rate of inflation to the rate of the preannounced devaluations. The initial rate of devaluation was deliberately set at a lower rate than ongoing inflation. This timetable was called the *tablita*, which the whole experiment came to be called (Fernandez, 1985).

Initially the introduction of the *tablita* brought about the expected results. In 1978 the rate of inflation was cut from 64 per cent to 30 per cent without a drop in production, which in fact expanded at a rapid rate. The important problem for the government, however, was the high rate of unemployment, which remained above 14 per cent. The military government, which had taken power after a brutal *coup d'état*, wanted spectacular economic success in order to gain some popularity. Consequently in 1979 it introduced three new elements into its economic policy:

- Implementation of a fixed exchange rate.
- Legalisation of a rigid backward indexation scheme.
- Relaxation of controls for capital movements.

The government assumed that foreign borrowing would finance investments that would lead to a reduction in unemployment. At first the new policy was extremely successful. The decision to allow commercial banks to increase substantially the ratio of foreign liabilities to equity induced a substantial capital inflow and a growth in investment. The rate of unemployment was reduced to 12 per cent.

This initial success overshadowed the fact that the 1979 policy package was inconsistent. The decision to implement 100 per cent wage indexation resulted in the overvaluation of the peso. This produced a swing in the trade balance towards a substantial deficit. Despite the overvaluation of the peso and the deterioration of the trade account, the stable exchange rate was able to be maintained because of the substantial foreign capital inflows.

The real appreciation of the Chilean peso placed important financial strains on most firms, which reacted by borrowing from the banking system. The government answered with a strict monetary policy because it wanted the demand for money to be satisfied through growth in exports or borrowing abroad, as prescribed by the monetary approach to the balance of payments. The result of this policy, however, was a hike in the level of interest rates, augmented by expectations of a devaluation. The markedly overvalued currency and the high interest rates produced a recession and the problem of bad loans. A large part of the demand for credit became 'false demand', consisting of the rolling-over of bad loans.

This situation was inconsistent with the long-run viability of the economic policy. The government, however, took a passive and overly dogmatic stance on macropolicy. The monetary authorities argued that the only effect of nominal devaluation would be to generate an equivalent domestic inflation without affecting relative prices or the real exchange rate. The monetary authorities also believed that an interest rate that equalised the supply of and demand for money was by definition an equilibrium rate. In fact, the positive interest real rates of 30 per cent or 40 per cent a year absorbed disequilibria in other sectors of the Chilean economy.

In mid-1981 interest rates continued to climb because of strong speculation against the peso. Many firms went bankrupt as they could no longer face foreign competition or pay their swelling interest bill. In 1982 the unemployment rate climbed to almost 20 per cent. This unsustainable situation finally burst because of an abrupt drop in foreign capital inflows. The Chilean experiment with the monetary approach to the balance of payments was terminated. The economy could no longer afford either trade liberalisation – cuts in imports became necessary to generate the trade surplus needed to repay the external obligation – or a fixed exchange rate. The peso was devalued. In December 1982 Chile declared the inconvertibility of its currency, imposed exchange controls and increased import tariffs substantially.

Argentina

At the end of 1979, Argentina followed the Chilean example and introduced the *tablita*. As in Chile, the implementation of the *tablita* was an experiment with the rational expectations approach. From a theoretical point of view, there is much merit in the rational expectations approach over the conventional stabilisation plan of monetary restriction, where the level of economic activity is initially reduced because real balances fall and interest rates rise. At the beginning, the experiment worked quite well. The declining trend of inflation was initially attained without affecting production or the rate of unemployment. After a short period, however, the Argentinean peso was overvalued and economic agents began to have doubts about the future of stabilisation plans. The main reason for this was the inconsistent economic policy.

In Chile, the nominal anchor of the exchange rate was supported by tight fiscal and monetary policies. In Argentina, the government did not move to reduce its budget deficit. Instead, it decided only to narrow the share of Central Bank credit in the financing of the deficit. From 1977–81, the share of Central Bank financing in overall financing of the budget deficit dropped from 12 per cent to 0.7 per cent of GDP. The government, however, was not following the main prescription of the monetary approach to the balance of payments; that is, it did not adjust the money supply to the changes in international reserves. Furthermore, a substantial part of the budget deficit was financed externally. This created a potentially explosive situation in which the build-up of international reserves and the strength of the domestic currency were the result of the budget deficit; that is, the large accumulation of reserves by the Central Bank was made possible by external financing of the fiscal deficit.

The second important reason for the inconsistency of the adjustment policy was that the Argentinean government abandoned plans to liberalise trade policy. Although trade liberalisation was an objective of the government's adjustment policy, the reforms were limited to reducing or eliminating export taxes. The plan to reduce import duties was only partially implemented. Accordingly, price arbitrage (the 'law of one price') could not support the stabilisation policy. Tariff protection remained high enough to sustain import-competing firms, so that the real appreciation did not force them to reduce profit margins. Rather than force down inflation for all sectors, the *tablita* caused the ratio of tradable to nontradable goods to fall by two thirds between 1977 and 1981 (Petrei and Tybout, 1985). The reason why the government neither reduced the budget deficit nor liberalised its trade policy was that it wanted to minimise the social costs of its economic policies. Fiscal and trade policies reflected the government's determination to reduce inflation without increasing unemployment. To achieve this goal, however, the government conducted an inconsistent economic policy that resulted in a substantial overvaluation of the exchange rate.

The overvaluation of the peso and the resulting deterioration in the trade account of the balance of payments created uncertainty about the future of the stabilisation plan. These doubts manifested themselves in very high interest rates related to devaluation expectations arising from a lack of confidence in the preannounced trajectory of devaluations. The premium for exchange rate risk created and increased the spread between domestic interest rates and international interest rates. This spread induced capital inflows, but at the same time it produced recession. As in Chile, firms were often caught in a vicious circle of falling earnings and rising debt obligations that forced distress borrowing. As a consequence of the lack of confidence in the continuity of the economic programme, many firms decided to go into debt in order to remain in operation while waiting for a change in economic strategy. The loss of profitability of enterprises increased the share of nonperforming loans in bank portfolios. The deteriorating situation in the real sector and expectations of devaluation and inflation provoked the flight of the peso into US dollars.

The government did not decide to devalue the peso because of the initial successes of its economic policy. In 1979–80 there was reduced inflation, economic growth and a gain in real wages. For wage earners it was a time of 'sweet money'. The choice was between buying cheap imported goods or depositing money at a high interest rate. The government wanted to defend the policy that had brought it some popularity. To defend the peso, authorities borrowed heavily abroad to intervene in the foreign exchange market. The actual situation, however, differed from that assumed by the government. What was going on was not traditional speculation against the peso. In fact, it was a capital flight as investors lost confidence in government economic policy.

The policy to defend the exchange rate facilitated capital flight. The overvalued exchange rate represented a subsidy for anyone shifting their wealth from domestic into real assets. Accordingly, by borrowing abroad the government was providing a supply of cheap foreign currency, which was used as a vehicle for capital flight. In 1981, the massive capital flight necessitated a real depreciation of the peso, which put an end to the experiment with the *tablita*.

Lessons

An important lesson that can be drawn from the Southern Cone experiment with the *tablita* is that in recently liberalised economies it is very difficult to keep relative prices in line. A previously repressed economy does not have a well-functioning system of developed goods and financial markets. Consequently economic liberalisation can produce a misalignment in relative prices; for example, overvaluation of the exchange rate and excessively high interest rates. The important lesson from the Southern Cone experience is that financial markets require a highly coherent economic policy, which is very difficult to achieve in recently liberalised economies. Accordingly, a series of nominal anchors were used in the transition period.

The related issue is the opening of the capital account. Southern Cone experience showed that, with a massive capital inflow, it is difficult to avoid overvaluation of the currency and a rise in interest rates. Both were almost unavoidable. In Chile, the monetary authorities attempted to neutralise the impact that the capital inflow exerted on the domestic money market. The result was a surge in interest rates. In Argentina, the monetary authorities did not attempt to neutralise fully the impact of capital inflows. The interest rate did not rise because of Central Bank intervention in the money market, but because of expectations of devaluation, and the lack of sterilisation augmented these expectations. The Argentinean peso was heavily overvalued after the first year of the *tablita* experiment.

The Southern Cone experiment also provides some lessons on the sequencing of liberalisation. Both in Chile and Argentina, liberalisation of the capital account was premature. It led to an unwarranted real appreciation of the exchange rate and an incorrect allocation of investment between tradable and nontradables. Reforms turned out to be biased against the sector the authorities had meant to promote. Profits of tradable goods were significantly reduced relative to those of other producers. The sequence of liberalisation was much better in Chile, where the capital account restrictions were relaxed after trade reform. This created space for a real devaluation of the Chilean peso in the 1970s, when it was necessary to offset the negative effect of cuts in the average level of protection. In Argentina, the plan to liberalise trade policy was partially abandoned and the liberalisation of the capital account was used to finance the fiscal deficit.

Probably the most important lesson that can be drawn from the Southern Cone experience is that fiscal deficit is the key element of an adjustment programme. The crucial difference between Chile and Argentina was that in Chile, before the *tablita* was adopted, the fiscal deficit had been substantially reduced. Accordingly the general public perceived government policy as consistent and credible. The consistency and credibility of the Chilean economic policy facilitated the success of the experiment with the *tablita* in 1978–79. The experiment did not produce an overvaluation of the peso. The rate of inflation did converge with the preannounced devaluation rates. The overvaluation of the peso resulted from the economic policy initiated in 1979.

In Argentina, the general public did not perceive the *tablita* as credible. The reasons for this were the massive budget deficit and inconsistent monetary policy. Economic agents were not convinced that the government would succeed in pushing down the rate of inflation to the rates of the preannounced devaluations. Accordingly, in Argentina the *tablita* did not gain the credibility it needed. The introduction of the *tablita* did not neutralise inflationary expectations. Shortly after its implementation it became obvious that the exchange rate and the fiscal policies were incompatible and that it was only because of the massive capital inflows that the *tablita* could be maintained. The overvalued exchange rate induced a hike in the real interest rate. This produced a recession and provoked a massive capital flight.

The Southern Cone experiments tried to establish a positive feedback between stabilisation policies and external liberalisation. Stabilisation policies were aimed at rectifying the balance of payments situation and enabling external liberalisation. The underlying assumption was that external liberalisation would preserve the results of stabilisation policies because of the influence of the 'law of one price'; that is, the arbitrage in goods and financial markets. To achieve such a goal turned out to be extremely difficult in the case of newly liberalised economies. The results of the adjustment policies in Chile, however, showed that a mixture of stabilisation policies and external liberalisation can produce positive results. Despite the termination of the Chilean experiment in 1982, it was successful in the sense that it paved the road to stabilisation of the economy through integrating it with the world market.

Adjustment Policies in the 1980s

In September 1982, the Mexican moratorium induced the debt crisis. Forthcoming loans to developing countries were cut drastically. Latin American countries could no longer service their already enormous external debt by means of new loans, but had to use their own resources. The turnaround from net capital inflow to a substantial net resource outflow created a severe balance of payments crisis in many countries. The debtor countries had to accommodate the external financial shock by reducing investment and increasing unemployment.

Brazil

There were two periods in the Brazilian adjustment policy in the 1980s: the period of orthodox stabilisation, from 1981 to 1985, and the period of heterodox stabilisation, from 1986 to 1987. In fact, balance of payments problems had been dominating Brazilian economic policy since 1980; that is, two years before the international debt crisis was sparked by the Mexican default. If one defined the indebtedness crisis as a situation in which economic policy had to be subordinated to an attempt to rectify the balance of payments, it would turn out that such a crisis began in Brazil not in 1982 but in 1980, when inflation reached three-digit levels and external creditors forced the Brazilian government to adopt a rigidly orthodox policy designed to reduce inflation and produce a trade surplus.

The Brazilian adjustment policy was a mix of a real devaluation and financial restrictions. The adjustment policies brought about an improvement in the trade account, which went from a US$2.8 billion deficit in 1980 to a US$1.2 billion surplus in 1981. The Brazilian economy, however, plunged into recession. In 1981, GDP fell by 4.4 per cent. In 1981 Brazilian international reserves grew by US$0.8 billion. Nonetheless Brazil was unprepared for the international debt crisis of 1982, when it was required to pay its creditors $12 billion. The trade surplus was insufficient to support these payments and, in 1982 Brazilian reserves fell by US$4.9 billion.

The Brazilian government then turned to the International Monetary Fund (IMF) for assistance. The IMF offered to extend stand-by credit, but this was conditional on Brazil devaluing the cruzeiro and tightening its stabilisation policies. In 1983, Brazil devalued the cruzeiro by 30 per cent. This devaluation and cuts in imports produced a substantial improvement in the balance of payments. The growing trade surplus and rescheduling of the external debt contributed to a spectacular improvement in the current account. From the balance of payments point of view, Brazilian adjustment policy was an impressive success. In 1982–4 the balance on the current account had improved by US$16.3 billion.

The price paid for this improvement was a recession and a budget deficit that was widening because of the necessity to issue new government paper to raise the funds needed to finance repayments on the external debt. Nonetheless, in 1984 the major goal of the IMF adjustment programme was achieved – the current account was balanced. Inflation, however, stayed at a stubbornly high level. Under the pressure of the IMF and external creditors, the government intended to change the rules of wage indexation to bring about a further cut in real wages. Opposition to such changes was widespread and included business groups, who demanded a cut in interest rates and argued that a further cut in real wages would further depress an already contracted domestic market.

Parliament rejected the changes to the economic policy as they would cause a prolonged recession. Recession seemed unwarranted after more than two decades of successful economic growth. Brazilians remembered the 'miracle' of the early 1970s, when economic reforms had enabled the resumption of stable economic growth, and were convinced that similar improvement was possible in the 1980s. Parliamentary dismissal of the government's proposals meant a break with the IMF. In 1984, however, Brazilian foreign exchange grew by US$6 billion. It was hoped that Brazil would be able to cope with the debt problem without the assistance of the IMF.

A year later, conditions to continue deflationary economic policy became even less politically viable. In 1985 Brazil had free presidential elections and the government did not want to disappoint society by imposing more recession and unemployment. Nevertheless, some form of stabilisation policy was required as inflation jumped to more than 200 per cent in 1985.

The Brazilian government was seeking an adjustment policy that would help to stabilise the economy and alleviate the social cost of the previous stabilisation programme. The proposed solution was a heterodox stabilisation plan. The concept of heterodox stabilisation assumed that the main reason for high inflation was inflationary expectations. Accordingly, the assumption was that the proper solution was to attack these inflationary expectations rather than continue a painful orthodox stabilisation through cutting production and government expenditure (Blejer and Cheasty, 1988).

Brazilians assumed that, to a large extent, the budget deficit was not the cause but the result of the high inflation. Two phenomena were highlighted. The first was the Olivera–Tanzi effect; that is, erosion of the real value of budget revenues in the time lag between the moment when taxes are due and the moment when tax revenues are used to finance budget expenditures (Tanzi, 1977). The second phenomenon was the inflationary component of budgetary interest payments; that is, an increase in the budget interest bill caused by the fact that nominal interest rates are being pushed up by a surge in prices (Diaz, 1986).

The proposed cure was a mixture of orthodox stabilisation policies and incomes policy; that is, price and wage controls. It was hoped that price controls would narrow the budget deficit through eliminating or reversing the Tanzi–Olivera effect and cutting down the swelling bill of budget interest payments. It was expected that the narrowing of the budget deficit (because of the neutralisation of inertial inflation) would reduce the costs of orthodox stabilisation.

In 1986, Brazil introduced a stabilisation programme that was structured according to the heterodox strategy – the Cruzado Plan, which was named after the new currency that was introduced to strengthen confidence in the programme. Similar to the *tablita*, the heterodox strategy had its roots in the theory of rational expectations, which says that a drastic and convincing change in government economic policy can influence people's inflationary expectations and break inertional inflation.

The fundamental element of the Cruzado Plan was a price and wage freeze. The wage freeze did not mean actual deindexation but rather the introduction of mechanisms to prevent real wage appreciation. Indexation was replaced by an automatic wage increase clause that was to be triggered when inflation reached a cumulative 20 per cent. The price and wage freeze was intended to avoid the effect of inflationary inertia and maintain the profitability of production, which would have been effected if prices and wages did not fall in line with the contraction of the money supply.

At the beginning, the Cruzado Plan worked well. In its first month, the plan showed that a proper combination of incomes policy with demand policies can produce a significant decline in inflation rates. Brazil enjoyed high rates of growth with relatively low rates of inflation. In 1986 Brazilians believed that the 'miracle' of the early 1970s had returned. Stable economic growth was believed to be restored. Confidence in the future was reflected by growth in the demand for money, which almost doubled, proving that the Cruzado Plan had changed people's inflationary expectations.

Unfortunately, the government's economic policy was inconsistent. The assumption was that the wage and price controls would allow adjustment of the rate of inflation to the rate of growth in the money supply. The growth in the money supply, however, was not effectively controlled. In 1986 prices rose by 145 per cent, whereas the money supply grew by 307 per cent, thereby creating strong inflationary pressures. The first signs that the success of the Cruzado Plan would not be sustainable were the shortages in different markets that appeared in the middle of 1986. The increase in the money supply exceeded the natural rise in money demand that followed disinflation.

To rescue the Cruzado Plan, in July 1986 the government announced the Cruzandinho Plan, which was a fiscal package designed to dampen consumption. It contained the imposition of new indirect taxes on the purchase of petrol, cars and foreign exchange. In June 1987 the authorities announced a New Cruzado Plan. This time, the goal was to increase the relative prices of public services and subsidised commodities. Both programmes brought about a significant increase in budget revenue, which, however, was not large enough to reduce the budget deficit to acceptable levels.

In 1987, inflationary tensions became so strong that people lost confidence in the government's stabilisation policies and the demand for money fell again. This proved that the Cruzado Plan had lost its impact on inflationary expectations. The government decided to loosen wage and price controls, and officially terminated the Cruzado Plan. Indexation was reintroduced and monthly inflation rates reached 20–30 per cent.

The failure of the Cruzado Plan was primarily because the fiscal policy was not strict enough and fiscal adjustment began too late. There is little question, however, that the external environment played a role. The most important reason for the failure of Cruzado Plan was that external debt service had evolved into a massive fiscal problem. The government had to issue more and more government paper in order to raise the resources needed to buy foreign exchange and service the external debt. Consequently, the mounting domestic debt was the outcome of the external debt service. Between 1984 and 1986, expenditure on servicing the overall public debt grew from 6.6 per cent to 12 per cent of GDP. This contributed substantially to the growth in the budget deficit from 4.8 per cent to 12.1 per cent of GDP. The increase in budget revenue could not outweigh the burden the external debt service imposed on the Brazilian budget. In 1988 alone, the net repayments on Brazil's external debt amounted to US$12 billion, which again added to inflationary pressures and caused an upsurge of inflation in 1989.

Mexico

The popular view of the reasons for the explosion of the external debt crisis is that it reflected unsound budgetary policies and unsustainable growth programmes. Mexico followed precisely such a pattern. In the 1970s Mexican external debt accumulated because of loose budgetary policies and an unsustainable growth programme that was to be financed from oil revenues. The budget revenues, however, were not enough to cover budget expenditure. The government had to borrow heavily, both abroad and domestically.

The large budget deficit resulted in inflation. Domestic prices gradually lost their competitive edge over external prices. In 1981 the combination of overvaluation and a budget deficit sparked off massive capital flight. Wealth holders used the underpriced foreign exchange as a vehicle to escape the consequences of expected devaluation and inflation. As in Argentina, capital flight was made possible by massive government intervention in the domestic foreign exchange market. In 1981 half of the Mexican budget deficit was financed by foreign borrowing, resulting in a substantial increase in public sector external debt. More serious than the amount itself was that the share of short-term credits climbed to 32 per cent. The deficit on the current account reached US$16 billion. Only 24 per cent of the deficit was the result of the trade deficit.

In 1982 the government announced that it would suspend repayment of the principal of its external debt. At the same time the budget deficit reached 14.4 per cent of GDP. The authorities could no longer use foreign borrowing to finance the budget deficit. Consequently the share of seigniorage in financing the deficit reached 63 per cent and the rate of inflation went up to 102 per cent.

In 1983 Mexico began a draconian adjustment policy. The real devaluation and tight monetary policies resulted in a more than 30 per cent drop in real wages. To obtain the resources needed to finance the trade surplus, Mexico managed to achieve a dramatic change in the noninterest balance of the budget. Between 1982 and 1983 it went from a deficit of 7.5 per cent to a surplus of 4.2 per cent of GDP. GDP, however, fell by 5.3 per cent. In 1983–5 Mexico continued the tight adjustment policies to achieve the trade surpluses needed to service the external debt. The fiscal costs of the external debt service did not allow for a balanced budget, despite the privatisation of many state firms and the scaling down of expenditure on social policy.

In 1986 the Mexican economy suffered severe terms-of-trade deterioration as the average dollar price of its crude oil exports fell by 53 per cent, thereby reducing oil export revenues by 58 per cent. One quarter of the country's fiscal income depended on oil revenues. To maintain the value of oil receipts in terms of domestic goods, the Mexican government devalued the peso heavily, to below the purchasing parity power level. The share of oil revenues in budget revenues stayed unchanged, however, at the cost of real income losses, which contributed indirectly to inflationary pressures. In 1986 real peso GDP fell by 3.8 per cent, whereas dollar GDP fell by 28.1 per cent. The budget deficit jumped from 8.3 per cent to 15.2 per cent of GDP. The 149 per cent devaluation and the budget deficit pushed the rate of inflation above 100 per cent. The most important reason for the budget deficit and inflation was continuing capital flight and growing leakage of real resources in the form of the foreign debt repayments. From 1984–6 Mexico's net debt repayments amounted to US$26 billion.

The IMF pressed Mexico to continue the orthodox stabilisation policies to reduce the fiscal deficit. Mexico, however, highlighted the fact that it had reached a balanced budget once adjusted for inflation; that is, the operational balance showed a surplus of 2.3 per cent of GDP. In 1986 Mexico reached an unprecedented agreement with the IMF, which accepted the concept of an operational deficit being a reliable indicator for evaluating the country's fiscal policy.

The difference between the nominal and the operational balance of the budget provided proof of the inertial character of inflation in Mexico. Thus Mexico decided to adopt a heterodox strategy, implementing a price wage exchange-rate freeze. Keeping in mind the previous Brazilian experience, however, Mexico waited for the right moment. Unlike in Brazil, Mexico's monetary and fiscal policies remained tight. Mexico postponed introduction of the stabilisation programme until the budget was in a sufficiently strong position because of cuts in expenditure, closing public firms, raising taxes and broadening the tax base. In short, Mexico did not make the same mistake as Brazil, which introduced a freeze on prices and wages without reducing the budget deficit, so that its freeze was bound to end in a renewed inflationary explosion.

The stabilisation programme was implemented in January 1988 and turned out to be successful. Inflation was substantially reduced and there was no rekindling of high inflation in Mexico. As had happened in Israel, an important reason for the success of the stabilisation programme was the government's agreement with the trade unions on wages (The Social Solidarity Pact), implemented in December 1987.

An important element of Mexico's stabilisation programme was trade liberalisation. In December 1987 the maximum tariff rate was reduced from 100 per cent to 20 per cent. Trade liberalisation helped to limit domestic price increases through international competition. Tariff reduction contributed to growth recovery as it enabled Mexican companies to import capital and intermediate goods at international prices, thus strengthening their export potential.

The difficult period was the poststabilisation recession. In a sense, Mexico could not afford economic growth. Growth would mean increased imports and reduced exports. This would mean that Mexico would have no foreign currency with which to pay the interest on its external debt. The Mexican government had to be careful not to provoke capital flight, which would trigger a negative feedback of devaluations and jumps in inflation. The price of this period was the necessity to keep interest rates at a high level in order to preserve the positive results of the stabilisation policy, and to convince foreign investors that the Mexican government was determined to continue its economic policies.

The key factor in the preservation of the results of the stabilisation programme was the government's agreement with the main sectors of the economy on a Pact for Stability and Economic Growth (PECE), which replaced the Economic Solidarity Pact. The renewed social pact was based on a negotiated agreement to adjust price and wage increases. Under the PECE, inflation dropped from 52 per cent in 1988 to 20 per cent in 1989, and there was an upturn in economic growth from 1.4 per cent to 2.9 per cent.

The accord that perhaps brought the most significant improvement was the agreement to reduce Mexico's external debt by 17 per cent. The actual results were smaller than expected, but the importance of the agreement was that it gave Mexico the chance to regain external equilibrium and the confidence of foreign investors. The reduction of the external debt reduced the level of the risk perceived by investors. This made it possible to lower interest rates, which took place in July 1989 immediately after the announcement of the agreement with creditors. The improvement in investor confidence resulted in an increase in the price of Mexican debt in secondary markets. The agreement with creditors also enabled Mexico to return to international financial markets. The subsequent capital inflows contributed to the restoration of economic growth.

Lessons

The comparison of adjustment policies in Brazil and Mexico does not offer easy conclusions because the situation in the two countries was different and policy makers were exposed to different sets of forces when forming their decisions. Some general conclusions, however, are relevant to economic policy in Eastern Europe.

First, painful stabilisation policies turned out to be unavoidable. Latin American economic experience shows that there is no way of circumventing postreform recession (Fanelli and Frenkel, 1992). What created the base for the spectacular success of the Mexican stabilisation policies in 1988 was the six years (1982–7) of painful orthodox stabilisation.

This highlights the issue of political constraints, which produced inconsistency in the implementation of the Cruzado Plan. Because of political pressure, the government did not want to provoke recession. Accordingly its monetary policy was not restrictive enough and the necessary fiscal adjustment was carried out too late. The efforts of the Central Bank to restrain monetary policy and raise interest rates faced strong political opposition.

Since the late 1980s the Mexican economy has continued to operate within a stable monetary and fiscal framework because of the social pacts agreed upon by the leaders of all the country's economic sectors. The successive extensions of the PECE pact have contributed to the recovery of investment, production and employment.

The second important lesson that can be drawn from the comparison of the Brazilian and Mexican experiences is that, in the case of a debtor country, cooperation with creditors is a necessary prerequisite for successful adjustment policies. In 1988 Mexico adopted a similar heterodox stabilisation scenario to that adopted earlier in Brazil. What brought about its success was not only the consistent implementation of the programme but also the support of the IMF and Mexico's creditors (Diaz, 1989). IMF-supported adjustment programmes usually require relatively tough measures that bring about recession. The Latin American experiences, however, show that cooperation with creditors is necessary. Adjustment programmes need to come to a reasonable compromise between the two parties.

As far as Mexico is concerned, cooperation with its creditors yielded a debt reduction agreement and subsequent capital inflows. Mexico could afford to increase its imports, which in 1988 grew from US$12.2 billion to US$18.9 billion and narrowed the trade surplus from US$8.5 billion in 1987 to US$1.8 billion in 1988. The changes in the balance of payments contributed to the success of the stabilisation programme.

As for Brazil, lack of support by its creditors was one of the causes of the failure of the Cruzado Plan. In 1986–7, when the plan was being implemented, Brazil's net repayments on its external debt amounted to US$17 billion. Such a huge capital outflow contributed to the failure of the stabilisation policy. Without the support of its creditors Brazil could not afford substantially to narrow its trade balance, which in 1987 amounted to US$11 billion, adding to the inflationary pressures that ultimately destroyed the Cruzado Plan. In 1988 the trade balance reached US$19 billion, an important factor in the renewed outbreak of high inflation.

Experiences of the Early 1990s

The 1980s have been called the lost decade for Latin American countries. The necessity to transfer a large part of domestic savings abroad suffocated economic growth and fuelled inflationary pressures. For a long time it seemed that the harsh adjustment policies that were followed would be unrewarded. Successive proposals aimed at solving the debt problem, such as the Baker Plan, did not seem very effective. The debtor countries were mired in economic recession at a time when only economic growth could help to alleviate the debt problem. The late 1980s and early 1990s brought about a spectacular turnaround of this situation. Capital began to flow back into the Latin American countries and net outflow was transformed into net inflow. In 1991 this amounted to 15 per cent of the region's exports of goods and services (Culpeper and Griffith-Jones,1992, p. 9).

The important reason behind the capital inflows into the Latin American countries was successful economic reform. To greater or lesser degrees, the various governments opened their economies to outside competition, curbed budget deficits, privatised state industry and increased the role of the market. The successful economic reforms offered foreign investors the prospect of stable and growing economies.

The underlying factor in the creation of investor confidence was the change of attitude of the Latin American governments towards economic policies. One spectacular symptom of the change was that the bold stabilisation programme in Argentina was initiated and successfully implemented under the rule of the Justicialist Party, which derived from the Peronist movement – the centre of populist economic policy!

In 1990–2 the structure of capital inflow mirrored the stage of economic reform in different countries. Long-term investment went mainly to those countries that had completed their reforms and embarked upon a stable growth path. This is why Mexico and Chile reported a particularly large amount of long-term investment. In Chile, the share of direct investment in foreign capital inflow accounted for 65 per cent of the total (Culpeper and Griffith-Jones, 1992, p. 15). A very high proportion of short-term flow went to Brazil as it had not managed to reduce its fiscal imbalance and stabilise the economy.

Other important reasons behind the capital inflow were the recession in the world economy and the relatively high level of interest rates in Latin

American countries. Recession in large parts of the developed world reduced the demand for investment. Low returns in established markets forced investors to look for new opportunities in Latin America and elsewhere. High interest rates in the countries of the region compensated investors for the perceived risks of investing there. Latin America offered a prospect of substantial capital gains because of the rapid increase in the US dollar stock prices of the main markets in the region. The other factors that helped to alleviate the debt crisis were the low interest rates in international financial markets and negotiated debt relief, both of which contributed to the reduction of debt overhang and eased the serviceability of foreign debt.

There is a positive feedback between the foreign capital inflow and the positive results of economic reforms in Latin American countries. On the one hand, the capital inflow helped to lift the financial constraints that had been imposed on Latin American countries since the beginning of the debt crisis. On the other hand, the inflow complicated economic policy in the region and produced phenomena similar to the Southern Cone experience form 1979 to 1982; that is, it forced an appreciation of the currencies and pushed up the level of interest rates.

Currency appreciation makes it difficult to increase exports, widens the current account and increases a country's dependence on international capital markets. A government can maintain the value of the exchange rate by intervening in the currency market, but in doing so it expands the money supply, adding to the inflationary pressures. This in turn creates the necessity to sell government debt to sterilise the impact of the capital inflow. Latin American governments did sterilise a considerable portion of the inflow but at the cost of pushing up interest rates, which deterred domestic investment and induced an even larger capital inflow.

The Southern Cone experiences show that a sudden inflow of capital can be destructive. There are significant differences, however, between the situation that prevailed before the outbreak of the debt crisis and the recent situation. The main problem of the late 1970s was swelling budget deficits financed by foreign borrowing. In the early 1990s, inflation was declining and the budgets of most Latin American countries were in balance. For example, in Mexico the fiscal surplus allowed internal debt to be paid back and interest rates to be lowered. This made it possible to sterilise foreign capital inflows without pushing up the interest rate level.

In the late 1970s, capital inflows were largely bank financed. In the early 1990s, the structure of inflows was significantly more varied and the funds went to the private sector. A substantial part went into investments that will be converted into tradables. Thus it is likely that future debt service will be financed without major problems.

In contrast to the late 1970s, capital inflows now going into Latin America do not reflect structural imbalances in the economies of these countries. This time, capital inflows reflect the integration of these countries with the world economy, which was made possible by their stabilisation policies and external liberalisation.

6.3   ADJUSTMENT POLICIES IN POLAND

Policies Before the Economic Transition

As in other debtor countries, Poland's external debt grew rapidly in the 1970s. The swelling refinancing component of external borrowing exploded in the late 1970s. In 1980, Poland borrowed US$8.7 billion, of which only 9 per cent was used to finance the trade deficit. In 1981, Poland went into default. In the 1980s, rescheduling agreements with creditors made possible the reduction of the actual debt repayments. Accumulation of arrears, however, produced rapid growth in the stock of external debt. From 1982 to 1989, despite net debt repayments, Poland's external debt almost doubled, reaching US$48 billion in 1990.

To rectify the balance of payments the government introduced some adjustment policies and implemented some partial economic reforms. An important element of these reforms was the introduction of the 'submarginal' exchange rate, which was indirectly indexed to the rate of inflation. The zloty was devalued to make 80 per cent of exports profitable; that is, only 20 per cent of exports were subsidised from the budget. Prices of tradables were linked to the exchange rate level, which contributed to some improvement in relative prices. The implementation of the submarginal rate implied a substantial real devaluation, as previously the exchange rate had been kept at an artificially overvalued level.

In the early 1980s there was a dramatic fall in imports due to the growth in their relative prices and the lack of availability of foreign credits. The drop in imports entailed, in turn, a substantial fall in exports. Nevertheless the real devaluation of the zloty enabled the revitalisation of exports. Consequently, Poland achieved a turnaround of the trade account of the balance of payments, which went from a US$0.8 billion deficit in 1980 to a US$1.4 billion surplus in 1984.

In the mid-1980s Poland introduced some additional measures to promote growth in exports. The package contained tax reductions for exporters and the right for exporters to retain part of their export earnings in order to finance their imports. Exporters could avoid the bureaucratic bargaining system necessity of putting their import requirements into the central plan. The system of retention quotas turned out to be quite effective. From 1985 to 1988 Poland's exports to the Western hemisphere rose by 40 per cent in US dollar terms.

Nonetheless, the growth in exports was the only positive result of the government economic policy. The adjustment policies of the 1980s were not supported by adequate financial restrictions. Supporting export-promoting reforms by pursuing consistent monetary and fiscal policies was impossible within the framework of a centrally planned economy, which implied a 'soft budget constraint' in the firms sector, resulting in chronic excess demand. In the 1980s, the excess demand could not be absorbed by imports, as had been the case in the 1970s. Consequently, inflationary pressures accumulated in the economy and generated a growing monetary overhang. The fiscal burden of the external debt service further fuelled inflation.

In the 1970s, Polish firms did not borrow from abroad to finance their imports, they bought imported goods from government trading companies. Importers paid prices that reflected artificially overvalued exchange rates. Consequently the mounting external debt was exclusively a government liability – only the government was responsible for the debt service. The introduction of the submarginal exchange rate implied substantial real devaluation. Consequently the government had to pay more and more to exporters for the foreign exchange it needed to service the external debt. In the 1980s the growing cost of servicing the external debt was a major reason for the fiscal deficit and inflation.[2] The government faced the problem of extracting resources from the public to finance the debt service and it had to resort to inflation tax as a means of overcoming the resistance of society to the internal transfer of resources to the budget. Large fiscal deficits were monetised, thereby generating additional inflationary pressures.

Shock Therapy

The early 1990s were a unique period in Poland's postwar history and economic policy. On the one hand, the country was faced with the necessity of stopping hyperinflation. On the other hand, the political changes made it possible to liberalise the economy as people were willing to make painful sacrifices in order to transform the country.

Hyperinflation and the reform package

In 1989, the communist government tried to gain some popularity and credibility before the intended power sharing with the democratic opposition. The goal of the government was to revitalise and liberalise the economy. It introduced some essential institutional reforms, the most important elements of which were the demonopolisation of the banking system and trade liberalisation. The lack of a coherent reform programme and constraints imposed by the lack of social support, however, put the government onto the path of a misaligned sectoral liberalisation and propelled the economy towards hyperinflation.

In the spring of 1989 the government liberalised food prices. In an economy of shortages, such a move unleashed strong inflationary pressures. At the same time the government was haphazardly liberalising trade policy. The unreasonable liberalisation of alcohol, tobacco and oil imports eroded the budget revenues obtained from the turnover tax. This contributed to the widening of the budget deficit, which was already growing because budgetary spending was used to boost demand and revitalise economic growth.

What planted the ticking timebomb of hyperinflation into the economy was the premature liberalisation of the foreign exchange market. The first element of foreign exchange liberalisation was the introduction of 'internal' convertibility of the domestic currency. Residents were free to buy and sell foreign currencies against the Polish zloty. This change coincided with accelerating inflation. Consequently the timebomb of dollarisation waited to be detonated by a surge in inflationary expectations, as had happened earlier in several other countries (McKinnon and Mathieson, 1981, pp. 17). The second component of foreign exchange liberalisation was alignment of the official exchange rate with the market rate. This implied a large real devaluation, which produced an additional strong inflationary stimulus. Then the official exchange rate depreciated roughly in line with inflation, which increased the inflation inertia.

The other factors that fuelled inflation resulted from the political events that took place in June 1989, when the communist government decided to organise partially free elections. The elections were overwhelmingly successful for the Solidarity trade union. The high expectations produced by this success and the accelerating inflation forced the new government to introduce wage indexation, the rationale for which was the same as in Latin American countries – to contain the fall in real income levels. The indexation formula that was used, however, was too generous, and it became an autonomous inflationary factor.

The mixture of budget deficit, rising food prices and wage indexation induced a surge in inflationary expectations. In an economy of shortages, people could not shield themselves against inflation tax by converting their money into goods and services. The liberalisation of the domestic foreign exchange market, however, opened the way for them to seek safety in US dollars and the timebomb of dollarisation exploded. The rapid decline in the demand for money produced runaway inflation in the same manner as occurred in Argentina in 1984 (Dornbusch and Tella, 1989, p. 6). In July 1989 the monthly rate of inflation was 9.5 per cent. A month later it jumped to 39.5 per cent.

In autumn 1989 the stabilisation plan was still not ready. The government introduced what it could at that moment – a restrictive monetary policy and a change in the rules of wage indexation. The former produced a rise in interest rates. This contained the dollarisation and pushed down the demand for domestic credit. The shift from domestic to foreign currency was halted. Without access to cheap credit firms could not afford to raise wages along with prices. The fall in absorption pushed down the monthly rate of inflation from 54.8 per cent in October to 17.7 per cent in December 1989.

In January 1990 the government launched a tough adjustment programme (the Balcerowicz Plan) aimed at stabilising and opening the economy. Initially the programme was a mixture of 46 per cent devaluation and restrictive financial policies. The major element of the programme was the introduction of a convertible currency with a stable exchange rate against the US dollar. Poland declared convertibility on the current account and subsequently fixed the nominal exchange rate in an attempt to provide an anchor for the price system. What was specific in the case of Poland, a previously centrally planned economy, was a price liberalisation aimed at correcting the misaligned relative prices. The price system was liberalised almost entirely, most prices being freed during the first week of January.

The real devaluation and the corrective inflation caused the monthly rate of inflation to shoot up to 79.6 per cent. This required very tough stabilisation measures that were only made possible by the democratisation of the country. People began to perceive the government as their own and consequently accepted its draconian incomes policy. The government implemented the rule that the rise in wages would compensate only 20 per cent of the rise in prices. The wage ceilings were enforced through a steeply progressive tax penalty. The result was a dramatic fall in real incomes. In March 1990 declining domestic demand dragged down the monthly rate of inflation to 4.3 per cent.

Results of the shock therapy

The main goals of the Balcerowicz Plan were to defeat inflation, establish external equilibrium and transform the economy from a tightly centralised system into a market-oriented one. The adjustment programme implemented in Poland bears some remarkable similarities to those undertaken in Brazil and Mexico in the early 1980s. The programme was a mixture of real devaluation and financial restrictions; that is, it followed the guidelines of the absorption theory approach to the balance of payments.

Absorption theory assumes that devaluation combined with financial restrictions brings about an improvement in the trade account of the balance of payments, because financial restrictions curb domestic demand (absorption) and support the devaluation to produce a proexport switch in domestic production. With tight monetary and fiscal policies firms are not able to raise wages along with the rise in prices produced by the devaluation. This produces a fall in domestic absorption, which releases resources for exports. Two principal conditions, however, have to be fulfilled to achieve such a proexport switch without causing recession.

First, the economy must be open. It should produce mainly tradables; that is, goods and services that can compete in international markets. In such an economy it is easy for domestic firms to respond swiftly to changes in the structure of demand. Consequently they are able to redirect their sales from domestic to foreign markets. The second condition is a high mobility of resources between sectors producing for domestic markets and those producing for external markets.

In Latin America these conditions were only partially fulfilled. The typical characteristics of Latin American economies were low mobility of resources and structural inflationary tensions stemming from the inward-oriented economic systems (Sachs, 1989, p. 21). These were the most important reasons why Latin American adjustment policies brought about recession. As far as the Polish economy is concerned, the structural imbalances were greater and the mobility of resources even lower. Consequently the drop in production was much greater.

The fall in production resulted from the restrictive financial policies and from domestic firms being affected by the hike in import prices but unable to switch their production rapidly into external markets. The important reasons for the drop in production were the disappearance of the previous artificial demand structures produced by central planning and a highly protected economic system.

For Polish firms, the adjustment policies were a real shock treatment. In an instant they were deprived of all they had enjoyed for decades; that is, government orders, cheap credit, and fiscal and trade privileges. More than a fall in production, this produced a kind of inward collapse of the previously inflated production levels. In many cases, the reaction of firms was similar to that of their Latin American counterparts: they waited for the collapse of the government stabilisation programme and restoration of the previous protective system. Such a 'survival strategy' deepened the fall in production, which was augmented by the collapse of trade with the USSR, previously Poland's largest trading partner. In 1990 all these factors produced a 26 per cent decline in domestic production. Of course, unemployment was also climbing rapidly.

Although the price was high, the adjustment programme had spectacular results. It stopped hyperinflation and produced a substantial improvement in the trade account of Poland's balance of payments. The surplus in the trade account restored exchange reserves, which enabled the government to maintain the convertibility of the Polish zloty and to use the exchange rate as the nominal anchor of the stabilisation policy.

However, the results of the stabilisation plan appeared more impressive than they actually were. On the plus side, the shock treatment made it possible not only to stop inflation but also to improve the budgetary situation. The stabilisation package contained a massive reduction in government expenditure, mostly through the elimination of subsidies to state-owned firms. While the initial fiscal adjustment was substantial, allowing a closing of the gap between revenues and outlays, its success was short-lived. The improvement in the budget was mostly the product of corrective inflation, although the rise in prices and the tough income policies produced a substantial increase in firms' profits.

The second factor behind the unexpected fiscal surplus was large capital gains on firms' dollar deposits after the 46 per cent devaluation of the zloty. Budget revenues grew substantially and, for a while, there was a surplus in the budget. The fall in production, however, caused a decline in budget revenues. As in Latin American countries, the growing budget deficit became the major problem to be faced by Poland's economic policy subsequent to the launch of the adjustment programme.

Southern Cone syndrome

As highlighted above, the initial package of Poland's adjustment policies was structured according to the prescriptions of the absorption approach to the balance of payments. A major component of the programme was real devaluation of the domestic currency. At the beginning it was not believed that the fixed exchange rate would be maintained for more than a couple of months. Contrary to expectations, the authorities managed to sustain a fixed exchange rate throughout 1990 despite the substantial real appreciation observed, particularly in the first months of the year. This gave the reform the credibility it needed. Furthermore, it afforded the opportunity to conduct adjustment policies following the guidelines of the monetary approach to the balance of payments. Subsequently, monetary policy became the main tool of the adjustment policies

In 1991–2, the events in Poland's economy unfolded in a way similar to those that took place in Chile and Argentina in the late 1970s and early 1980s. Although the sequence of events did not exactly follow the Southern Cone pattern, some similarities do stand out. The relevant interactions are depicted in Figure 6.1. Whilst, given its budget deficit, the Polish situation seemed similar to that of Argentina, a distinct feature of Polish economic policy was that the Central Bank was very strict in adjusting its monetary policy to changes in the balance of payments, as was the case in Chile.

Figure 6.1 focuses on the budget deficit because, since the second half of 1990, it has been the main problem of Poland's economic policy. In 1991, the government increased the tax burden imposed on firms to halt the deterioration in the budget. The tax burden, however, turned out to be unsustainable. Firms' profits had already been eroded by the recession, high interest rates and the real appreciation of the zloty. The final result of the enlarged tax burden was a further drop in production and a further decrease in budget tax revenues (Bolkowiak and Majewicz, 1992). Poland was on the wrong side of the Laffer curve with respect to corporate taxes.

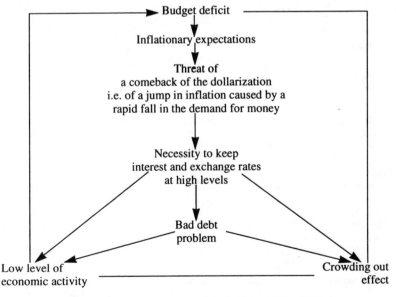

Figure 6.1   Consequences of the budget deficit, 1991–2

In 1990, Poland experienced a real exchange rate appreciation that reduced the competitiveness of exports. In May 1991, the deteriorating trade balance forced the government to devalue and float the zloty. The exchange rate was adjusted by 15 per cent and pegged to a basket of five currencies. The adopted system was similar to a preannounced crawling peg.

The exchange rate began to depreciate at a daily rate of nine zlotys per US dollar, resulting in a monthly depreciation rate of about 2 per cent (Table 6.1). The programme was similar to that of the *tablita* – the initial rate of devaluation was deliberately set at a rate lower than existing inflation in order to provide a clear signal to the general public that the

Table 6.1   Zloty exchange rate, 1991–2 (December 1989 = 100)

	Official rate	Nominal effective rate	Real effective rate (prices)	Real effective rate (wages)
1991:				
January	175.1	192.8	49.0	78.6
February	175.1	189.9	45.2	68.9
March	175.1	175.2	39.9	61.3
April	175.1	174.2	38.7	61.7
May	188.8	188.2	40.7	68.3
June	210.0	202.1	41.6	74.3
July	211.2	208.3	42.9	71.3
August	208.0	205.3	42.0	70.4
September	205.6	206.7	40.5	67.4
October	205.5	207.1	39.3	62.1
November	204.8	211.9	30.0	59.0
December	204.1	216.2	38.6	54.1
1992:				
January	207.3	218.7	36.3	60.4
February	217.8	225.7	36.8	62.8
March	247.8	252.3	40.4	65.3
April	251.1	257.2	39.7	63.6
May	252.6	262.2	38.9	67.6
June	252.6	257.5	39.1	65.8
July	249.3	273.6	39.4	61.6
August	250.5	279.5	39.2	61.6
September	255.1	284.6	38.9	59.7
October	264.6	289.6	37.4	58.6
November	280.7	293.6	37.1	58.2
December	284.8	297.9	36.8	54.0

Source: Wyczanski (1993a).

government was determined to push down the rate of inflation to the rate of the preannounced devaluations. The new exchange rate mechanism, in combination with monetary disinflation, led to further real appreciation.

For several reasons, the government was not in a position to lower the interest rate or substantially devalue the zloty. The main reason for this was the fragility of the public's confidence with respect to the domestic currency. What was undermining confidence in the zloty was the budget deficit. Any sign of weakness on the part the monetary authorities could have produced a surge in inflationary expectations. This could have provoked dollarisation and runaway inflation.

There were also fiscal reasons for not devaluing the domestic currency; that is, the necessity to push down the costs of servicing the external debt. In 1990–2, the real appreciation of the Polish zloty greatly reduced budget expenditure on the debt. The trouble was that, under such circumstances, a growing part of the debt service was indirectly financed by exporters as they were getting less and less for their export earnings.

The decision to devalue the zloty and increase the cost of the external debt service would have been very difficult to take given the situation of rapidly growing internal debt. The widening budget deficit forced the government to increase its issue of domestic debt instruments. In a situation in which the real interest rate was higher than the rate of economic growth, the issuing of government securities produced a snowball effect of rapidly accumulating domestic debt. Further nominal devaluations would add to the fiscal burden of the external debt service.

The real interest rate (Table 6.2) reflected a mixture of tight credit and risk premiums, reflecting the possibility of exchange rate depreciation. High interest rates led to a rapid increase in nonperforming loans. It was not possible for firms to pay high real interest rates when output was falling. They were not borrowing to invest or to finance working capital, but to avoid bankruptcy. The deterioration of firms' debt-to-equity ratios eroded the soundness of the banking system. By the end of 1991, bad loans constituted a substantial part of commercial banks' capital and reserves.

The high interest rate produced an increase in domestic savings and growth in the liquidity of the banking system. As a result of the bad debt problem, however, the banks were afraid to lend money to the enterprises. Instead, they bought government securities. Therefore, domestic savings were financing the budget deficit rather than production.

The situation in Poland has been particularly difficult because of a massive crowding-out effect. The shift from money to debt finance with a growing budget deficit led to crowding out, which was severely deflationary. In 1990–2, the entire growth of domestic credit was absorbed by

Table 6.2   Interest rates, Poland, 1991–2

	Refinancing rate	Leading rate	Deposit rate	Inflation rate
1991:				
January	55	55–68	55–66	320
February	72	76–90	73–85	118
March	72	76–90	73–85	70
April	72	76–90	73–85	38
May	59	66–72	60–72	38
June	59	66–72	60–72	78
July	50	57–68	49–63	1
August	44	51–62	42–56	7
September	40	48–62	42–54	66
October	40	46–58	38–54	46
November	40	46–58	38–54	46
December	40	46–58	38–52	44
1992:				
January	40	46–58	38–52	138
February	40	46–58	38–52	24
March	40	46–58	38–56	27
April	40	46–58	38–58	55
May	40	46–58	38–58	60
June	40	46–58	38–58	21
July	38	45–60	38–49	18
August	38	45–60	38–49	38
September	38	45–60	38–49	86
October	38	45–48	38–49	43
November	38	45–48	38–50	38
December	38	45–48	38–52	31

Source: Wyczanski (1993a), p. 99.

budget deficit financing. The nominal growth of credit extended to firms reflected almost exclusively the rate of inflation and the capitalisation of interest payments on the banking system's bad-loans portfolio.

All this created the danger that economic recovery would eventually be aborted as firms would accumulate debt at an unsustainable pace. Nevertheless, there was some hope because of the relatively low rate of inflation and the unexpected resumption of growth in 1992, when industrial production grew by 3 per cent. At the beginning of 1993, the government tried to encourage the budding recovery by cautiously lowering the interest rate level.

External Economic Policies

Poland's adjustment programme was a real shock therapy for firms as they were practically cut off from credit and deprived of the financial privileges they had enjoyed in the past. Under such circumstances the only source of funds available for firms was export earnings. Consequently, the development of the trade account of the balance of payments was a crucial determinant of the level of production.

Trends in the balance of payments

In 1990, the fall in domestic absorption produced a forced switch effect in the industrial sector of the economy. There was a spectacular turnaround on the trade account of the balance of payments. The trade surplus increased from US$0.2 billion in 1989 to US$2.2 billion in 1990. At the beginning of the programme, the only way to finance production was to use up foreign exchange balances, which exporters had been allowed to hold under the previous economic system. Accordingly, from the very start of the adjustment programme, only exporters had the chance to maintain previous production levels. In 1990 the result was a spectacular 43 per cent growth in exports. The large trade surplus, however, was a short-lived phenomenon. Liberalisation of trade flows produced rapid growth in consumer imports. The main reason for this growth was the real appreciation of the domestic currency – as in Chile and Argentina in the early 1980s. This entailed a deterioration of the trade account.

The implementation of the preannounced crawling peg temporarily stopped the deterioration of the trade account. In 1991, however, the trade surplus narrowed to US$51 million, mainly because of continuous growth in imports. In 1992, imports rose by 47 per cent. The surge in imports is probably explained for the most part by the opening up of the economy and the exchange rate appreciation. In 1992 the balance of payments data, based on banking system statistics, showed a US$0.5 billion surplus on the trade account. Nevertheless, the trade balance will probably go into the red, as eventually happened in Mexico after the liberalisation of its external sector (Dornbusch, 1988).

In the early 1990s, Poland's situation was much more difficult than in Latin American countries. As shown in Table 6.3, in the case of Poland there was no substantial inflow of credit or direct investment. Furthermore, there are no grounds for expecting a large capital inflow in the immediate future. There are investment opportunities in Poland, but the risk perceived by the investors is still high. In Mexico and other Latin American countries,

Table 6.3   Poland's balance of payments: main indicators (millions of US dollars)

	1988	1989	1990	1991	1992
Exports	7248	7575	10863	12760	13997
Imports	-6307	-7336	-8649	-12709	-13485
Trade surplus	941	240	2214	51	512
Effective debt repayments	-1586	-1563	-740	-1235	-1538
Private transfers	1422	1144	1676	308	230
Drawings of credit	259	226	428	786	526
Direct investments	-	-	10	117	284
Official reserves					
Increase	561	259	1938	-	473
Decrease	-	-	-	1183	-

Source: National Bank of Poland.

stabilisation policies induced a return of capital into their more familiar markets. In the case of Poland and other East European countries, it will take time for investors to familiarise themselves with the new markets.

The rapid growth of Poland's exports was the result of the forced switch policies. For the growth to continue there is need for a substantial increase in investment. The question is how to release resources for domestic investment when there is no significant capital inflow and domestic credit is being absorbed by the budget deficit. The success of the reform has depended crucially on elimination of the debt overhang and the reduction of resource transfers.

Debt reduction

Poland was able to stop the accumulation of debt because of its agreement with the Paris Club, an accord made possible by the positive results of the IMF-supported adjustment programme. The agreement with the Paris Club, signed in April 1991, envisaged a two-stage 50 per cent debt reduction in real (present value) terms. A 30 per cent reduction was made after IMF approval of the three-year economic programme. The second (20 per cent) stage will be effected after the successful completion of the programme. This unprecedented debt reduction has been made possible by the unique structure of Poland's external debt, with a 66 per cent share of the credit being guaranteed by other governments.

Without this massive debt reduction, by 1995 Poland's external debt would have reached US$100 billion (Antowska-Bartosiewicz and Malecki 1991, pp. 11) and the debt overhang would have deterred the foreign capital inflow so vitally needed to finance the restructuring of the economy (Antowska-Bartosiewicz and Malecki, 1992a). The agreement with the Paris Club provided new breathing space and improved investor confidence, which should result in increasing capital inflow.

The large debt repayments will start at the end of the 1990s. The burden of these repayments, however, will probably ease with economic growth and the expected capital inflows. This process has already started: in 1989 and 1992 the amount of the debt repayments was almost the same; in 1989, however, interest and principal payments amounted to 21 per cent of exports, whereas in 1992 they were only 11 per cent.

As shown in Table 6.4, the agreement with the Paris Club led to a cessation of growth in the stock of debt. In the 1980s, Poland's external debt accumulated because of arrears, but the agreement with the Paris Club adjusted the debt service to conform with Poland's ability to repay the debt. Accordingly there will be no accumulation of arrears, excluding debt under renegotiation.

The debt reduction agreement brought down net external transfers to a level consistent with the restoration of growth at a pace reflecting the country's potential. If the trade account balances in 1994–5, a yearly inflow of about US$2 billion in 1994–5 and US$2.5 billion from 1995–8 will be sufficient to service Poland's eternal debt (Gotz-Kozierkiewicz and Malecki, 1993). Taking into account the results of the adjustment policies and the country's economic potential, there are good reasons to expect an even larger capital inflow.

Table 6.4   Debt service, Poland (billions of US $)

	1989	1990	1991	1992
Total debt	41.4	48.5	48.4	47.0
Interest due	3.5	3.9	3.4	4.7
Interest paid	1.1	0.4	0.9	1.1
Interest paid to exports (%)	14	3.9	6.9	7.8

Source: National Bank of Poland.

There is a positive feedback between the results of adjustment policies and the agreement with the Paris Club. The agreement alleviated the debt burden considerably and the economic reforms of the early 1990s provided the potential to finance the debt service.

One positive result of the economic reform in Poland is that the disappearance of the previously inflated demand structures provided the opportunity to revalue the Polish zloty. Under the previous economic system, domestic production was easily absorbed by inflated demand. It was necessary for the government to keep the exchange rate at a relatively low level in order to create an incentive to export. Consequently, foreign exchange was overpriced and the country had to overpay for the foreign exchange it needed to service the external debt.

Under the new liberalised system, the overpricing of foreign exchange to stimulate exports was no longer necessary because the stabilization policy forced firms to find external markets. Consequently, the share of expenditure on external debt servicing as a proportion of overall budget expenditure has fallen considerably. Thus Poland's ability to finance and service the external debt is improved but not absolute. The real appreciation of the Polish zloty, however, has created the potential to finance this debt when the economy recovers and budget revenues grow.

Poland's improved ability to service the external debt enhanced discussions with commercial banks on the restructuring and reduction operation, as reflected by the rising price of Polish debt in the secondary market. Poland is continuing negotiations with Russia based on the cancellation of mutual claims. Poland's indebtedness to Russia came about in the 1980s because of the rising cost of oil imports. Russia's debt to Poland accumulated in the late 1980s and the early 1990s as a result of declining Russian exports to Poland.

Trade liberalisation

For decades Poland applied a protectionist development strategy based on import substitution to promote industrialisation. Poland's foreign trade system was typical of centrally planned economies. The gist of the system was a state monopoly in foreign trade and strict foreign exchange regulation. Firms did not buy goods and services abroad. Their requirements for imports were established by the central plan. State foreign trade enterprises imported goods according to the guidelines of the plan. Firms would then make payments in domestic currency at the official exchange rate.

In 1990 the government initiated an ambitious and comprehensive programme of trade liberalisation. There was a rapid elimination of the licensing system and a convertible currency was introduced. Trade policy liberalisation was an integral part of stabilisation policy. The government hoped that the 'law of one price' (price competition) would help push down the domestic rate of inflation as much as was possible in the case of an inward-oriented economy.

From 1989 to 1992 imports rose by 84 per cent, a major part of which were consumer goods. Growth in consumer imports played an important role in the government's incomes policy. The progressive appreciation of the domestic currency made imported goods cheaper for domestic consumers, and consequently the appreciation helped to cushion the fall in real incomes caused by the stabilisation policies.

In 1990 trade and fiscal surpluses enabled the implementation of a liberal trade policy. The trade surplus made it possible to avoid the imposition of import duties as an instrument to protect Poland's international reserves. The fiscal surplus made it possible to avoid the imposition of import duties as a source of budget revenues. Accordingly, in 1990 the average level of import duties was temporarily reduced from 18 per cent to 5 per cent.

As described earlier, 1991 brought a deterioration in both the trade account of the balance of payments and the fiscal budget. In addition, imports contributed to the fall in domestic agricultural and industrial production as profit margins fell after tariff reduction. All these factors forced the government to raise import duties to 18 per cent and impose additional tariff protection for some specific branches of production. In August 1991 tariff rates were raised and different levels were established for different commodities: 5 per cent for raw materials, 10–15 per cent for intermediate goods, 20 per cent for agricultural products and textiles, and 35–45 per cent for luxury products.

An additional reason for the increase in tariffs was to have higher tariffs in place before completion of negotiations on association with the European Union – the transition agreement required both parties to refrain from raising the degree of protection once the agreement had come into effect.

The restoration of import barriers was only a temporary phenomenon. The agreement, which was signed in December 1991, envisages the establishment of a free trade area between Poland and the EU (Jasinski and Kotynski, 1992, p. 30). In March 1992, Poland lowered its tariffs on non-agricultural imports from the EU. In coming years, other duties will be reduced under the transition agreement. The process of this reduction is asymmetric. The EU is obliged to reduce its import duties earlier and some protection of Polish industry during the transition period will be maintained. Poland has also been given the right to impose temporary import barriers to protect newly emerging industries or branches that are undergoing deep restructuring. As a result of the economic recession, the EU has delayed its decision to open its market to Polish steel, textiles and food exports. The expected recovery in the world economy, however, will probably pave the way for further integration of the East and West European markets.

The economic transformation required Poland to change its status in the General Agreement on Tariffs and Trade (GATT). Poland joined GATT in 1967 as a centrally planned economy that did not impose import duties. Instead it relied on import licences and foreign exchange controls. Consequently Poland's obligation to GATT was not to reduce the level of import duty barriers but to increase imports. Liberalisation of Poland's trade policy created the need to change this quantitative obligation into an agreement on the level of tariffs and Poland is committed to a long-term policy of lowering tariff levels. It has proposed that it will set the majority of its tariffs in the context of the current renegotiation of its protocol of accession to GATT, which should allow Poland to participate fully in the multilateral trading system as a market economy.

As far as internal economic policy is concerned, it is difficult to define exactly what is adequate protection. As a result of the partial external liberalisation of the 1980s, some branches of production are relatively competitive in international markets. Consequently these branches 'deserve' tariff protection during the period of economic transition. Others, however, need deep restructuring in order to become internationally competitive. In their case, an inflow of foreign capital and foreign management skills are much more essential than trade protection.

The emerging foreign exchange market

The opening up of Poland's economy produced the need to create a foreign exchange market. Firms' profits depend more and more on exports and as a consequence they are more and more exposed to exchange rate risk. This has produced a demand for hedging; that is, a need to develop forward markets.

There are two basic conditions for the establishment of forward markets. The first is an operational interbank spot market. The second is a stable interest rate to enable calculation of interest rate parity. Neither of these conditions were fulfilled at the beginning of Poland's economic reform. Interest rates floated with the rate of inflation. The interbank foreign exchange market was nonexistent. Commercial banks could only sell foreign exchange to the Central Bank. There were two reasons for keeping the foreign exchange market under the control of the Central

Bank. The first was the necessity to protect the official international reserves and the convertibility of the Polish zloty; the second was the fragility of the economic stabilisation.

As mentioned above, the government used the exchange rate as the nominal anchor of its stabilisation programme. Accordingly, it could not afford to be exposed to the risk of uncontrollable devaluations, which could happen if the exchange rate were to be determined in the free inter-bank foreign exchange market. The adopted solution was to control the foreign exchange market and keep the exchange rate at a predetermined level. The rate in the parallel market was kept on a short leash simply by price arbitrage. People could buy and sell foreign exchange in banks at the official rate. Accordingly, the parallel market quotations had to converge with the Central Bank's exchange rate policy.

The floating interest rate and Central Bank control over the foreign exchange rate was a necessity only at the beginning of the stabilisation pro-gramme. Since 1991, the foreign exchange policy of the Central Bank has become more and more liberal. Commercial banks have been allowed to retain more and more foreign exchange, which has enabled the emergence of an interbank foreign exchange market. In addition banks have started to quote and sell forward contracts, which was made possible by the develop-ment of a securities market that provided funds with fixed interest rates.

The interest rate in the interbank money market is still floating with inflation. Transactions in the secondary securities market, however, use fixed interest rates for contracts with different maturities. The fixed inter-est rates allow for the calculation of interest rate parities and fixed exchange rates for transactions in the forward market (Antowska-Bartosiweicz and Malecki, 1992b, p. 30).

Dilemmas of the liberalisation of capital flows

It has been widely accepted that one of the reasons why the Southern Cone experiments with the *tablita* did not bring the expected results was the pre-mature liberalisation of the capital account of the balance of payments. One has to take into account, however, that the liberalisation of the capital account was a logical consequence of adopting the guidelines of the mone-tary approach to the balance of payments. The monetary approach demands that, because of the liberalisation of the capital account, interna-tional capital flows become the major factor in adjusting the supply of money to the demand for money. The price to be paid for the fulfilment of this promise is the necessity to adjust monetary policy to changes in the balance of payments.

This may work in the case of open economies that are fully integrated with the world market. In the late 1970s, however, the economies of Chile and Argentina were still inward-oriented and unbalanced. The massive inflow of capital that took place in both countries after liberalisation of capital flows was not a monetary phenomenon; it mainly reflected the demand for capital. Consequently, Chile and Argentina were exposed to the pressure of massive capital inflows. This resulted in overvaluation of both currencies, which raised the interest rate to an unsustainable level.

In Chile, the Central Bank attempted to neutralise the monetary effects of the foreign capital inflow. Due to the shallow domestic financial market, however, it had to raise interest rates to an extremely high level, which was a major factor in the ensuing recession. In Argentina, the overvaluation of the exchange rate provoked massive capital flight.

Is there a threat that liberalisation of the capital account of Poland's balance of payments could produce similar results as in the Southern Cone of Latin America in the late 1970s? In the case of Poland a massive capital inflow is rather a hypothetical situation. Furthermore, the authorities have set an upper limit on the contracting and guaranteeing of new, nonconcessional external debt with a maturity of more than a year.

Likewise, is there a threat that the real appreciation of the Polish zloty and capital liberalisation will provoke capital flight? Such a situation also seems to be rather hypothetical. What is possible is an inflow of short-term capital looking for profits from interest rate arbitrage.

The general lesson that can be drawn for Eastern Europe from Latin American experiences is the importance of proper sequencing of external liberalisation. The question is, how can liberalisation be sequenced in a situation in which the budget deficit is absorbing the entire real growth in domestic credit? The deterioration in Poland's budget has forced the government partially to liberalise the flows on the capital account in order to sell government paper to foreign investors. This will release a portion of domestic credit for the firms sector. Such a move is against the Latin American lessons as far as the sequencing of liberalisation is concerned and is a product of the narrow breathing space left for Poland's economic policy.

In all probability the inflow of foreign capital to Poland will be somewhat smaller than to Latin American countries. Nevertheless, it will pose a number of risks, including exchange rate appreciation and a widening trade deficit. Latin American experience provides reasons for government supervision and regulation at the stage when flows expand in order to discourage an excessive inflow of certain types of capital. For example, Poland should follow the Latin American experience in discouraging excessive short-term inflows via the use of taxes or reserve requirements.

Latin American Experience and Poland's Economic Policy

In many respects, policy makers in Poland utilised the Latin American experience to structure their package of adjustment policies. The main lesson of the Southern Cone experience is that stabilisation policy must harmonise the movements of all principal economic variables: prices, wages, exchange rates and interest rates. In 1990, Poland adopted a series of nominal anchors, including credit rationing. The exchange rate was supported by the use of consistent monetary and fiscal policies. The system of forward-looking fixation of the nominal exchange rate proved successful. There were only two minor discretional devaluations – in May 1991 and February 1992. In the spring of 1993, the rate of inflation converged with the rate of preannounced nominal devaluations. This made possible the stabilisation of the real exchange rate and allowed the government to lower interest rates.

The main lessons from the Latin American adjustment policies in the 1980s are as follows. First, implementation of policy reforms and the eventual positive economic outcome is a slow process measured in years. Second, governments must take political constraints into account. These lessons are especially difficult to follow in a country without a middle class (a natural base for any stabilisation policy), where the government is under a constant pressure from various social groups wishing to reconstruct the network of trade and monetary and fiscal privileges they had been enjoying for decades.

Poland is experiencing a stabilisation recession that is testing the sociopolitical fibre of the country. Much depends on political stability. Slow economic growth produces a temptation to abandon the fight against inflation. Despite such pressures, successive governments have managed not to change the economic policies adopted in 1990, which priorised stabilisation and external liberalisation. This reflects the general political consensus to continue the policy, the expected reward of which is an inflow of foreign capital.

Another general lesson that can be derived from Latin American experiences is that economic liberalisation is the method of solving the debt problem. There are two major reasons for this. First, stabilisation and external liberalisation create investor confidence. The second is that economic liberalisation has made possible the deflation of previously inflated domestic demand structures. This has enabled a real appreciation of domestic currencies and reduced the fiscal burden of debt service. On a number of occasions in the 1980s Poland devalued its currency to make exports attractive to producers. The successive devaluations, however, augmented the fiscal burden of the debt service. Each devaluation forced the government to pay more for the foreign exchange it needed to service the external debt. Although Latin American countries had similar experience, this 'magnifying' problem was even more difficult for East European countries.

In the shortage economies of Eastern Europe it was necessary to keep the exchange rate at a very low level in order to induce exports. In the case of Poland, the financing of the debt imposed a large burden on budget expenditure. Economic liberalisation deflated the previously excessive domestic demand structures and it was no longer necessary to overprice foreign exchange to induce exports. This change resulted in a large fall in the fiscal burden of the debt service, which opened the opportunity for cooperation with creditors and paved the way for the integration of Poland's economy with the world market.

6.4   CONCLUSION

The key problem of Polish economic policy is that, with a large budget deficit and a shallow money market, control over the money supply can be exercised only at the cost of keeping interest rates at a high level. The authorities have managed to converge the inflation rate with the nominal rate of preannounced devaluations, which alleviated the need to use high interest rates to support the exchange rate. The worsening of the trade account produced by trade liberalisation, however, induced expectations of devaluations that have made it difficult to lower interest rates.

The persistence of high interest rates poses a serious threat to Poland's stabilisation programme. Margins obtained from foreign debt negotiations may not materialise. The gains stemming from reduced resource transfers can be outweighed by rapidly growing budget interest payments on domestic public debt. In 1991–2 interest payments on domestic public debt surged from 11 to 42 trillion zlotys, which accounted for 60 per cent of the budget deficit. Interest payments were crowding out other government expenditures. Low public investment has built up dangerous bottlenecks that stand in the way of an ultimate resumption of growth.

In 1991–2, interest payments on domestic debt kept mounting because the real interest rate was below the growth of output. In 1993 the situation began to reverse itself, because the growth of output climbed above the real interest rate. Consequently the restarting of growth will help to weaken the negative feedback between recession and the budget deficit.

It is believed that the financial constraints imposed by debt financing of the budget will eventually be lifted by foreign capital inflows. In 1991–2 the flow of foreign direct investment was relatively small, but there are good reasons to assume that it will increase substantially. The main reason for this optimism is that there is no threat of a rekindling of inflation or of reimposition of exchange controls.

Poland has made major and costly efforts at very successfully restoring macroequilibrium under very difficult circumstances. The government introduced a number of structural reforms that have dramatically increased the country's export potential. Furthermore, in 1992 the economy improved, despite low foreign capital inflows and a very restrictive policy of disinflation that resulted in a 23 per cent real decline in credit extended to the firms sector (Gotz-Kozierkiewicz and Malecki, 1993, p. 19). The resumption of growth was made possible by the liberalisation of the economy. Although scarce, capital was at least able to move to the most attractive investment opportunities.

It is hoped that the opening of the economy will be successful in attracting foreign capital inflows. In 1994, Poland eliminated all remaining restrictions under Article VIII of the Fund's Articles of Agreement, and the zloty is now eligible to become a fully-fledged convertible currency (and is expected to do so in 1995).

The expected inflow of foreign capital will support economic recovery and increase government revenues, thus providing the funds urgently needed to balance the budget. The resulting improvement in the budget will enable reforms aimed at enhancing domestic savings, for example transforming the social security system from 'pay-as-you-go' to a capitalisation system that will stimulate domestic capital markets and reduce dependence on foreign capital, as was the case in Chile.

Notes

1. The author would like to thank Professor Marcelo De Paiva Abreu for his comments and suggestions.
2. The situation was analogous to that of Argentina and Chile in the 1970s, when the Central Banks of both countries were extending exchange rate guarantees to domestic firms.

References

Abreu, M. P. (1992) 'Trade policies in a heavily indebted economy: Brazil, 1979–1990', discussion paper (Departamento De Economia, Pontificia Universidade Catolica do Rio De Janeiro).

Amadeo, E. J. and J. M. Camargo (1990) 'The political economy of budgets cuts: A suggested scheme of analysis', discussion paper (Departamento De Economia, Pontificia Universidade Catolica do Rio De Janeiro).

Anonymous (1987) *Theoretical Aspects of the Design of Fund-supported Adjustment Programs* (Washington, DC: IMF).

Antowska-Bartosiewicz, I. and W. Malecki (1991) 'Porozumienie z Klubem Paryskim w sprawie polskiego zadluzenia' (The agreement with the Paris Club on Poland's external debt reduction), mimeo (Warsaw: Institute of Finance).

Antowska-Bartosiewicz, I. and W. Malecki (1992a) 'Naplyw kapitalu zagranicznego a wzrost gospodarczy – przypadek gospodarki polskiej' (Foreign capital inflow and the Economic Growth – the case of Poland), mimeo (Warsaw: Institute of Finance).

Antowska-Bartosiewicz, I. and W. Malecki (1992b) 'Terminowy rynek walutowy – propozycje wprowadzenia w Polsce' (A proposal of establishing the forward foreign exchange market in Poland) (Warsaw: Institute of Finance), p. 33.

Bacha, E. L. (1986) 'External Shocks and Growth Prospects: The case of Brazil, 1973–89', *World Development*, vol. 14, no. 8.

Bacha, E. L. (1992) 'Savings and Investment for Growth Resumption in Latin America: The Cases of Argentina, Brazil and Colombia, discussion paper (Departamento De Economia, Pontificia Universidade Catolica do Rio De Janeiro).

Balcerowicz, L. (1992) *800 dni: szok kontrolowany* (800 days: The shock under control) (Warsaw: Polish Printing House, BGW).

Blejer, M. and A. Cheasty (1988) 'High Inflation, Heterodox Stabilisation, and Fiscal Policy', *World Development*, vol. 8.

Blejer, M. and Ke-Young Chu (1989) *Fiscal Policy, Stabilization and Growth in Developing Countries* (Washington, DC: IMF).

Boguszewski, P. (1991) 'Stabilizacja wybranych gospodarek hiperinflacyjnych' (Stabilization in some hyperinflation economies), *Materialy i studia* (Materials and analysis), vol. 12 (Warsaw: National Bank of Poland).

Bolkowiak, M. and A. Majewicz (1992) 'Polityka fiskalna w okresie transformacji a zalamanie sytemu dochodów panstwa' (Fiscal policy in the transformation period and the fall in the budget revenues), mimeo (Warsaw: Institute of Finance).

Bonelli, R., G. Franco and W. Fritsch (1992) *Macroeconomic Instability and Trade Liberalisation in Brazil: Lessons from the 1980s to the 1990s* (Washington, DC: Inter-American Development Bank).

Bruno, M. (1992) 'Stabilization and Reform in Eastern Europe', *IMF Staff Papers*, vol. 4, (Washington, DC), p. 768.

Bruno, M., E. Dornbusch, S. Fisher, and G. Tella (1988) *Inflation Stabilization. The Experience of Israel, Argentina, Brazil, Bolivia and Mexico* (Cambridge, MA: MIT Press).

Cardoso, E. A. and R. Dornbusch (1989) 'Brazilian Debt: A requiem for muddling through', In S. Edwards and F. Larrain (eds), *Debt adjustment and recovery, Latin America's prospects for growth and development* (Oxford: Basil Blackwell).

Corbo, V. (1992) 'Development Strategies and Policies in Latin America: A historical perspective', Occasional Papers (San Francisco: International Center for Economic Growth), p. 22.

Corbo, V.(1992) 'Economic Transformation in Latin America. Lessons for Eastern Europe', *European Economic Review*, vol. 36.

Corbo, V., F. Coricelli and J. Bossak (1991) *Reforming Central and Eastern European Economies: Initial results and challenges* (Washington, DC: World Bank).

Culpeper, R. and S. Griffith-Jones (1992) 'Rapid return of private flows to Latin America: New trends and new policy issues', mimeo (Ottawa: International Development Research Centre).

Diaz, Francisco Gil (1986) 'Government Budget Measurement under Inflation in LDCs', in B. P. Herber (ed.), *Public Finance and Public Debt* (Detroit: Wayne State University Press).

Diaz, Francisco Gil (1989) 'Mexico's Debt Burden', in Sebastian Edwards and Filipe Larrain (eds), *Debt Adjustment and Recovery: Latin American's Prospects for Growth and Development* (London: Basil Blackwell).

Dornbusch, R. (1988) 'Mexico: Stabilization, debt and growth', Economic Policy, no.7.

Dornbusch, R., F. Leslie and C. H. Helmers (1986) *The Open Economy: Tools for policy makers in developing countries,* EDI Series in Economic Development (Oxford University Press).

Dornbusch, R. and G. Tella (1989) *The Political Economy of Argentina: 1946–83* (London: Macmillan).

Edwards, S. (1984) *The Order of Liberalisation of the External Sector in Developing Countries,* Essays in International Finance (Princeton University).

Edwards, S. (1991) 'Stabilization and Liberalization for Policies in Transition: Latin American lessons for Eastern Europe', in Ch. Clauge and G. C. Rauser (eds), *The Emergence of Market Economies in Eastern Europe* (Cambridge, Mass: Blackwell).

Edwards, S. and A. Cox-Edwards (1987) *Monetarism and Liberalization* (New York: Ballinger).

Fanelli, J. M. and R. Frenkel (1992) *On Gradualism, Shock and Sequencing in Economic Adjustment* (Bueno Aires: CEDES).

Fernandez, M. (1985) 'The Expectations Management Approach to Stabilization in Argentina during 1976–82', *World Development,* vol. 13, no. 8.

Fisher, S. (1992) 'Socialist Economy Reform: Lessons of the first three years', mimeo (Cambridge, Mass: MIT).

Frenkel, J. A. and H. G. Johnson (1976) *The Monetary Approach to the Balance of Payments* (London: George Allen & Unwin).

Fritsch, W. and G. H. B. Franco (1991) 'Trade policy issues in Brazil in the 1990s', discussion paper (Pontificia Universidade Catolica do Rio De Janeiro).

Galvez, J. and J. Tybout (1985) 'Microeconomic Adjustment in Chile 1977–81', *World Development,* vol. 13, no. 8.

Gotz-Kozierkiewicz, D. (1992) 'Polityka kursu walutowego a wzrost gospodarcz' (Exchange rate policy and the economic growth), mimeo (Warsaw: Institute of Finance).

Gotz-Kozierkiewicz, D. and W. Malecki (1993) 'Kurs walutowy i zadtuzenie zagraniczne w procesie osiagania równowagi pienieznej' (Exchange rate and external debt during the period of regaining monetary equilibrium), mimeo (Warsaw: Institute of Finance).

Grabowski, B. (1990) 'Monetarne podejscie do teorii bilansu platniczego' (The monetary approach to the balance of payments theory), *Ekonomista,* vol. 2–3.

Gray, C. W. (1991) 'Tax Systems in the Reforming Socialist Economies of Europe', *Communist Economies and Economic Transformation,* vol. 3, pp. 63–79.

Jasinski, L. J. and J. Kotynski (1992) 'Polska polityka handlowa – jaki liberalizm, jaka protekcja? w Otwieranie polskiej gospodarki na wspolprace z zagranica: Mozliwosci i ograniczenia' (Poland's trade policy: How to dose liberalism and protection?) in *Opening of Poland's Economy: Opportunities and barriers* (Warsaw: *IKC*).

Kalicki, K. (1991) 'Polityka pieniezna w okresie realizacji prgramu dostosowawczego' (Monetary policy during the implementation of the adjustment program), *Bank i Kredyt,* vol. 5–6, International economic report (Warsaw: World Economy Research Institute).

Long, M. (1988) *Crisis in the Financial Sector* (Washington, DC: World Bank).

McKinnon, R. I. and D. Mathieson (1981) 'How to Manage a Repressed Economy', *Essays in International Finance* (Princeton, NJ: Princeton University Press).

Meller, P. (1991) 'The Chilean Trade Liberalization and Export Expansion Process (1974–90)' mimeo (Santiago: CIEPLAN).

Meller, P. (1992) *Latin American adjustment and economic reform: Issues and recent experience* (Santiago: CIEPLAN).

Petrei, A. H. and J. Tybout (1985) 'Microeconomic adjustments in Argentina during 1976–1981: The importance of changing levels of financial subsidies', *World Development,* vol. 13, no. 8.

Ramos, J. (1986) *Neoconservative Economics in the Southern Cone of Latin America, 1973–1983* (Baltimore, MD: Johns Hopkins University Press).

Rosati, D. (1990) *Teoria i polityka progamow stabilizacyjnych MFW* (The theory and policy of the IMF adjustment programs) (Warsaw: Institute of Conjuncture and Foreign Trade Prices).

Sachs, J. D. (ed.) (1989) *Developing Country Debt and Economic Performance* (Chicago, IL: University of Chicago Press).

Simonsen, M. H. (1988) 'Price Stabilization and Income Policies: Theory and the Brazilian case study', in Bruno *et al.,* pp. 259–86.

Slawinski, A. (1992) *Polityka stabilizacyjna a bilans platniczy* (Stabilization policy and the balance of payments) (Warsaw: PWN).

Tanzi, V. (1977) 'Inflation, lags in collection and real value of tax revenue', *IMF Staff Papers,* vol. 24.

Wernik, A. (1992) 'Budzet panstwa a transformacja i wzrost' (State budget, transformation and growth), mimeo (Warsaw: Institute of Finance).

Wyczanski, P. (1993a) 'Polityka kursowa na lata dziewiecdzisiate' (Exchange rate policy in the 1990s), *Material and studies* (Warsaw: National Bank of Poland).

Wyczanski, P. (1993b) *Polski system bankowy: 1990–1992* (Polish banking system: 1990–1992) (Warsaw: Fredrich Ebert Stiftung).

7 Stabilisation Lessons for Eastern Europe from Latin America: The Perspective of Monetary and External Sector Policy

Marcelo de Paiva Abreu and José María Fanelli

7.1 INTRODUCTION

Over the last thirteen years, since the beginning of the so called 'debt crisis', the Latin American countries have been undergoing a difficult period of economic adjustment. At the onset of the crisis, these countries tried to attack macro-instability by resorting to traditional short-run adjustment policies. From the mid-1980s onwards, however, it became increasingly clear that adjustment policies alone would not be able to do the job of stabilising the economy. The crisis had induced structural imbalances that were so deep that they not only impeded stabilisation but had also become independent sources of instability. In such a context, policy makers in one Latin American country after the other realised that structural reform policies aimed at attacking the existing imbalances in the fiscal, external and financial fronts were absolutely necessary. Therefore, stabilisation policies began to be complemented with structural reform measures. The general orientation of the reform was, and still is, towards liberalisation, deregulation and the reduction of the role of the state in the economy.

The need to implement structural reforms together with macroeconomic adjustment represents a difficult challenge from the economic policy point of view. There are important interactions between stabilisation and structural reform measures that are largely unknown. The only antecedents in Latin America of these kinds of policies were the programmes implemented in the late 1970s in Argentina, Uruguay and Chile, which resulted in complete failure. In recent years, however, because of the acceleration of the process of transformation, a great deal of knowledge (mostly of the learning-by-doing type) about the interaction of stabilisation and structural reform has accumulated in Latin America.

The purpose of this chapter is to draw some lessons from the recent Latin American experiences with stabilisation and structural reform that could be useful to East European countries, who, in their transition to a market economy, are facing somewhat similar problems to those that have arisen in Latin America since the beginning of the debt crisis.

It must be taken into account, however, that this chapter is just part of a much wider project comprising this objective.[1] Consequently, our treatment of the issue will not be a systematic one. Our main purpose is to complement – from the 'Latin American point of view' – two of the chapters of this book: Karagodin's comparison of the experiences of Russia and Argentina on stabilisation and monetary policy (Chapter 5) and Slawinski's comparison of the experiences of Poland and Brazil on adjustment and the evolution of the external sector (Chapter 6). In doing so, our arguments will emphasise economic policy issues.

Section 7.2 analyses the issues relating to stabilisation that were raised by Slawinski and Karagodin. Section 7.3 assesses the questions posed by these authors regarding the process of structural reform, with emphasis on the financial and external sectors.

7.2   STABILISATION

From the analysis of the Latin American experience regarding the stabilisation-cum-structural reform process, the most important lessons that can be drawn are as follows (Fanelli and Frenkel 1992):

- The achievement of a reasonable degree of macroeconomic stability during the process is crucial in determining the probability of success of the reform package.
- The transitional period is very long and difficult to manage. During this period the economic policy role is decisive in designing the speed and attributes of each stage of liberalisation, especially regarding trade, the decontrolling of the capital account and the financial system.
- The state has a vital role to play with regard to the regulation of the economy. For example, the analysis of the financial crisis in the Southern Cone of Latin America shows that the financial system must be tightly supervised by the authorities, including, eventually, credit rationing and the control of interest rates.
- During the transitional period, there is likely to be an increment in the demand for external credit to finance the restructuring of the economy.

- The transitional period can be very painful and the government has to take political and social constraints into account.

In this section, we analyse the issues relating to stabilisation that were raised in chapters 5 and 6, taking these lessons as our frame of reference. Two of the most important conclusions that Karagodin and Slawinski draw from their analyses of stabilisation in Latin American and Eastern European countries are, first, that pure monetarist policies are inefficient in highly indexed economies and, second, that external support is crucial. We fully agree with these conclusions, but some points deserve to be stressed and expanded on.

According to Karagodin, orthodox stabilisation tools such as monetary restraint and effective demand management are not suitable for fighting inflationary processes because of the presence of 'inertial' elements. Likewise he believes that foreign aid is a necessary condition for a successful stabilisation. There is a link, however, between these two factors. The Latin American experience provides enough evidence to show that the availability of external support and the 'selection' of an orthodox stabilisation strategy by the authorities are not usually independent, specifically because the financial support of the IMF and the World Bank has normally been necessary to the implementation of an orthodox stabilisation programme. In fact, it seems that this is currently the case in Russia. As McKinnon noted in his critical review of the stabilisation experience in Russia, where the reform authorities implemented an extremely orthodox package at the beginning of 1992, they were 'acting in good faith and seemed to be following the advice of international agencies like the IMF and the World Bank and most Western economists' (McKinnon, 1993, p. 14). It is obvious that the authorities' expectation was that by acting in that way, they would increase the probability of receiving substantial external support from the Western countries.

Indeed, more often than not countries that were able to launch 'heterodox' programmes – such as the current ones in Mexico and Argentina – could be innovative in economic policy making because they were able to launch the programmes without the need for external support, at least in the initial stages of the implementation. In Mexico, the *'Pacto'* was launched in December 1987 after the country had accumulated a sufficient amount of reserves as a consequence of the previous recession. In Argentina, the huge trade surplus generated by the 1989 hyperinflation-induced recession led to a significant accumulation of reserves in 1990. This, together with the capital inflows stemming from privatisation, rendered a prior agreement with the IMF unnecessary. The size of Brazilian reserves in 1994 allowed not only the conclusion of debt negotiations without an explicit blessing from the IMF but also the implementation of a new stabilisation programme with a reasonable chance of success if complemented by fiscal discipline as well as structural reforms in the midterm.

It follows, then, that until Russia is able to establish minimal control over foreign exchange flows, and therefore impede the depletion of international reserves through capital flight, it is very unlikely that it will have sufficient degrees of freedom to introduce important innovations in the traditionally recommended orthodox package.

This, however, does not mean that the accumulation of reserves is a sufficient condition for stabilisation. We completely agree with Karagodin when he says that one important lesson to be drawn from Latin America is that external support plays a key role in ensuring the sustainability of the reform process. The availability of reserves only makes the implementation of a stabilisation programme possible. It cannot guarantee its sustainability in the medium run. The experience of countries suffering from high inflation is that, if the stabilisation programme initially succeeds, there is a subsequent marked increment in the demand for foreign credit. This has occurred in countries such as Mexico and Argentina where high inflation regimes existed.

One point that deserves to be mentioned is that, in many Latin American countries, when a significant increase in reserves makes stabilisation feasible, it is usually an endogenous byproduct of instability: reserves accumulated because the highly uncertain context typically generated a macroeconomic scenario characterised by a deep recession and a real-exchange rate level that tended to overshoot its 'equilibrium' value (as is currently the case in Russia). Once the economy is stabilised, however, domestic absorption tends to increase and relative prices begin to change in favour of nontradables. It is during this second stage that the availability of foreign funds becomes critical in supporting the stabilisation process. The increase in the domestic activity level tends to widen the current account disequilibrium and augment the financing needs of the economy. An additional factor with the same effect is that, within a more stable environment, there is usually a recomposition of the internal demand for money; that is, a remonetisation of the economy. If, as in the case of Argentina, the government is reluctant to issue money to finance either itself or the domestic financial system in order to strengthen the programme's credibility, the only remaining source for the creation of money is the accumulation of reserves. Consequently, there will be an additional increase in the use of foreign funds fueled by the economy's remonetisation.

The experience of Latin American countries in the 1990s is a clear example of the key role that the availability of foreign credit plays in the stabilisation process. Inflation and stagnation could only be overcome when the situation of the external capital market changed greatly. The rationing of external credit tended to disappear in a context of falling interest rates, and consequently the stability could be maintained because it was possible to finance the increasing current account deficit that accompanied the gradual stabilisation of many economies in the region. The only case of a country stabilising and growing before this change in the foreign capital market was Chile. However, Chile was not the exception to the rule. Its only particularity was that, while private sources of credit were still being rationed for other countries in the region, Chile received significant amounts of 'nonmarket' external funds from multilateral agencies. It was this privileged treatment that made possible the financing of the current account deficit generated during the stabilisation-cum-structural reform process.

External support is as important to Russia or Poland as it was to Latin America for ensuring sustainability for one important reason: in both cases the occurrence of a sizable negative external shock severely aggravated the disequilibria created by the ongoing disarticulation of the public sector and the monetary system. In the case of Russia, Karagodin correctly calls attention to tight external credit rationing and capital flight as factors exerting pressure on the external gap. From our point of view, however, insufficient emphasis is given to another factor that heavily contributed to worsening Russia's (and the Eastern European countries') external position: the complete disarticulation of the CMEA trading regime. This obliged the country completely to reorganise its commercial flows (and consequently its economic structure) in a context of both instability and scarcity of external financing.

To a certain extent, a comparison of the cases of Poland and Russia also shows the importance of external support during stabilisation. Poland achieved a much greater degree of stability than Russia, but the former country (together with some of the smaller economies in the former Soviet Union's sphere of influence) was able to obtain relatively favourable treatment in relation to foreign debt and trade. Indeed, because of the fact that the bulk of external credit in Latin America in the 1990s was provided via market sources, there is no Latin American counterpart of the Paris Club decision to halve Poland's foreign debt (ironically with a sizable Brazilian contribution as a creditor). Regarding the external sector, it should also be mentioned that another factor that could greatly help the future evolution of Eastern European economies is that access to developed markets is recognised as a legitimate right of these new market-oriented economies even if there are many problems of adjustment, especially commercial relations with the European Union.

The previous arguments emphasised the importance that a reasonable level of reserves and access to external credit markets have in achieving stabilisation, but it was not intended to downgrade the relevance of other factors. Specifically, two additional factors are extremely important in determining the evolution of stabilisation: the fiscal and the political. It is very difficult for a country to maintain a minimum degree of stability without a sustainable fiscal adjustment. The attainment of a minimum degree of political stability and a consensus on the characteristics of economic adjustment are also necessary.

The evolution of the Brazilian economy in recent years is very illustrative regarding the role of fiscal factors. Since the mid-1980s, Brazil has had no special difficulty in adjusting the balance of payments, given that the United States' macroeconomic policies helped to improve demand for exports and reduce the foreign debt burden through a reduction in interest rates. Because the bulk of foreign indebtedness had been transferred to the government before 1982, the relevant constraint in the adjustment process became fiscal rather than foreign exchange because of the failure of successive attempts to close the fiscal gap. As a consequence, since 1981 Brazil's economic performance has continued to be little short of disastrous, periods of high inflation alternating with short periods of stable prices following stabilisation efforts based first on a monetarist outlook and then on different nuances of inertial interpretations of inflation causality.

Difficulties with the fiscal constraint were the main reasons for the failure of the Cruzado Plan in 1986, as the initial success in reversing inflationary expectations was squandered because of the government's reluctance to adjust public accounts. The Collor Plan in 1990 failed for similar reasons – the premature, *ad hoc* thawing of frozen assets and the inability to put public finances in order – together with a credibility crisis due to widespread government corruption. In spite of Brazil's much better position regarding the current account, compared with Argentina or Mexico, the persistence of fiscal disequilibrium meant that Brazil was still in deep trouble thirteen years after the beginning of the economic crisis that had been prompted by difficulties with the debt service in 1981. The effect that this lack of stability has had on growth is impressive: per capita GDP in 1992 was 8 per cent below its 1980 level.

Regarding the role of political factors, Brazil's experience with stabilisation is also very relevant, especially for Russia and other transition economies suffering from political instability. In the case of Brazil, in addition to the influence of strictly economic determinants, the evolution of political instability became an independent factor impeding successful fiscal adjustment. The political turmoil that led to President Collor's impeachment resulted in the acceleration of inflation, and there is no clear indication that it will be politically possible to reach the necessary agreement on the fiscal package to reverse this situation. In such a context, foreign reserves have been increasing in recent years as a result of a good export performance and a significant inflow of foreign capital attracted by high domestic interest rates. However this alone will not stabilise the economy. In addition, because of political and macroeconomic uncertainty, not much of this inflow is long-term capital, in contrast with that invested in Latin American economies that did manage to achieve a greater degree of stability.[2]

Indeed, what the Brazilian experience suggests is that the sequencing of political and economic reforms is as important as the sequencing of strictly economic reform measures. In almost all the often quoted successful Latin American episodes of economic stabilisation and structural reform, the economic reform package preceded political reform. It is markedly so in Chile and Mexico, where political reform is proceeding at a slower pace than economic reform, and where either the military is preserving an important political position or single-party political power still prevails. In contrast Brazil's political reform advanced at a much faster pace than economic reform. In Eastern Europe there was considerable additional political scope in the implementation of tough economic policies, given the massive political support for a change in policies associated with communist governments. A taxonomy similar to that applied to Latin American economies would position Poland with Chile and Mexico, while Russia would be most akin to Brazil.

While the rewards of economic reform are very concrete in terms of its impact on decisions by the international financial community, international businesses, relevant international organisations and foreign governments, political good behaviour is less likely to be well rewarded. This is especially the case in Brazil, where such advances have been marred by a marked deterioration in social conditions and signs exist of a governance crisis. In addition, opposition to liberalising reforms in Brazil was more significant, as from the beginning of the century until 1980 the model based on import substitution (or repression from the 1970s) and export promotion had been spectacularly successful, even if compared with high-growth countries such as Japan and South Korea. In this sense, another lesson provided by the Brazilian experience is that the design of the structural reform process must take into account the fact that history matters. Unlike other primary exporters, the lack of a *laissez faire* tradition in Brazil was an additional factor against reform.

One last lesson we would like to stress regarding the stabilisation process – taking into account not only the current Brazilian experience but also that of many Latin American countries during the debt crisis (notably Argentina and Peru) – is that the failure of one stabilisation plan makes the next one all the more difficult. Repeated 'shock' stabilisation efforts are by definition increasingly less effective because economic agents learn how to protect their interests, making it increasingly difficult to reverse inflationary expectations.

The persistence of macroeconomic instability not only tends to reduce the effectiveness of an adjustment programme, it also makes structural reforms less likely to succeed. In the case of Brazil, for example, of the broad economic reform package attempted in 1990, only the trade liberalisation and privatisation elements survive, and even they are facing increasing pressure from unfavourably affected lobbies. The longer high inflation persists, the more likely it is that these efforts will be reversed or paralysed. In Chapter 6 Slawinski also noted that Poland's experience shows that external liberalisation comes only after a long period of domestic stabilisation. While it may not always be true that stabilisation is a precondition for liberalisation, it is certainly true that high inflation is likely to have an adverse effect on structural reforms.

7.3　STRUCTURAL REFORMS

Both Slawinski and Karagodin mention that there is much to be learned from the Latin American experience regarding the problem of the proper sequencing of economic policies. Specifically, these authors make some important remarks on the relationship between the opening of the trade and capital accounts. We agree about the relevance of the stylised facts of the sequencing of economic reforms in Latin America as a frame of reference when designing structural reforms in Eastern European transition economies. We will make some comments on this as they may complement Karagodin's and Slawinski's remarks, especially regarding the relationship between stabilisation and structural reform.[3]

Russia is presently undergoing a process of extreme macroeconomic instability and therefore a profound reform of the economic structure is badly needed. Without the dramatic features of Russia's current situation, other Eastern European economies are also implementing (or need to implement) deep structural reforms, consisting of privatisation, financial liberalisation and the opening of the economy. This situation is very similar to that which prevailed in most Latin American countries after the debt crisis of the early 1980s when, unlike the experience of other reforming countries (for example, Spain), the structural reforms oriented towards market 'liberalisation' had to be implemented in a situation of marked macroeconomic disequilibrium. It is precisely the existence of a disequilibrium context that makes the Latin American experience with stabilisation and structural reform highly relevant to Russia and other transition economies. The collection and systematisation of the available empirical evidence regarding Latin America can be of great help as a first step to a better understanding and design of the sequence of economic policies in Eastern European countries, because we do not have sound theoretical models to assess *a priori* the effects of liberalisation when pervasive market disequilibria exist.

Given the lack of sound theoretical bases, in the current mainstream approach to the problem of sequencing there is a common sense-based sharp distinction between two stages of the reform.[4] During stage one, economic policy should focus almost completely on establishing a sound macroeconomic setting. Achieving control of fiscal and monetary variables and correcting relative prices should be the priority at this stage. For the alignment of relative prices, devaluation and domestic price decontrol are typically recommended. Once the economy has achieved an acceptable degree of macroeconomic stability, stage two should be launched; that is, implementation of the market friendly package (privatisation, elimination of nontrade barriers and tariff reduction, decontrol of the domestic financial system, and so on).

Although it is true that structural reform is not possible without achieving a minimum degree of stability, the framework based on the distinction between stabilisation and liberalisation reforms may be inappropriate as a guide to policy making in Russia and other transition economies. In this respect, the experience of the (up to now) more successful Latin American countries has highlighted two important points. First, stabilisation and structural reforms are not independent; indeed there are complicated interactions between the two. Second, because of the constraints posed by macroeconomic imbalances, the reforms implemented did not always imply a move towards market liberalisation.

In the case of countries such as Argentina, Mexico and even Chile, stabilisation and structural reform were not independent for one important reason: more often than not, market-friendly reforms were implemented because they could significantly contribute to the reduction of existing macroeconomic imbalances and not because the authorities were pursuing – independently of the aim of stabilising – greater efficiency in resource allocation. In Argentina, for example, privatisation was initially conceived of as a means of simultaneously closing the fiscal and external gaps. This means that, when maximisation of fiscal revenues and/or foreign funds originating in the privatisation process conflicted with efficiency, the former objective took precedence. The same kind of trade-off has been faced by the authorities of Latin American countries that have implemented debt–equity swap schemes – the authorities have always chosen that which was more favourable to macroeconomic stability. A second important reason why macroeconomic policy and structural reform are not independent is that the transformation process is long lasting and tends to generate important disequilibria. Consequently, if stability is hampered by structural reform it is very likely that the reform process will be interrupted. The Latin American experience provides rich examples of this, especially if one takes into account the Southern Cone liberalisation attempts of the late 1970s.

This kind of interaction between stability and reform in a disequilibrium context explains why not all the reforms are market friendly, irrespective of the authorities' convictions. In Latin America, the need to ensure a minimum level of fiscal and monetary control has often led to the implementation of 'structural reforms' that do not favour market liberalisation; indeed they may be viewed more as 'market repression'. As a first step to regaining control over the monetary base in the period prior to the launch of the ongoing Convertibility Plan, the Argentine government implemented the so-called Bonex Plan, which involved the expropriation of a significant part of domestic financial assets. In Chile, after the financial crisis of the early 1980s, there was a massive *de facto* nationalisation of the financial system. The banking sector was not privatised, but gradually liberalised until the government had 'cleaned' the banks' balance sheets and property rights. In Mexico, in spite of the overall movement of economic policy towards market liberalisation, together with the launching of stabilisation, a 'social pact' was signed that implied tight control on the evolution of key nominal prices and wages. For strictly macroeconomic reasons, neither Chile nor Mexico even considered the possibility of privatising the state-owned copper and petroleum firms, which are primary sources of fiscal revenue.

These kinds of stylised facts regarding the Latin American experience of reforming in a context of marked disequilibrium speak favourably of a pragmatic approach to economic policy making. From our point of view, such an approach can greatly help in designing economic policy in Russia, especially taking into account the discouraging results of the big-bang approach adopted in the design of the stabilisation programme launched in January 1992, which Karagodin has described so well in Chapter 5.

The questions posed by the present transitional period in Russia, Poland and other Eastern European economies, nonetheless, seem to be much more complex than those pertaining to Latin America. The most important factor is that there are many more 'missing' markets in the transitional Eastern European economies than in the Latin American ones. The absence of a well-structured market system implies that market failures are more pervasive in Russia than in Latin America. For instance, in Latin America one important market failure is the narrowness of the long-run market for credit, but in Russia there are no financial markets in the true sense of the word, even ones for financing short-term borrowing needs. This, in turn, makes the problem of capital flight even worse. In a highly inflationary context, the nonexistence of short-run financial assets implies that agents have no financial assets but foreign currency to hedge against inflation.

In addition, market failures interact perversely with coordination failures at the macroeconomic level. The absence of a long-run market for government bonds, for example, makes the smoothing of the adjustment effort impossible. Not only is financing the structural change of the economy difficult, but also the public sector cannot finance its own restructuring and hence has to resort to money creation in a systematic way.

This weakness in the existing market structure implies that – notably in Russia but also in the other Eastern European economies – market creation seems to be a much more important task than market liberalisation. However market creation is not only economic in character. It implies deep institutional reform that range from the clarification of property rights to the creation of a true capitalist financial system. The existence of these problems in the transition economies renders meaningless many of the questions traditionality examined under the heading of 'stabilisation policy'.

For example, in the Latin American context, as Karagodin mentions, adjustment primarily implies tightening the budget constraint of both the public and the private sector – in the case of the former by means of fiscal adjustment and in the latter by means of monetary restriction. In the case of Russia and other Eastern European economies, the uncertainty regarding the division of public/private and property rights makes the budget constraints each agent faces, either in the public or the private sector, extremely soft. This is so, for example, in the case of the budget constraint of firms when they can avoid paying their debts without going bankrupt. It is easier to incur arrears in a context in which there is no clear enforcement of contracts because it is not known who the parties to such a contract are.

It follows that, unlike Latin American countries, Eastern European countries need to clarify the structure of property rights and to define the responsibilities of each part of the government regarding expenditures and taxes before implementing strong fiscal or monetary policies. That is, it is necessary to define the budget before hardening the budget constraint which economic agents face in both the private and the public sector. This means that the role of the state will be crucial in the coming years, and consequently both stabilisation and structural reform should focus on fortifying the state's autonomy. To be sure, this does not mean that the ongoing process to reduce the economic influence of the state and to strengthen the private sector should be interrupted. Nor does it imply that we ignore the fact that government failures can be as distortive to economic efficiency as market ones.

Precisely because it is not possible to induce an immediate and once-and-for-all liberalisation of an economy and there is a long transitional period of which very little is known, we believe that the approach to economic policy design and implementation must be very pragmatic. Instead of beginning from a rather abstract notion of a fully liberalised economic setting, and examining the supposedly correct sequence of steps needed to reach it without difficulty, it would be more fruitful to examine concrete reform steps and to analyse the specific dynamics they generate in a disequilibrium context. It is necessary to make room for the potential role that both government and market failures could play in determining the effects of specific measures.

An additional reason why the approach during the implementation of reforms should be pragmatic is that the possibility that the dynamic path generated by the reform could be explosive should not be overlooked. The Latin American experience shows that in a disequilibrium and a highly unstable economic setting it is unlikely that the economic behaviour of individuals will be flexible and rapid enough to adapt to radical changes in the economic environment induced by structural reform policies. In a highly uncertain context, defensive and conservative behaviour can be highly profitable to the extent that it guarantees a greater flexibility in the decision-making process. The lack of rapid adaptation to the new rules established by policy makers is, indeed, a typical source of coordination failure. If the agents' behaviour does not change in the right direction when the government radically modifies the economic setting, the consequences in terms of instability can be severe.

This has typically been the case of the cycles of protection/opening/balance-of-payment crisis/protection in Argentina, Chile and other Latin American countries. In order to make the programme more credible, the authorities launch quick and ambitious measures to open the economy. It is expected that the private sector will take the new setting as a permanent one, and consequently will invest in restructuring firms to enable them to cope with external competition. However, due to the fact that the impact-effect of these kinds of programmes generates a significant increase in imports, the current account begins to show wide and increasing deficits. Taking into account this new piece of information about the widening of the external gap, the private sector anticipates that the new policy will not last long, and consequently does not invest in restructuring. Private agents choose to maintain a greater degree of flexibility in decision making and hold their assets in a liquid form in anticipation of macroeconomic turmoil. In such a situation, it is very likely that exports will stagnate because of the lack of investment in the tradable sectors and, given the upward trend in imports, the current account deficit could become unsustainable. In order to avoid an external payments crisis the authorities are forced to increase tariffs and/or reestablish quantity controls, and to implement complementary measures such as strict control on capital account transactions. *Ex post*, economic policy validates the conservative behaviour of private agents to the extent that the programme of opening the economy is reverted. The appearance of destablising trends in the evolution of the current account during the reform process becomes the most important factor explaining the failure of the attempt at structurally transforming the economy.

The current situation in Russia is a case in point regarding the role of explosive trends during the adjustment process, but it is a fact that many liberalisation attempts have given rise to explosions. Given this tendency, if destablising trends are identified when a reform package is implemented, the authorities in charge of the reform should be prepared to face that fact as quickly as possible. In designing the proper instruments to deactivate explosive trends, an ideological rather than pragmatic approach may result in not only greater instability but also in reversion of the structural reform process.

Notes

1. On the characteristics of the project, see Chapter 1 of this volume.
2. In the last few months of 1994 and the beginning of 1995 significant success has been obtained in Brazil in the battle to reduce the fiscal deficit, eliminate high inflation and attract productive investment. While the war is certainly not over, observers are mostly optimistic that this situation will continue.
3. The problem of sequencing is more systematically treated in Chapter 1 of this volume.

4.   See, for example, Guitián (1987), Williamson (1990) or the 1991 World
      Development Report (World Bank, 1991), which analyses the relationship
      between stabilisation and structural reform.

References

Fanelli, José María and Roberto Frenkel (1992) 'On Gradualism, Shock Treatment
     and Sequencing', in *International Monetary and Financing Issues for the 1990s*,
     vol. 2 (New York: UNCTAD, United Nations).
Guitián, Manuel (1987) 'Adjustment and Economic Growth: Their Fundamental
     Complementarity', in V. Corbo *et. al.* (eds), *Growth-Oriented Adjustment
     Programs* (Washington, DC: International Monetary Fund and World Bank).
McKinnon, Ronald I. (1993) 'Gradual versus Rapid Liberalization in Socialist
     Economies: Financial Policies and Microeconomic Stability in China and Russia
     Compared', Annual Bank Conference on Development Economics (Washington
     DC: World Bank).
Williamson, John (1990) 'What Washington Means by Policy Reform', in John
     Williamson, *Latin American Adjustment. How Much has Happened?*
     (Washington: Institute for International Economics).
World Bank (1991) *World Development Report* (Washington: World Bank).

Bibliography

Abreu, Marcelo P. (1992) 'Trade policies in a heavily indebted economy: Brazil, 1979–1990', discussion paper (Departmento De Economia, Pontificia Universidade Catolica do Rio De Janeiro, June).

Abreu, Marcelo and José María Fanelli (1994) 'Stabilization Lessons for Eastern Europe from Latin America: The Perspective of Monetary and External Sector Policy', mimeo (Pontificia Universidade Catolica do Rio de Janeiro, Brazil, and CEDES, Buenos Aires, Argentina).

Agrawal, Pradeep *et al.* (1995) *Economic Restructuring in East Asia and India: Lessons in Policy Reform* (London: Macmillan).

Amadeo, E. J. and J. M. Camargo (1990) 'The political economy of budgets cuts: A suggested scheme of analysis', discussion paper (Departamento De Economia, Pontificia Universidade Do Rio De Janeiro).

Anonymous (1987) 'Theoretical aspects of the design of fund-supported adjustment programs' (Washington: IMF).

Antowaska-Bartosiewicz, I. and W. Malecki (1991) 'Porozumienie z Klubem Paryskim w sparawie polskiego zadluzenia' (The agreement with the Paris Club on Poland's external debt reduction), mimeo (Warsaw: Institute of Finance).

Antowska-Bartosiewicz, I. and W. Malecki (1992) 'Naplyw kapitalu zagranicznego a wzrost gospodarczy – przypadek gospodarki polskiej' (Foreign capital inflow and economic growth – the case of Poland), mimeo (Warsaw: Institute of Finance).

Antowska-Bartosiewicz, I. and W. Malecki (1992) 'Terminowy rynek walutowy – propozycje wprowadzenia w Polsce' (A proposal of establishing the forward foreign exchange market in Poland) (Warsaw: Institute of Finance), p. 33.

Arrow, K. (1991) 'Transition from Socialism', *Estudious Económicos*, vol. 6, pp. 5–22.

Bacha, E. L. (1986) 'External shocks and growth prospects: The case of Brazil, 1973–89', *World Development,* vol. 14, no. 8.

Bacha, E. L. (1992) 'Savings and investment for growth resumption in Latin America: The Cases of Argentina, Brazil and Colombia', discussion paper (Departamento De Economia, Pontificia Universidade Catolica do Rio De Janeiro).

Balcerowicz, L. (1992) *800 dni: szok kontrolowany* (800 days: The shock under control) (Warsaw: Polish Printing House, Bqw).

Banco de Mexico (1992) *The Mexican Economy* (Mexico City: Banco de Mexico).

Bird, R. (1992), 'Tax Reform in Latin America', *Latin American Research Review,* vol. 27, no. 1, pp. 7–36.

Bitran, E. and Sáez, R. E. (1994) 'Privatization and Regulation in Chile', in B. Bosworth, R. Dornbusch and R. Labán (eds), *The Chilean Economy: Policy Lessons and Challenges* (Washington, DC: The Brookings Institution).

Blejer, M. and A. Cheasty (1988) 'High Inflation, Heterodox Stabilization, and Fiscal Policy, *World Development,* vol. 8.

Blejer, M. and Ke-Young Chu (1989) *Fiscal Policy, Stabilization and Growth in Developing Countries* (Washington, DC: IMF).

237

238   Bibliography

Boguszewski, P. (1991) 'Stablizacja wybranych gospodarek hiperinflacyjnych' (Stabilization in some hyperinflation economics), *Materialy i studia* (Materials and analysis), vol. 12 (Warsaw: National Bank of Poland).

Bolkowiak, M. (1992) 'Majewicz, polityka fiskalna w okresie transformacji a załamanie sytemu dochodów panstwa' (Fiscal policy in the transformation period and the fall in the budget revenues), mimeo (Warsaw: Institute of Finance).

Bolton, P. and G. Roland (1992) 'Privatization Policies in Central and Eastern Europe', *Economic Policy* (15 October).

Bonelli, R., G. Franco and W. Fritsch (1992) *Macroeconomic Instability and Trade Liberalization in Brazil: Lessons from the 1980s to the 1990s* (Washington, DC: Inter-American Development Bank).

Borensztein, Eduardo (1993) 'The Strategy of Reform in the Centrally Planned Economies of Eastern Europe: Lessons and Challenges', *Papers on Policy Analysis and Assessment Series* (Washington, DC: IMF).

Bresser Pereira, Luiz Carlos (1993) 'Economic Reforms and Economic Growth: Efficiency and Politics in Latin American', in L. C. Bresser Pereira, J. M. Maravall and A. Przeworski (eds), *Economic Reforms in New Democracies* (New York: Cambridge University Press).

Bruno, Michael (1992) 'Stabilization and Reform in Eastern Europe', *IMF Staff Papers*, vol. 39, no. 4, pp. 741–77.

Bruno, M., R. Dornbusch, S. Fisher and G. Tella (1988) *Inflation Stabilization: The experience of Israel, Argentina, Brazil, Bolivia and Mexico* (Cambridge, MA: MIT Press).

Burgess, Robin and Nicholas Stern (1993), 'Taxation and Development', *Journal of Economic Literature*, vol. 31, no. 2, pp. 762–830.

Canavese, A. (1991) 'Hyperinflation and convertibility-based stabilization in Argentina', mimeo (Buenos Aires: Instituto Torcuato di Tella).

Caprio, Gerard Jr. and Ross Levine (1994) 'Reforming Finance in Transitional Socialist Economies', *The World Bank Research Observer*, vol. 9, no. 1, pp. 1–24.

Cardoso, Eliana (1991) 'La Privatización en América Latina', in J. Vial (ed:), *Adónde Va América Latina: Balance de las Reformas Económicas* (Santiago: CIEPLAN), pp. 79–100.

Cardoso, E. (1992) 'Privatization in Latin America', paper prepared at the annual meeting of the 'Red de Centros Latinamericanos de Investigation en Macroeconomia', Cartagena, Colombia, 18–20 April.

Cardoso, E. A. and R. Dornbush (1989) 'Brazilian Debt: A requiem for muddling through', in S. Edwards and F. Larrain (eds), *Debt Adjustment and Recovery, Latin America's prospects for growth and development* (Oxford: Basil Blackwell).

Cho, Yoon-Che and Deena Khatkhate (1989) 'Lessons of Financial Liberalization in Asia: A Comparative Study', World Bank Discussion Paper no. 50 (Washington, DC: World Bank).

Cooper, Richard N. (1991) 'Economic Stabilization in Developing Countries', International Center for Economic Growth Occasional Paper no. 14 (San Francisco: ICEG).

Corbo, V. (1992) 'Development Strategies and Policies in Latin America: A historical perspective', International Center for Economic Growth, Occasional Papers (San Francisco: ICEG), p. 22.

Corbo, V. (1992) 'Economic Transformation in Latin America. Lessons for Eastern Europe', *European Economic Review*, vol. 36.

Corbo, V., F. Coricelli and J. Bossak (1991) *Reforming Central and Eastern European Economies: Initial results and challenges* (Washington, DC: World Bank).

Culpeper, R. and S. Griffith-Jones (1992) 'Rapid return of private flows to Latin America: New trends and new policy issues', mimeo (Ottawa: International Development Research Centre).

Damill, M., J. M. Fanelli and R. Frenkel (1991) 'Shock externo y desequilibrio fiscal: Brazil', mimeo (Buenos Aires: CEDES, December).

Devlin, R. (1992) 'Privatization and social welfare in Latin America', unpublished (Santiago).

Diaz, Francisco Gil (1986) 'Government Budget Measurement under Inflation in LDCs' in B. P. Herber (ed.), *Public Finance and Public Debt* (Detroit: Wayne State University Press).

Diaz, Francisco Gil (1989) 'Mexico's Debt Burden', in Sebastian Edwards and Filipe Larrain (eds), *Debt Adjustment and Recovery: Latin America's Prospects for Growth and Development* (London: Basil Blackwell).

Diaz, F. G. and R. R. Tercero (1988) 'Lessons from Mexico', in M. Bruno, *et al.*, *Inflation, Stabilization* (Cambridge, MA: MIT Press).

Dornbusch, R. (1988) 'Mexico: Stabilization, debt and growth', *Economic Policy*, no. 7.

Dornbusch, Rudiger (1990) 'Policies to Move from Stabilization to Growth', *World Bank Economic Review* (Supplement), pp. 19–56.

Dornbusch, R., F. Leslie and C. H. Helmers (1986) 'The Open Economy: Tools for policy makers in developing countries', *EDI Series in Economic Development* (Oxford University Press).

Dornbusch, R. and A. Reynoso (1989) 'Financial Factors in Economic Development', NBER Working Paper no. 2889.

Dornbusch, R. and M. Simonsen (1987) *Inflation Stabilization with Income Policy Support: A review of the experience in Argentina, Brazil, and Israel* (New York: Group of Thirty).

Dornbusch, R., F. Sturzenegger and H. Wolf (1989) 'Extreme Inflation: Dynamics and stabilization', *Brookings Papers on Economic Activity*, no. 1.

Edwards, Sebastian (1984) 'The order of liberalisation of the external sector in developing countries', *Essays in International Finance* (Princeton University).

Edwards, Sebastian (1991) 'Stabilization and Liberalization Policies in Central and Eastern Europe: Lessons from Latin America', mimeo, NBER Working Paper no. 3816.

Edwards, Sebastian (1991) 'Stabilization and Liberalization for Policies in Transition: Latin American lessons for Eastern Europe', in Ch. Clauge and G. C. Rauser, (eds), *The Emergence of Market Economies in Eastern Europe* (Ballinger).

Edwards, Sebastian (1992) 'The Sequencing of Structural Adjustment and Stabilization', ICEG Occasional Paper no. 34 (San Francisco: ICEG).

Edwards, S. and A. Cox-Edwards (1987) *Monetarism and Liberalization* (New York: Ballinger) US.

Fanelli, J. M. and J. Machines (1994) 'Capital Movements in Argentina', mimeo

Fanelli, José and María and Roberto Frenkel (1992) 'On gradualism, shock and sequencing in economic adjustment', Paper prepared for the G-24 (Buenos Aires: CEDES).

Fanelli, José María and Roberto Frenkel (1992) 'On Gradualism, Shock Treatment and Sequencing', in *International Monetary and Financial Issues for the 1990s*, vol. 2, (New York: UNCTAD, United Nations) pp. 73–100.

Fanelli, J. M., R. Frenkel and G. Rozenwurcel (1990) 'Growth and structural reform in Latin American. Where do we stand?', CEDES document no. 57 (Buenos Aires: CEDES).

Fanelli, J.M., R. Frenkel and G. Rozenwurcel (1992) 'Growth and Structural Reform in Latin America. Where we Stand', in A. Zini Jr., *The Market and the State in Economic Development in the 1990s* (Amsterdam: North Holland).

Fanelli, J. M., R. Frenkel and L. Taylor (1992) 'The World Development Report 1991: A critical assessment', CEDES Document no. 78 (Buenos Aires: CEDES).

Fernandez, M. (1985) 'The Expectations Management Approach to Stabilization in Argentina during 1976–82', *World Development*, vol. 13, no. 8.

Fischer, Stanley (1991) 'Privatization in East European Transformation', NBER Working Paper no. 3703 (Cambridge MA: NBER).

Fischer, Stanley (1992) 'Socialist economy reform: Lessons of the first three years', mimeo (Cambridge, Mass: MIT).

Floyd, R., Gray, C. and Short, R. (1984) *Public Enterprises in Mixed Economies*, International Monetary Fund, Washington, DC.

Frenkel, R. (1992) 'Comment on "Latin American adjustment and economic reforms: Issues and recent experience" by Patricio Meller', mimeo (Brunswick, NJ: Rutgers University).

Frenkel, J. A. and H. G. Johnson (1976) *The Monetary Approach to the Balance of Payments* (London: George Allen & Unwin).

Fritsch, W. and G. H. B. Franco (1991) 'Trade policy issues in Brazil in the 1990s', discussion paper Pontificia Universidade Catolica Do Rio De Janeiro.

Galel, A., L. Jones, P. Tandom and I. Gogelsang (1992) 'Synthesis of cases and policy summary, paper presented to a conference on the welfare consequences of seedling public enterprises', World Bank, Washington, DC, 11–12 June 1992.

Galgóczi, B. (1992) 'Strategies of privatization in Hungary' (Budapest, Hungary, unpublished).

Galvez, J. and J. Tybout (1985) 'Microeconomic Adjustment in Chile 1977–81', *World Development*, col. 13, no. 8.

Gelb, A. H. and C. W. Gray, (1991) 'The Transformation of Economics in Central and Eastern Europe', *Policy and Research Service*, no. 17 (Washington, DC: The World Bank).

Gerchunoff, P. and Castro, L. (1992) 'La Racionalidad Macroeconomica de las Privatizaciones: El Caso Argentina', mimeo, CEPAC, Santiago, Chile.

Glade, W. (1991) *Privatization of Public Enterprises in Latin America*, International Center for Economic Growth, Institute of the Americas and Centre for USA–Mexican Studies (San Francisco, CA: ICS Press).

Gotz-Kozierkiewics, D. and W. Malecki (1993) 'Kurs walutowy i zadłużenie zagraniczne w procesie osiagania równowagi pieniężnej' (Exchange rate and external debt during the period of regaining monetary equilibrium), mimeo (Warsaw: Institute of Finance).

Government of Brazil (1987) 'Retarturio de Atividades Desemolvidas', Conseho de Privitizacão, Brasilia, Brazil.

Government of Brazil, *Annual Reports*, Secretaria de Controle de Empresas Estalas, 1980–86, Brasilia, Brazil.

Grabowski, B. (1990) 'Monetarne podejscie do teorii bilansu platniczego' (The monetary approach to the balance of payments theory), *Ekonomista*, vols. 2–3.

Gray, C. W. (1991) 'Tax Systems in the Reforming Socialist Economies of Europe', *Communist Economies and Economic Transformation*, vol. 3, pp. 63–79.

Greenaway, David and Chris Milner (1991) 'Fiscal Dependence on Trade Taxes and Trade Policy Reform', *Journal of Development Studies*, vol. 27, no. 3, pp. 95–132.

Guitian, Manuel (1987) 'Adjustment and Economic Growth: Their Fundamental Complementarity', in V. Corbo *et al.* (eds), *Growth-Oriented Adjustment Programs* (Washington, DC: International Monetary Fund and The World Bank).

Hachette, D. and R. Lüders (1992) *La Privatizacion an Chile* (San Francisco: Centro Internacional para el Desarrolla Economico, CINDE).

Helleiner, G. K. (1990) 'Trade Strategy in Medium-Term Adjustment', *World Development*, pp. 879–97.

Hoós, Janos (1992) 'The main features of privatization in Hungary', mimeo, Budapest University (Budapest, Hungary).

Horton, Susan, Ravi Kanbur and Dipak Mazumdar (1991) 'Labour Markets in an Era of Adjustment: An Overview', *Economic Development Institute* WPS 694 (Washington, DC: World Bank).

International Monetary Fund (1993) 'Transition to a Market Economy: Lessons from the IMF's Experience', *IMF Survey*, 26 July.

Jasinski, L. J. and J. Kotynaski (1992) 'Polska polityka handlowa – jaki liberalizm, jaka protekcja?' Otwieranie polskiej gospodarki na wspolprace z zagranica: Mozliwosci i ograniczenia' (Poland's trade policy: How to dose liberalism and protection?), in *Opening of Poland's Economy: Opportunities and barriers* (Warsaw: IKC).

Kalicki, K. (1991) 'Polityka pieniezna w okresie realizacji programu dostosowawczego' (Monetary policy during the implementation of the adjustment program), *Bank i Kredyt*, vols. 5–6 (Poland, 1993), *International economic report* (Warsaw: World Economy Research Institute).

Kaufman, R. (1987) 'Politics and inflation in Argentina and Brazil: The Austral and Cruzado packages in historical perspective', mimeo (Santiago: CIEPLAN).

Kaufman, R. (1990) 'Stabilization and Adjustment in Argentina, Brazil, and Mexico', in J. Nelson, (ed.), *Economic Crisis and Policy Choice: The politics of adjustment in the Third World* (Princeton, NJ: Princeton University Press).

Khalilzadeh-Shirazi, J. and Anwar Shah (1991) *Tax Policy in Developing Countries* (Washington, DC: World Bank).

Kiguel, M. and N. Liviatan, (1988) 'Inflationary Rigidities and Orthodox Stabilization Policies: Lessons from Latin America', *The World Bank Economic Review*, vol. 2 (September).

Kiguel, M. and N. Liviatan (1991) 'Stopping Inflation: The experience of Latin America and Israel and the implications for Central and Eastern Europe', in V. Corbo, F. Coricelli and J. Bossak, (eds), *Reforming Central and Eastern European economies* (Washington, DC: World Bank).

Kopits, G. and D. Mihaljek (1993) 'Fiscal Federalism and the New Independent States', in V. Tanzi (ed.), *Transition to Market: Studies in Fiscal Reform* (Washington, DC: International Monetary Fund).

Kornai, J. (1990) *The Road to a Free Economy* (New York: W. W. Norton).

Kuznetsov, Yevgeny (1993) 'Adjustment of the Russian Defence-Related Enterprises: Macroeconomic Implications', mimeo (Moscow: Institute for Economic Forecasting).

Larrain, F. (1991) 'Public Sector Behaviour in a Highly Indebted Country', in F. Larrain and M. Selvosky (eds), *The Contrasting Chilean Experience: The public sector and the Latin American crisis* (San Francisco: International Centre for Economic Growth).

Leite, Sérgio Pereira and V. Sundararajan (1990) 'Issues in Interest Rate Liberalization', *Finance and Development*, pp. 46–8.

Levine, Ross and David Scott (1993) 'Old Debts and New Beginnings: A Policy Choice in Transitional Socialist Economies', *World Development*, vol. 21, no. 3, pp. 319–30.

Lipton, D. and J. Sachs (1990) 'Privatization in Eastern Europe: The Case of Poland', *Brookings Papers on Economic Activity*, vol. 2, pp. 293–341.

Litvack, J. and I. Wallich (1993) '¿Son decisivas para la transformación de Rusia las finanzas intergubernamentales', *Finanzas y Desarrollo*, (June).

Long, M. (1988) *Crisis in the Financial Sector* (Washington, DC: World Bank).

Lüders, R. (1991) 'Massive Divesture and Privatization: Lessons from Chile', *Contemporary Policy Issues*, vol. ix (October).

McKinnon, Ronald I. (1991) *The Order of Economic Liberalization, Financial Control in the Transition to a Market Economy* (London: Johns Hopkins University Press).

McKinnon, Ronald I. (1993) 'Gradual versus Rapid Liberalization in Socialist Economies: Financial Policies and Macroeconomic Stability in China and Russia Compared', Annual Bank Conference on Development Economics (Washington, DC: World Bank).

McKinnon, R. I. and D. Mathieson (1981) 'How to Manage a Repressed Economy', *Essays in International Finance* (Princeton, NJ: Princeton University Press).

McLure, C. E., Jr (1992) 'Tax policy lessons for LDCs and Eastern Europe, Occasional Papers No. 28 (San Francisco: International Centre for Economic Growth).

McLure, C. E., Jr (1992) 'A Simpler Consumption-Based Alternative to the Income Tax for Socialist Economies in Transition', *World Bank Research Observer*, vol. 7, pp. 221–37.

McMahon, Gary and Klaus Schmidt-Hebbel (1995) 'Macroeconomic Adjustment and Tax Reform in Developing Countries', in G. Perry and J. Whalley (eds), *Fiscal Reform and Structural Change* (London: Macmillian, forthcoming).

Meller, P. (1991) 'The Chilean trade liberalization and export expansion process (1974–90)', mimeo (Santiago: CIEPLAN).

Meller, P. (1991) 'Adjustment and Social Costs in Chile during the 1980s', *World Development*, vol. 19, no. 11.

Meller, P. (1992) 'Latin American adjustment and economic reforms: Issues and recent experience', paper presented at the Conference Economic Reforms in Market and Socialist Economics, Madrid, Spain, 6–8 July 1992. Organized by Pensmiento Iberoamericano and the World Bank.

Meller, P. (1992) 'La Apertura Comerical Chilena: Enseñanzas de Política', Working Paper No. 109 (Washington, DC: Banco Interamericano de Desarrollo).

Morales, Juan Antonia A. (1991) 'Reformas Estructurales y Crecimiento Económico en Bolivia', Working Document No. 4 (IISEC).

Morales, Juan Antonio A. and Gary McMahon (eds) (1995) *Economic Policy in the Transition to Democracy in Latin America* (London: Macmillan).

Nair, G. and Filippides, A. (1988) 'How Much Do State-Owned Enterprises Contribute to Public Sector Deficits in Developing Countries – and Why?', World Bank WP 45, Washington, DC.

Nelson J. (1989) *Fragile coalitions: The politics of economic adjustment in the Third World* (New Brunswick, CA, and Oxford : ODC).

O'Connel, A. (1992) 'The Argentine economy: Short-and-middle-run prospects', mimeo (Buenos Aires: Centro de Economía Internacional).

OECD (1991) *OECD Economic Survey*, Czech and Slovak Federal Republic (Paris: OECD).

OECD (1992) *OECD Economic Survey* (Mexico and Paris: OECD).

Ofer, Gur (1992) 'Macroeconomic Stabilization and Structural Change: Orthodox, Heterodox, or Otherwise?', mimeo (Washington, DC: World Bank).

Ortiz, G. (1991) 'Mexico beyond the Debt Crisis: Toward sustainable growth with price stability', in M. Bruno, *et al.* (eds), *Lessons of Economic Stabilization and its Aftermath* (Cambridge, MA: MIT Press).

Perry, Guillermo (1992) ' Finanzas Públicas, Estabilización, y Reforma Estructural en América Latina', mimeo (BID).

Petrei, A. H. and J. Tybout (1985) 'Microeconomic Adjustments in Argentina during 1976–81: The importance of changing levels of financial subsidies', *World Development*, vol.13, no. 8.

Ramos, J. (1986) *Neoconservative Economics in the Southern Cone of Latin America, 1973–1983* (Baltimore, MD: Johns Hopkins University Press).

Remmer, K. (1986) 'The Politics of Economic Stabilization: IMF standby programs in Latin America, 1954–1984', *Comparative Politics*, vol. 19, no. 1.

Richet, X. (1993) 'Transition Towards the Market in Eastern Europe: Privatization, Industrial Restructuring and Entrepreneurship', *Communist Economies and Economic Transformation*, vol. 4, pp. 229–43.

Ritter, A. R. M. (1992) 'Development Strategy and Structural Adjustment in Chile', *From the Unidad Popular to the Concretion 1970–92* (Ottawa: The North–South Institute).

Rosati, D. (1990) 'Teoria i polityka progamow stabilizacyjnych MFW' (The theory and policy of the IMF adjustment programs) (Warsaw: Institute of Conjuncture and Foreign Trade Prices).

Ross, J. (1993) 'The fundamental error in principle of Mr. Fyodorov's economic package', mimeo (Moscow).

Rostowski, J. (1993) 'The Inter-enterprise Debt Explosion in the former Soviet Union: Causes, Consequences, Cures', *Communist Economies and Economic Transformation*, vol. 5, pp. 131–53.

Ruprah, I. (1992) 'Divestiture and Reform of Public Enterprises: The Mexican Case', mimeo, CIDE, Mexico City, Mexico.

Sachs, Jeffrey (1989) *Developing Country Debt and Economic Performance* (Chicago, IL: University of Chicago Press).

Sachs, Jeffrey (1994) 'La derrota reformista en Rusia es culpa del FMI', *Ambito Financiero* (January).

Sáez, R. (1992) 'An overview of privatization in Chile: The episodes, the results and the lessons', unpublished (Santiago).

Schwartz, G. and P. Silva Lopes (1993) 'La privatización: expectativas, ventajas y desventajas, concesiones y resultados', *Finanzas y Desarrollo* (Junio).

Simonsen, M. H. (1988) 'Price Stabilization and Income Policies: Theory and the Brazilian case study', in Bruno *et al.*, *Stabilization* (Cambridge, MA: MIT Press) pp. 259–86.

Situación Latinoamericana (1993) various issues (Santiago, Chile).

Slawinski, A. (1992) 'Polityka stabilizacyjna a bilans platniczy' (Stabilisation policy and the balance of payments) (Warsaw: PWN).

Slemrod, J. (1990) 'Optimal Taxation and Optimal Tax-systems', *Journal of Economic Perspectives*, vol. 1.

Solimano, Andrés (1990) 'Macroeconomic Adjustment, Stabilization, and Growth in Reforming Socialist Economies', WPS 399 (Washington DC: World Bank).

Solimano, Andrés (1992) 'Diversity in Economic Reform: A Look at the Experience in Market and Socialist Economies', WPS 981 (Washington, DC: World Bank).

Standing, Guy (1994) 'Employment Restructuring in Russian Industry', *World Development*, vol. 22, no. 2, pp. 253–60.

Standing, Guy (1994) 'Labour Market Implications of "Privatization" in Russian Industry in 1992', *World Development*, vol. 22, no. 2, pp. 261–70.

Stiglitz, Joseph E. (1993) 'The Role of the State in Financial Markets', Annual Bank Conference on Development Economics (Washington DC: World Bank).

Tait, A. A. (1992) 'A Not-So-Simple Alternative to the Income Tax for Socialist Economies in Transition: A Comment on McLure', *World Bank Research Observer*, vol. 7, pp. 239–48.

Tanzi, Vito (1977) 'Inflation, Lags in Collection and Real Value of Tax Revenue', *IMF Staff Papers*, vol. 6, no. 24.

Tanzi, Vito (1989) 'The Impact of Macroeconomic Policies on the Level of Taxation and the Fiscal Balance in Developing Countries', *IMF Staff Papers*, vol. 36, no. 3, pp. 633–56.

Tanzi, Vito (1992) 'Fiscal Policy and Economic Reconstruction in Latin America', *World Development*, no. 5.

Tanzi, Vito (1993) 'Financial Markets and Public Finance in the Transformation Process', in V. Tanzi (ed.), *Transition to Market: Studies in Fiscal Reform* (Washington, DC: International Monetary Fund).

Tirole, J. (1991) 'Privatization in Eastern Europe: Incentives and the Economics of Transition', in O. J. Blanchard and S. Fischer (eds), *NBER Macroeconomics Annual 1991* (Cambridge, MA: MIT Press).

UN (1994) *Human Development Report* (New York: Oxford University Press). DP

Urzúa, C. M. (1994) 'An Appraisal of Recent Tax Reforms in Mexico', in G. McMahon and G. Perry (eds), *Tax Reform and Structural Change* (London: Macmillan).

Vicker, J. and G. Yorrow (1991) 'Economic Prospective on Privatization', *Journal of Economic Perspective*, vol. 5.

Vuylsteke, C. (1988) 'Techniques of Privatization of State-owned Enterprises', Vol. I, *Methods and Implementation*, World Bank Technical Paper, no. 88 (Washington, DC: World Bank).

Waterbury, J. (1989) 'The Political Management of Economic Adjustment and Reform', in J. Nelson (ed.), *Fragile Coalitions: The politics of economic adjustment* (New Brunswick, CA, and Oxford: ODC).

Wernik, A. (1992) 'Budzet panstwa a transformacja i wzrost' (State budget, transformation and growth), mimeo (Warsaw: Institute of Finance).

Whitehead, L. (1989) 'Democratization and Disinflation: A comparative approach', in J. Nelson (ed), *Fragile Coalitions: The politics of economic adjustment* (New Brunswick, CA, and Oxford: ODC).

Williamson, John (1990) 'What Washington Means by Policy Reform', in John Williamson, *Latin American Adjustment. How Much has Happened?* (Washington, DC: Institute for International Economics).

World Bank (1982, 1991, 1994) *World Development Report* (Washington, DC: World Bank).

World Bank (1992) *Russian Economic Reform: Crossing the Threshold of Structural Change*, a World Bank Country Study (Washington, DC: World Bank).

World Bank (1992) *Privatization: The lessons of experience* (Washington, DC: World Bank Country Economic Department).

Wyczanski, P. (1993) 'Polityka kursowa na lata dziewiecdzisiate' (Exchange rate policy in the 1990s), *Materials and studies* (Warsaw: National Bank of Poland).

Wyczanski, P. (1993) 'Polski system bankowy: 1990–1992' (Polish banking system: 1990–1992) (Warsaw: Fredrich Ebert Stiftung).

Zhukov, Stanislav (1994) 'Russian Ecological Challenges', mimeo (Moscow: Institute of World Economy and International Relations).

Index

Index